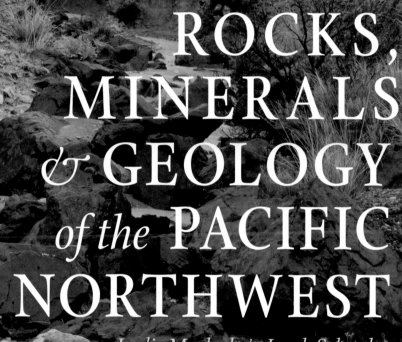

ROCKS, MINERALS & GEOLOGY of the PACIFIC NORTHWEST

Leslie Moclock & Jacob Selander

TIMBER PRESS FIELD GUIDE

for Rowan —LM
for Dad —JS

Page 1: Wire gold, Liberty, Washington
Pages 2–3: Blue Basin, John Day Fossil Beds National Monument, Oregon

Published in 2021 by Timber Press, Inc.
The Haseltine Building
133 S.W. Second Avenue, Suite 450
Portland, Oregon 97204-3527
timberpress.com

Printed in China
Text design by Michelle Owen, based on a series by Susan Applegate
Cover design by Vincent James, based on a series by Susan Applegate

ISBN 978-1-60469-915-9
A catalog record for this book is available from the Library of Congress.

CONTENTS

HOW TO USE THIS BOOK

One of the great joys of studying geology is learning how to uncover the "why" of the natural landscape around you. Why is there a mountain here, and a valley over there? Why do I find agates in one place and garnets in another?

The answers to these questions lie in the land itself. Rocks tell their own stories; they record evidence of their birth and tell us how the world around them has changed as they have passed through time. Learning how to read these stories is as simple as knowing what observations to make and what features to investigate.

This book begins with an overview of the major geologic theories that structure our current understanding of geologic processes and introduces the major geophysiographic regions of the Pacific Northwest.

Next come chapters on geology at many scales, from tiny crystals to vast plateaus. Each identification chapter—minerals, rocks, structures, landscapes—can be approached independently depending on your object of interest. These are the chapters to visit if you're holding a rock in your

hand and you just want to know what it is. They also provide a scientific framework for understanding rock features as well as tools for making identifications in the field. This includes information on where you're likely to find what—for example, the name of a physiographic region and particular mountain range known to contain good examples of a certain mineral. Note however, that any location information is for general reference only and not intended to provide directions to specific sites.

For the fullest understanding of geology in the field, we recommend you familiarize yourself with each section of the book and see how they integrate with one another. Individual minerals affect the shapes of mountains, and mountains have a say in the formation of a beach.

In the final chapter, we'll discuss how to put your observations together and tell a geologic story. This section also contains a summary of the Northwest's geologic history—stories generated by the work of thousands of scientists over many decades in the field.

INTRODUCTION TO GEOLOGY AND THE PACIFIC NORTHWEST

Minerals, rocks, structures, landscapes— these elements are all part of a unified whole. Our planet is a dynamic body of rock in motion, constantly creating and consuming the features we see on its surface. The science of geology is the study of these features and the processes that affect them. And there is no better place to see geology in action than the Pacific Northwest.

This chapter introduces some planet-sized geologic concepts such as plate tectonics to help you understand the big forces at work on our corner of the continent. Throughout the rest of the book, you'll learn not only how to identify geologic features but also how to connect them to these larger concepts—to see the history written in our rocks. Some other big ideas such as the geologic time scale are also discussed.

Finally, this chapter describes our regional setting, dividing the Northwest into thirteen physiographic provinces based on a combination of geography, geology, and climate. These provinces are referenced heavily throughout the rest of the book so it's a good idea to get familiar with them and refer to the regional map as needed.

Primer on Plate Tectonics

The concepts and processes described by plate tectonics provide an overarching, unifying framework through which most of modern geology can be understood. The basic idea is that the rigid outermost shell of Earth, its crust, is broken into over a dozen pieces referred to as tectonic plates. These plates move about the Earth's surface, continually rearranging themselves over long geologic periods of time. At their boundaries, the plates collide, move apart, or slide past each other, creating a variety of geologic activities. For example, the grinding of one tectonic plate against another creates earthquakes, and two plates colliding can build a mountain range.

To truly understand all the ways the plate-tectonics system affects Earth's surface, it's helpful to take a look beneath the surface. We'll examine our planet's internal structure, what makes a plate, and what happens when plates interact with one another.

Earth's Interior

The inside of our planet is not a hodge-podge of random materials; instead it comprises discretely organized layers of specific materials. This organization came about during Earth's infancy, over 4.5 billion years ago. When Earth first formed, it was so incredibly hot that all its components were in a liquid state. Over time, heavier elements such as iron and nickel sank toward the center of the early Earth, and lighter elements floated to the surface.

This process is called density stratification, or the layering of materials according to their densities. We often use the term *strata* (from the Latin *stratum*, meaning "layer") in geology to describe layers of sediments or rocks, and the term *stratification* to describe the processes by which the layers formed. A bottle of salad dressing provides a great example. Salad dressings often contain multiple ingredients of different densities—left still on the shelf, these ingredients will settle out, or in geologic terms, stratify, into layers with the denser ingredients on the bottom and the less dense ingredients on top. Of course, the early Earth was not composed of oil and vinegar, but its elements behaved in a similar fashion. The end result of density stratification within our planet is a set of interior layers that can be classified based on their elemental, or chemical, composition.

Starting at the center of the Earth, its core, we find the densest material, primarily an iron-nickel alloy. Surrounding the core and making up roughly 80 percent of Earth's interior volume is the mantle, which is composed of iron- and magnesium-rich silicate minerals (minerals containing silicon and oxygen). The crust is Earth's outermost layer. It is the least dense but most varied, comprising oxygen, silicon, aluminum, iron,

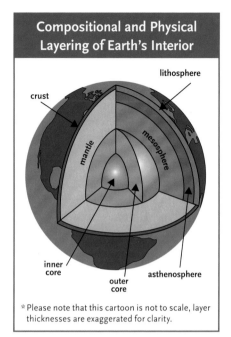

Compositional and Physical Layering of Earth's Interior

lithosphere

crust

mantle

mesosphere

inner core

outer core

asthenosphere

*Please note that this cartoon is not to scale, layer thicknesses are exaggerated for clarity.

calcium, potassium, sodium, magnesium, and more.

Chemical composition is not the only way to describe how the inside of our planet works. A separate but related classification scheme divides the Earth's interior into layers based on physical properties. For example, is the layer solid? Liquid? Does the layer break easily or does it deform slowly? This second classification system is referred to as the physical or mechanical layers of Earth's interior.

In the mechanical system, Earth's core is subdivided into an inner and outer layer, creatively named the inner core and the outer core. The inner core is solid, its temperature estimated to be around 9800°F, roughly the same as the surface of our Sun. While these temperatures are extreme, intense pressure from thousands of miles of surrounding rock prevents the inner core from melting. The outer core, under slightly less pressure, is liquid at temperatures ranging from 7200°F to 10,800°F, and its flow creates the dynamo responsible for Earth's magnetic field.

The mantle is also subdivided based on its mechanical properties. Above the outer core is the mesosphere (meso = "middle"), which corresponds with the lower mantle. The mesosphere is solid, and its temperature ranges between 4500°F and 9000°F. Surrounding the mesosphere is the asthenosphere (from the Greek for "weak"), a region of the upper mantle that is solid but also readily able to flow, similar to warm putty. Its temperatures vary from 1800°F to 4500°F. The very outermost part of the mantle, however, is cool enough to be rigid. It, along with the crust above it, makes up Earth's outermost mechanical layer: the lithosphere (from the Greek for "rock").

The rigid lithosphere is broken into plates that fit together like a puzzle wrapping around the outside of Earth. These plates float on the flowing, or ductile, asthenosphere, and their relative motions are described as plate tectonics.

Plates and Plate Boundaries
When describing plate tectonics, we are analyzing the motions of the Earth's rigid outer shell (the lithosphere) as it glides on top of the asthenosphere. The lithosphere has two compositional layers: the crust and the cool sphere of uppermost mantle. Many aspects of plate motion and interaction can be attributed to differences in the crustal part of the lithosphere,

which comes in two distinct types: oceanic and continental.

Oceanic crust is composed primarily of iron- and magnesium-rich silicate minerals. It has an average density of about 3 grams per cubic centimeter, and a thickness ranging from 3 to 6.5 miles. Continental crust is composed of aluminum-, calcium-, and potassium-rich silicate minerals. It's lighter than oceanic crust, with an average density of about 2.7 grams per cubic centimeter, but much thicker, ranging in thickness from 20 to 30 miles. The thinner, denser oceanic crust underlies deep ocean basins while the thicker, less dense continental crust makes up landmasses and tall mountains. Individual plates may contain only oceanic crust or a combination of both oceanic and continental crust.

These differences in crustal density and thickness matter particularly when plates are interacting with one another along their boundaries. These properties, along with the kinds of motion the plates experience, determine what kinds of features form where plates interface.

Plate boundaries can be divided into three general categories:

- Divergent, or spreading, in which plates are moving away from each other
- Convergent, or collisional, in which plates are moving toward each other
- Transform, or sliding, in which plates slide laterally past each other

Divergent Boundaries
Just as the name implies, at a divergent boundary, also known as a spreading center, the tectonic plates on either side

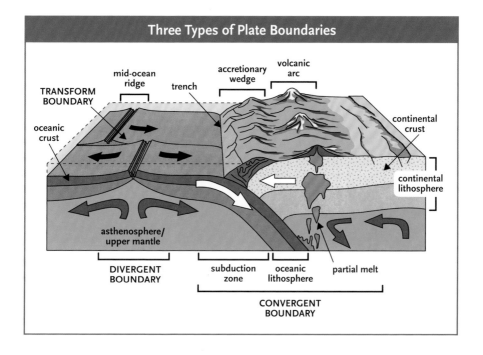

are moving away from each other. As they part, partially molten material from the upper mantle wells up and fills in the gap. This material cools to form new crust and is in turn pushed away from the boundary by new material welling up from the mantle. As this process repeats, the plates on either side of a divergent boundary are continually pushed apart. The most common divergent boundaries on Earth are the mid-ocean ridges, a 40,000-mile-long undersea mountain chain, in which the active plate boundary is centered at the ridges' crest. Mid-ocean ridges produce new oceanic crust and wrap around Earth like the seams on a softball.

Part of the mid-ocean ridge system lies 150–300 miles offshore from Oregon and Washington in the Pacific Ocean. The roughly north-south trending Juan de Fuca and Gorda Ridges are the divergent boundary between the Pacific Plate and the Juan de Fuca Plate. The Pacific Plate is moving roughly west-northwest, and the Juan de Fuca Plate east-southeast. In detail, the Juan de Fuca Plate can be subdivided into smaller micro-plates, with the Explorer Plate to the north, and Gorda Plate to the south.

On continents, divergent boundaries create long, linear rift valleys. Over time, given enough spreading and production of dense crust, continental rifts can potentially develop into ocean basins.

Convergent Boundaries

The opposite of spreading centers, at convergent boundaries the plates involved are moving toward each other in a process of collision. When tectonic plates collide,

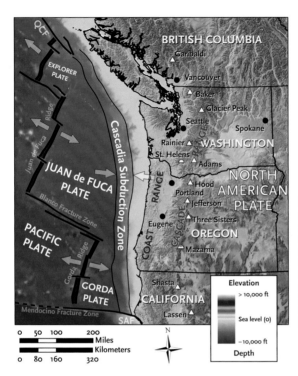

Map of the Pacific Northwest and the major tectonic plates, plate boundaries, and Cascades volcanoes. Abbreviations QCF and SAF are the Queen Charlotte Fault and San Andreas Fault, respectively. Both the QCF and SAF are large transform boundaries at the northern and southern ends of the Cascadia Subduction Zone.

one of two things happens. First, if the two colliding plates are both continental and have a somewhat equal density, the collision will cause the crust to become thickened along the plate boundary, which creates large mountain belts at the Earth's surface (think of the Himalayas). Second, if the colliding plates are of differing densities, the denser of the two is forced underneath the other in a process of subduction. This can occur when an oceanic and continental plate collide, because the oceanic plate is frankly denser, but it can also happen when two oceanic plates collide. Of two oceanic plates, one will be older and colder, and therefore denser than the other, and the older plate will subduct beneath the younger.

Regions around the globe where subduction is taking place are referred to as subduction zones. They are associated with multiple major features, particularly trenches, volcanoes, and accretionary wedges.

The largest features are trenches—narrow, deep parts of the ocean floor at the interface between the colliding plates. At trenches, the subducting plate dives into the upper mantle underneath the non-subducting plate. Once the subducting plate has reached a certain depth, any water present in the rock is released, which lowers the melting point of the solid mantle above it. This produces blobs of partial melt, which migrate upward through the mantle and crust due to their lower density. Where these blobs of partial melt reach the surface, they make volcanoes. These volcanoes will form in a line roughly parallel to the trench itself called a volcanic arc.

At convergent boundaries between oceanic and continental plates, sediments that were deposited on the ocean floor aren't dense enough to subduct along with the plate they've settled on. The continental plate acts like a giant bulldozer, scraping off these sediments and forming them into a wedge above the subduction zone. This is known as an accretionary wedge, a quasi-triangular-shaped body of material that has been added to a continental plate. If an accretionary wedge is large enough, it can rise above sea level to form a smaller range of mountains parallel to the volcanic arc.

Parallel to the coastline of Oregon and Washington, and about 50–100 miles offshore, the oceanic Juan de Fuca Plate is colliding with the continental North American Plate. This convergent boundary is named the Cascadia Subduction Zone (abbreviated CSZ) and has produced the numerous volcanoes, all part of the Cascade Volcanic Arc, for which the Pacific Northwest is famous. The Coast Ranges of Oregon and Washington, along with the Olympic Peninsula, are the results of a large accretionary wedge that has developed above the CSZ.

Transform Boundaries
Our third type of plate boundary involves the sideways, or lateral, motion of two plates past each other. Think of cars driving in opposite directions on a two-lane highway. Transform boundaries are present on ocean floors, connecting mid-ocean

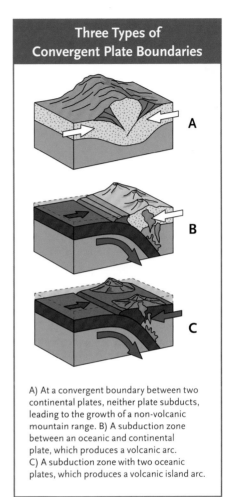

Three Types of Convergent Plate Boundaries

A) At a convergent boundary between two continental plates, neither plate subducts, leading to the growth of a non-volcanic mountain range. B) A subduction zone between an oceanic and continental plate, which produces a volcanic arc. C) A subduction zone with two oceanic plates, which produces a volcanic island arc.

ridge segments, and on continents, connecting spreading boundaries to convergent boundaries. For example, the San Andreas Fault is a continental transform boundary that connects a spreading center in the Gulf of California to the southern end of the Cascadia Subduction Zone. The other major transform boundaries in the Pacific Northwest exist on the floor of the Pacific Ocean. To the south, a transform boundary called the Mendocino Fracture

14

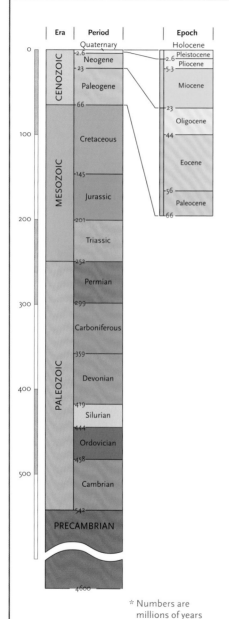

* Numbers are
millions of years

The study of geology is in many ways a study of time. Geologists reconstruct past sequences of events to understand how mountains formed and what ancient climates were like, so we need a way to refer to time periods long before human calendars had meaning. For this purpose, we use two geologic timescales, one relative and the other absolute.

The relative timescale uses no numbers and is concerned with the relative relationships between rocks and fossils, specifically ordering them from oldest to youngest. It grew out of early work by English canal surveyor William Smith around the turn of the nineteenth century. He spent many years examining rock layers as canals were dug and observed that many recognizable layers stacked up in the same order in different locations across the country. Moreover, many of those layers contained fossils, and the order of fossils in the layers also remained the same no matter the location. If he came across any one identifiable layer, he could predict what fossils he would find in the layers below or above. This led to the profound insight that the layers were arranged chronologically; that is, the deepest layers and their fossils were older than the higher layers.

Based on these observations, Smith proposed the principle of faunal succession, or the idea that fossils can be used to order time. Throughout Earth's history, many species have only existed for brief periods before becoming extinct, so fossils from these short-lived species can serve as markers for particular stretches of time. As Smith's ideas caught on, geologists began to study and group fossils around the world according to their relative ages. They gave certain groupings names like Cambrian or Jurassic and listed the groups from old to young.

The relative timescale used today is based off the work of thousands of scientists over the past 200 years. Earth's history is divided into eras, which are then further subdivided into periods, epochs, and ages. The boundaries between each grouping are commonly related to significant changes in the fossil record; for example, the Mesozoic era is famously the time of dinosaurs, while the Cenozoic is known as the time of mammals.

Prior to the twentieth century, we had no way of knowing how old any fossil was in an absolute sense—that is to say, its age in numbers. The discovery of radioactivity changed this, and scientists learned to use trace amounts of radioactive elements trapped within certain crystals to determine how long ago those crystals formed. This process, known as radiometric dating, allows scientists to figure out exactly how old a rock is (so long as it has the right kinds of crystals for analysis). Scientists have since used these techniques to match absolute ages to the relative geologic timescale.

Both ways of thinking about time—relative and absolute—remain useful. Some rock units contain no fossils, so they can't be placed on the relative scale, while others lack the crystals necessary for radiometric dating and can't be assigned a numerical age. These timescales are therefore used together to draw the fullest picture of Earth's changes over time.

Zone connects the San Andreas Fault to the CSZ and links with the southern end of the Gorda Ridge. At the northern end of the Gorda Ridge the Blanco Fracture Zone connects to the Juan de Fuca Ridge, which is in turn connected via transform boundary at its northern edge to the Queen Charlotte Fault, which extends north to a subduction zone in Alaska. The figure on page 12 illustrates how each plate and boundary in the region links together.

Physiographic Provinces of the Pacific Northwest

The geography of Oregon and Washington is incredibly diverse, spanning temperate rainforests, glaciated mountain peaks, semi-arid deserts, and productive agricultural regions. It would be difficult to picture one single style of landscape to best represent the Pacific Northwest. In fact, in many places it is possible to drive through multiple regions you might consider "classic Pacific Northwest" within less than three hours.

The reason behind the wide variation in geographic regions is simple—geology. The high topography of the Cascade Range and Olympic Mountains, produced by subduction-related volcanic processes, catches weather systems moving inland from the Pacific Ocean. This leads to high amounts of precipitation (places in the Olympic Mountains receive as much as

150 inches of rain annually), deep river valleys, and snow- and glacier-covered peaks. Move across the Cascades into eastern Oregon and Washington, and it's a stark transition to a semi-arid landscape, much of it shaped by massive lava flows and glacial outburst floods of gargantuan proportion. In the geologic present, tectonic forces are stretching southern Oregon like an accordion, perhaps to someday resemble northeast Washington, which in the geologic past was stretched so much that rocks formed over 12 miles below the surface of the crust are now exposed at the surface.

Because of its wide range in geography and geology, the Pacific Northwest can be divided into distinct physiographic provinces based on location, geology, regional climate, and topography. In this book, we've named thirteen distinct provinces in Oregon and Washington. You'll find descriptions of each in this chapter and see them referenced as notable localities in the rock and mineral entries. The descriptions here are meant to give you a basic understanding of which rocks you'll find where. We do use some terminology introduced more completely in later chapters. If you find yourself wanting more details about the how and why of any province's geology, please turn to our final chapter, Telling the Story.

Coast Ranges

The Coast Ranges province (COR) stretches north-south along the Pacific coastline from the Willapa Hills in Washington, across the Columbia River, and south through the Coast Ranges of Oregon. We're defining the northern boundary of the COR province as the Chehalis River valley in Washington; its southern border stretches between Cape Blanco and Roseburg in Oregon, and it's bounded on the east by the Willamette Valley and Puget Lowlands. The vast majority of the COR landscape is high relief and rugged, though relatively low elevation compared to other mountainous regions in the Pacific Northwest. Most high ridges in the COR have less than 3000 feet elevation, the exception being Marys Peak in Oregon at 4100 feet.

Most of the rocks in the Coast Ranges originated as sediments on the floor of the Pacific Ocean, deposited during Neogene and Paleogene times. Through tectonic convergence, they were scraped off the subducting plate onto North America. In many places these sediments and sedimentary rocks are cut by igneous rocks created through tectonic activity. Additionally, some igneous rocks that were once part of the oceanic crust detached during subduction and are exposed within the COR.

Olympic Peninsula

The Olympic Peninsula (OLY) is located in northwest Washington, north of the Chehalis River and west of the Puget Lowlands. The OLY could be considered a northern extension of the Coast Ranges, but because the topography and geology are quite distinct from the COR, we are separating the OLY as its own unique province. The dominant topographic feature of the OLY are the Olympic Mountains, many of whose peaks reach elevations greater than 6500 feet. These mountains have steep ridges separating deeply incised valleys and form a formidable topographic barrier to weather systems moving inland from the Pacific Ocean. Portions of the

Physiographic Provinces of Oregon and Washington

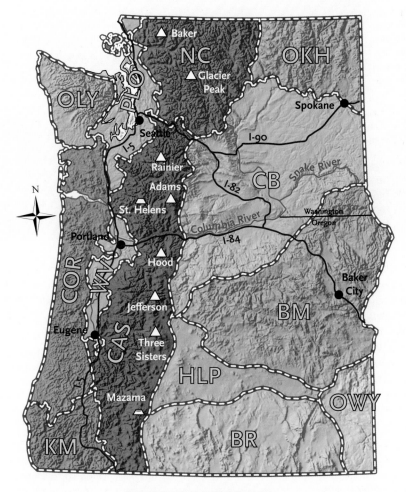

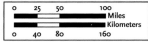

COR: Coast Ranges
OLY: Olympic Peninsula
KM: Klamath Mountains
WV: Willamette Valley
PLO: Puget Lowlands

CAS: Cascade Range
NC: North Cascades
CB: Columbia Basin
OKH: Okanogan Highlands
BM: Blue Mountains

HLP: High Lava Plains
BR: Basin and Range
OWY: Owyhee Plateau

View of the Coast Ranges province (COR) in Oregon, looking south from Marys Peak near Corvallis

OLY receive upward of 150 inches of precipitation annually. Higher elevations within the OLY also contain some of the only landscapes in the Pacific Northwest west of the Cascade Range to have been shaped by alpine glaciation in the recent geologic past.

Rocks in the Olympic Peninsula are similar in history and age to rocks in the Coast Ranges (sediments and igneous rocks that originated on top of or as part of the oceanic crust). However, some rocks within the Olympic Mountains display low-grade metamorphism, indicating a history of slightly more intense deformation as these rocks were added to the North American continent.

Klamath Mountains

The Klamath Mountains province (KM) sits south of Oregon's Coast Ranges and west of the Cascades. This mountainous region is characterized by steep, high-relief topography, with ridge and peak elevations reaching 5900–6500 feet. Unlike the Olympic Mountains, high elevations within the KM show no signs of glaciers in their past.

The Klamath Mountains have a slightly different geologic history than their northern counterparts along the Pacific coast. Many rocks in the KM could be considered "exotic," meaning the rocks come from someplace other than the North American continent. These exotic rocks are generally classified into terranes—groups of related rocks added to North America at similar times within the geologic past. The terranes that make up the KM are Paleozoic to Jurassic in age, and consist of a wide range of compositions, from sections of oceanic crust to oceanic sedimentary rocks to volcanic island arcs. Some rocks in the KM retain their initial composition

View of the Olympic Mountains (OLY), looking west across the Puget Sound from Whidbey Island

Glacially shaped peaks in the core of the Olympic Mountains (OLY), viewed from Hurricane Ridge in Olympic National Park

The Illinois River valley in the Klamath Mountains (KM)

and properties, and others display metamorphism. Scattered among the various terranes are small instances of igneous rock from the Jurassic and Cretaceous. The KM is one of the most geologically diverse regions in the Pacific Northwest.

Willamette Valley and Puget Lowlands

Nestled between the Coast Ranges and the Cascade Mountains of Oregon and Washington are the Willamette Valley (WV) and Puget Lowlands (PLO), respectively. Though these two regions are not directly connected, since the geographic location, topography, and general geology of the Willamette Valley and Puget Sound are similar we are describing them as a single physiographic province. Both regions are fairly low-relief, lower-elevation valley and river floodplains covered in deposits of recent (Quaternary) sediments. The WV in Oregon extends from Eugene to Portland and comprises primarily the floodplains of the Willamette River and its tributaries. Isolated pieces of higher topography within the valley are composed of erosion-resistant basalts, either local intrusions or remnants of the Columbia River Basalt Group.

The PLO flank the I-5 corridor from south of Tacoma to the Canadian border. Unlike in the WV, most of the Quaternary sediment covering the PLO has a glacial origin, stemming back to approximately 15,000 years ago when most of this region was covered in a sheet of ice. Southward motion of this ice sheet carved out the north-south oriented valleys and hills that

The Willamette Valley's (WV) fertile soils support abundant agriculture.

are ubiquitous to the Puget Sound region near Seattle.

Cascade Range

When most people think of the Pacific Northwest, they're likely to picture a snow-covered volcano resting atop a plateau of evergreen ridges. It's a classic representation of the Cascade Range province (CAS).

The Cascade Range forms the spine of the Pacific Northwest, extending south to north from the Oregon-California border to the I-90 corridor in central Washington. The bulk of the CAS is composed of igneous rocks, which formed as a result of subduction between the North American and Juan de Fuca Plates.

Capping the CAS are the numerous high volcanic peaks for which the Pacific Northwest is famous. This is the Cascade Volcanic Arc, a result of the Juan de Fuca Plate subducting beneath North America. The main volcanic peaks in the CAS reach elevations from 10,000 to over 14,000 feet, well above the surrounding mountains. These larger volcanoes and the volcanic rocks associated with them and their eruptions can be subdivided into the High Cascades, though here we keep the volcanoes and their products as part of the CAS province.

Many large volcanoes in the CAS are still active; the eruption of Mt. Saint Helens in Washington on 18 May 1980, is the most recent major example. During this eruption, the mountain lost about

A view south through the Puget Sound toward Mt. Rainier, a CAS volcano

Looking south in the Cascade Range (CAS) toward the Tatoosh Range and Mt. Adams in the distance. While you might think of the Cascades as just the large volcanoes, it's important to remember that these volcanic peaks are built on top of a broader mountain range.

Diablo Lake, Colonial Peak (left), and Pinnacle Peak (right) in the North Cascades (NC)

1300 feet of height and produced a lateral blast that leveled dozens of square miles of forest. Much of the aftermath of the eruption is still visible today, though vegetation in the blast zone is making quite a comeback.

North Cascades

While the North Cascades (NC) could be considered a northern extension of the Cascade Range proper, the topography and geologic history of the region north of the I-90 corridor differ significantly enough from the more southern region that it deserves its own designation. The topography of the NC is quite varied, ranging from very rugged, high (greater than 10,000 feet) glaciated peaks to deep valleys to steep-sided islands in the San Juan archipelago. Many of the valleys in the NC were intermittently occupied by glaciers during the past 2 million years and display classic features associated with mountainous glaciation.

Aside from two volcanoes associated with the Cascade Volcanic Arc, Mt. Baker and Glacier Peak, the NC is a veritable mishmash of igneous and metamorphic rocks, ocean crust, mantle rocks, and continental sedimentary rocks—all ranging in age from Precambrian to Oligocene.

Columbia Basin

East of the Cascade Range, the Columbia Basin (CB) encompasses over 258,000 square miles of eastern Washington and northern Oregon. The rain shadow of the Cascades makes most of the Columbia Basin into high desert, though with water supplied by aquifers and the Columbia

The Columbia River and Columbia Basin (CB) near Tri Cities, Washington

Rolling hills, alfalfa fields, and windmills are typical of the eastern portion of the Columbia Basin (CB).

Roadcut through the Grande Ronde Basalt, part of the Columbia River Basalt Group in the Columbia Basin

and Snake Rivers, much of the CB is very agriculturally productive. In general, the CB is fairly low relief, with landscapes of broad rolling hills separated by steep gorges. An exception is along I-82 near Yakima where tectonic compression has produced a series of roughly east-west oriented ridges.

Parts of the CB are underlain by crystalline igneous and metamorphic rocks, but these are rarely seen as most of the region is covered in the infamous Columbia River Basalt Group, massive basalt lava flows that erupted around 17–14 million years ago, in total, over 300 individual flows with an estimated volume of over 40,000 cubic miles of material, over 11,000 feet thick in some places (see page 314 for more).

These large floods of basalt were not the only floods to shape the Columbia Basin. Around 14,000 years ago enormous glacial outburst floods sent hundreds of cubic miles of water across the landscape, carving deep valleys into the flood basalts (see page 284 for more).

Okanogan Highlands

North of the Columbia Basin and east of the North Cascades are the Okanogan Highlands (OKH), where some of the oldest rocks in the Pacific Northwest can be found. The topography of the OKH is relatively high mountain peaks (elevations reaching 7600 feet) and north-south oriented ridges and parallel valleys with rivers draining into the Columbia River proper. The landscape contains much more

Highway roadcut of crystalline metamorphic rock along US-20 in the Okanogan Highlands (OKH)

Exposed deep crustal rocks in the Okanogan Highlands (OKH) show a history of extension.

relief than the adjacent Columbia Basin; as a result the OKH receives slightly more annual precipitation and supports temperate alpine forests.

Rocks in the OKH range from Precambrian sediments that have been slightly metamorphosed to igneous and high-grade metamorphic rocks that formed at a depth of over 12.5 miles within the crust. Overall the rocks in the OKH represent multiple episodes of extension and compression beginning with the breakup of a supercontinent that existed long before any other rocks in the Pacific Northwest.

Blue Mountains

South of the Columbia Basin and covering a large area of eastern Oregon are the Blue Mountains (BM). This region, as you might guess, is primarily mountainous. It boasts a lot of relief between its valleys

Early fall in the Wallowa Mountains, part of the greater Blue Mountains province (BM)

High Lava Plains

East of the central Oregon Cascades and south of the Blue Mountains are the High Lava Plains (HLP) of Oregon. The name of this province comes from its relatively high average elevation (about 4500 feet) and low-relief topography that is intermittently broken by volcanic centers of varying size. Much of the HLP is underlain by flood basalts that erupted at approximately the same time as the Columbia River Basalt Group, but are topped with ash flow and fall deposits, recent Quaternary volcanic rocks, and intermittent lakes.

Much of the volcanism in the HLP comes from basaltic cinder cones and small lava flows that get progressively younger from east to west across the province. Some of the youngest volcanism in the HLP is associated with the Newberry Caldera, southeast of Bend, Oregon (see page 248 for more).

Around 14,000 years ago, during the last ice age, large parts of the HLP were covered in shallow lakes, which have since drained or dried up. Many volcanic centers, such as Fort Rock, show an interesting interaction between volcanism, lakes, and wave-driven erosion.

and adjacent ridges, with mountain peaks exceeding 9000 feet in places. Higher areas in the BM were glaciated in the past, but only landscape records of the glaciers remain.

The geology of the Blue Mountains is similar to that of the Klamath Mountains, as the BM is underlain by accreted terranes and exotic island arcs. Much of the region is covered with Columbia River Basalts, but in places the basalts did not reach, or where they have eroded, these exotic terranes are exposed at the surface. Many of these terranes contain slightly metamorphosed sedimentary and volcanic rocks. In places igneous intrusions "stitch" different terranes together. Near the John Day area, sedimentary rocks and deposits preserve a fossil record of Eocene mammals and flora that once lived in the region.

Basin and Range

South of the High Lava Plains is the Basin and Range province (BR). As the name implies, this region's topography comprises mountain ranges separated by relatively flat basins. They are north-south oriented with, in places, over a mile of relief between range crests and valley floors. Steens Mountain, the highest peak in the BR, is the southernmost area in the Pacific Northwest outside of the high

View to the east across the High Lava Plains (HLP) from the summit of Paulina Peak in Newberry National Volcanic Monument. Each separate mound in the photo is an individual cinder cone volcano.

peaks of the Cascade Range to have been glaciated in the past. Much of this region is internally drained, meaning rivers that form during rainy or snowmelt seasons do not flow into the Pacific Ocean. Rather, the rivers flow into basins that fill with seasonal lakes, which dry up during summer.

Rocks in the BR are primarily volcanic, both from local eruptions and those associated with flood basalts. The region has been undergoing tectonic extension—stretched in a roughly east-west direction. This extension is not localized to Oregon; the BR province here is the northern extension of the much larger Basin and Range that encompasses most of Nevada, eastern California, and parts of western Utah.

Owyhee Plateau

In the far southeast corner of Oregon lies the Owyhee Plateau (OWY). The plateau proper refers to parts of this region's low-relief, high-elevation (ranging from 4500 to 5500 feet) topography. The Owyhee River and its tributaries have carved deep, narrow gorges into the landscape.

Bedrock in the OWY represents a violent volcanic history of flood basalts and large caldera-forming eruptions. Most of the Columbia River and other flood basalts in the Pacific Northwest originated from vents near the OWY, and areas around the plateau not covered in basalt have thick rhyolites or large ash-flow tuffs that erupted locally during the Eocene and Miocene.

View from the Steens mountain range overlooking the basin of the Alvord Desert in the BR province

Rhyolite tuffs in Leslie Gulch, Owyhee Plateau (OWY)

MINERALS

Minerals are quite simply the building blocks of geology. Individually, they are tiny, but together they make up mountains. Learning to identify and understand different kinds of minerals is like learning the letters in an alphabet for a new kind of language; discovering their shapes, properties, and occurrences is the first step toward understanding larger-scale geology.

So what's the difference between a rock and a mineral? Simple—rocks are made of minerals.

A mineral is anything that is all of the following:

• Naturally occurring—formed in nature and not through human effort or activity.
• Formed by physical and chemical processes; never alive. For example, salt is a mineral because it forms when seawater evaporates, while sugar—a molecule that comes from plants—is not.

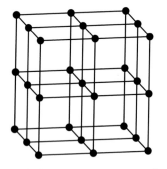

A simple cubic lattice demonstrating a regular, repeating structure

• A crystalline solid—a solid with its atomic building blocks arranged in a regular repeating pattern like a scaffold. Some solids, like glass, are amorphous, meaning their building blocks are scattered randomly rather than stacked. Amorphous solids are not minerals.
• Has a definite chemical composition—is made of known atomic ingredients. For example, quartz is made of silicon and oxygen atoms in a ratio of 1:2, and its chemical formula is SiO_2. Hematite, a naturally occurring "rust" mineral, is made of iron and oxygen with the formula Fe_2O_3.

Each official mineral recognized by the International Mineralogical Association has its own unique name, chemical formula, and crystal structure. The atomic ingredients in the formula and the shape of the structure determine what a mineral looks like and how it behaves.

Minerals with structural and chemical similarities are classified into groups that often have similar defining physical properties. Some group members may be so similar they cannot be differentiated without microscopic study. Conversely, some minerals can have such a wide range of appearances that different varieties have gained their own informal names.

A crystal is any individual specimen of a mineral, for example, a quartz crystal or a calcite crystal. Not all crystals are beautiful; many are opaque or dull and appear unremarkable. A gem is any crystal that is valued by people, often for shininess or transparency.

MINERAL CHEMICAL FORMULAS

A mineral's chemical formula tells us not only what the mineral is made of, but also a little bit about how it's put together. The mineral quartz, for example, has the chemical formula SiO_2, because it's made of the elements silicon (Si) and oxygen (O) in a ratio of 1:2. That ratio is represented by the subscript attached to each element. If, like silicon in this formula, an element has no subscript, it's the same as saying it has a subscript of 1.

Some formulas have greater complexity and variability. Consider alkali feldspar, $(K,Na)AlSi_3O_8$. The silicon and oxygen at the end of the formula tell us that this is a silicate, by far the most common group of minerals (see page 42). They also, along with aluminum (Al), make up the framework of the mineral the same way that walls and floors make up the structure of a house.

The elements enclosed in parentheses are a bit different. The parentheses tell us that there is a place in the structure where another atom can go, like putting furniture in an empty room. The elements listed inside the parentheses are those that are able to fit into that room—in this example, potassium (K) or sodium (Na). As a mineral grows, it can put either element in the available spot.

Because a mineral's structure is repeated over and over, it's really more like a high-rise apartment complex. Each unit has a room capable of housing an atom of K or Na. Some individual crystals may fill all their units with one

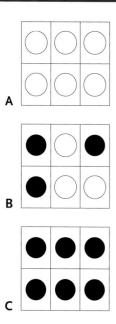

Three simplified crystals showing structures filled with (A) only K atoms, (B) a mix of K and Na atoms, and (C) only Na atoms

element or the other, but many fill them with a mix—for example, 60 percent K and 40 percent Na. Another crystal may have a 70/30 split or an even 50/50.

All of these crystals are alkali feldspar. The formula tells us that its composition has an inherent variability, ranging from pure $KAlSi_3O_8$ to pure $NaAlSi_3O_8$, though it's usually a mix.

Besides K and Na, other common atomic pairs or substitutes include iron (Fe) and magnesium (Mg), silicon and aluminum, and calcium (Ca) and magnesium.

A pyrite crystal on a quartz crystal

Basalt rock

A rock is an aggregate (group) of mineral crystals that have grown together into a unified solid. A rock may be made of many different kinds of minerals (like granitic rocks) or many individual crystals of one mineral (like quartzite). Rocks can also contain material other than minerals, such as animal shells, plant material, and coal.

Sunstone, a gem variety of feldspar

Finding Crystals

The word *crystal* invokes images of tall, pointed, shining beauties that sparkle in the light or show off a deep color. In reality, crystals are often more mundane; they are individual pieces of any mineral. Because all rocks are made of minerals, all rocks are made of crystals.

Rocks are identified in part by the kinds of minerals they contain, and individual crystals can range in size from as large as a car to smaller than the eye can see. So how do you know when you're looking at a crystal?

Start by looking for splotches of color. Most individual crystals are one color throughout. Each splotch or shape in a rock may be a crystal or cluster of identical crystals. Well-formed crystals can have sharply defined edges and shapes; others have more irregular boundaries. The former are described as euhedral, and the latter as anhedral. Anhedral minerals are often called grains rather than crystals to indicate that they don't have flat crystal faces.

Crystals also commonly have these properties:

- 3D shape. All crystals, even flat ones, have a three-dimensional shape within whatever rock they're in. Make sure a color splotch isn't just a surface stain by looking at the rock from all directions and examining both freshly broken and weathered surfaces.
- Limited variety. Most rocks contain only one to four kinds of minerals large enough to identify with the naked eye, and the rock will usually have multiple crystals of each mineral type. Try to find multiple examples of the 3D color splotch you started with.
- Flashes of light. On a freshly broken rock face, many crystals will reflect light from flat or dish-shaped surfaces when the rock is rotated back and forth.

Each splotch in this image is a crystal in a rock. Some are euhedral, making sharp blocky shapes, and others are anhedral. The crystals have three-dimensional shapes and there are only about four different kinds visible. If turned, many crystal faces would give off flashes of light.

Often, part or all of a rock may comprise crystals too small to see individually. A body of microscopic crystals is usually a single color that is dull on both weathered and freshly broken surfaces (except for some silica-rich rocks like chert, which can have waxy or shiny, dish-shaped fractures). In some rocks, the microcrystalline zones may appear to surround larger crystals or fill in gaps—this is called a rock matrix. In other rocks, the entire specimen may be microcrystalline.

A microcrystalline rock specimen made of crystals too small to see. Notice the relatively uniform color and the granularity of the broken surface.

Once you have identified individual mineral crystals within a rock, you can do tests on their physical properties to identify which minerals they are.

Mineral Properties for Identification

Each mineral's unique chemical makeup and crystal structure give it distinctive physical properties that can be observed and tested in order to tell minerals apart.

Habit The visible shape a mineral specimen takes. Many minerals have a small range of characteristic habits. A specimen may be a single crystal with a perfect form or an aggregate of crystals in different arrangements. Different habits come from the shape of a mineral's crystal structure interacting with the specific environment in which each crystal grows.

Individual crystals may be generally described as equant (same size in all dimensions), elongate, flat, or branching. Within these categories there are additional, more specific terms (illustrated below). Sometimes crystals grow in pairs or multiples that are mirrored or rotated with respect to one another. These are

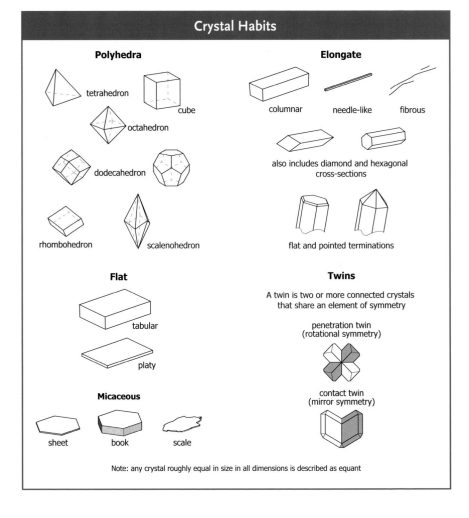

Crystal Habits

Polyhedra
- tetrahedron
- cube
- octahedron
- dodecahedron
- rhombohedron
- scalenohedron

Elongate
- columnar
- needle-like
- fibrous

also includes diamond and hexagonal cross-sections

flat and pointed terminations

Flat
- tabular
- platy

Micaceous
- sheet
- book
- scale

Twins

A twin is two or more connected crystals that share an element of symmetry

penetration twin
(rotational symmetry)

contact twin
(mirror symmetry)

Note: any crystal roughly equal in size in all dimensions is described as equant

called twins; most twinning happens on a microscopic scale, but some large crystals may grow with characteristic twinned forms.

Crystals do not always grow in their most perfect forms. When they are constrained by their neighbors, they may end up taking a generally rounded shape called a bleb or a grain.

Groups of crystals also have specific descriptors. Elongate crystals arranged in a starburst pattern are called radiating. Some radiating crystals are packed so tightly together they form spherical balls, also called globular aggregates. Another rounded shape, called botryoidal, describes crystal groups that resemble a bunch of grapes. Crystal aggregates that lack any particular arrangement and have no internal features are simply called massive.

Hardness The ability of a mineral to scratch or resist being scratched. Usually described with the system known as Mohs Hardness Scale, a unitless scale from 1 to 10, with 1 being the softest (talc) and 10 the hardest (diamond). When comparing two materials, the material with the higher hardness number can scratch the material with the lower number.

Hardness is important because some minerals can look virtually identical but have very different hardnesses, so testing hardness can help distinguish between them.

Luster The manner in which a crystal reflects light. Luster can be earthy, dull, silky, greasy, pearly, vitreous (glassy), metallic, and so on—there are many words to describe it.

A mineral's luster is determined by basic properties of its crystal structure

HOW TO TEST HARDNESS

Don't worry about determining a mineral's exact hardness number—it's much more useful to figure out what materials it will scratch or will scratch it. The hardness numbers in each mineral entry will simply help you predict this. Use an unknown mineral to try to scratch an object of known hardness or vice versa. Some common testing tools include:

2–2.5 Fingernail
3 Copper penny
5.5 Glass
5–6.5 Steel (regular steel like that in a nail has a hardness of 5.5, while hardened steel like that used in most knife blades and rock hammers can have a hardness up to 6.5)

Example: Quartz and calcite can look very similar, but quartz has a hardness of 7, while calcite has a hardness of 3. Quartz is able to scratch glass and the flat edge of a knife blade, but calcite cannot. Calcite can leave a faint scratch on a copper penny because their hardnesses are the same; quartz leaves a deep scratch on a penny because its hardness is much higher.

Note: When you're in the field you may be less likely to have a plate of glass handy than something like the flat of a knife blade or the head of a hammer. However, because steel hardness is variable in a way that glass is not, glass is always listed as the test object for minerals in the 5–6 hardness range. If you know the hardness of your knife blade, you can use it to test this range instead.

and how well it reflects light, but an individual specimen's luster can be affected by its specific habit or by its growth and history. For example, a single, large crystal of quartz can have a reflective, vitreous luster, but a mass of quartz in a rock vein may be greasy or even dull. This is because the highest possible reflectiveness occurs when a specimen is a perfectly formed crystal with faces like mirrors. Specimens with imperfect crystals or pitted or etched faces will not reflect as much light.

Cleavage A mineral has cleavage if it breaks readily along planes of weakness in the crystal's structure. The number of cleavage planes and the angle(s) at which

Illustrations of crystals with three cleavage planes: cubic (left) and rhombohedral (right). The different angles between the planes cause the crystals to break into different shapes.

Stair-step cleavage. To determine whether a flat surface is a cleavage plane, look on broken faces for other flat surfaces in the same orientation.

they intersect can help distinguish one mineral from another.

Fracture If a mineral breaks without cleavage, the broken surface is described as a fracture. Some fracture types have names, like conchoidal (dish-shaped), splintery, or hackly (jagged). For most minerals, either their cleavage or their fracture stands out as an identifying feature—we list the more useful of the properties in individual entries.

Conchoidal fracture in obsidian

Color The color of a mineral visible to the naked eye. This is a mineral's most deceptive property. Many minerals can be many different colors, so color is a poor tool to use for identification.

Mineral color can come from a variety of different sources. Some minerals are "self-colored" by their essential atomic ingredients. A few, like gold and pyrite, exhibit only one color, but most self-colored minerals have a range of possible colors due to small differences in the exact atomic makeup of a particular specimen. For example, minerals that contain a lot of iron and magnesium are often darker in color when they contain more iron and lighter in color when they

A metallic yellow pyrite crystal and its dark gray-black streak

have more magnesium. The minerals of the amphibole group are good examples of these variations.

Other minerals are colored by trace atomic impurities. These impurities act like a small drop of food coloring within the crystal. Some common impurities include iron (responsible for red, yellow, orange, brownish, and occasionally purple, green, and light blue colors), manganese (pink, red), copper (blue, green). Unlike food coloring, though, the color a trace element generates depends on how exactly it fits into the mineral's crystal structure, which is why one element like iron can produce many different colors in different kinds of minerals.

Mineral color can also be affected by optical effects. For example, some crystal structures cause light to bounce and split within the crystal, resulting in an iridescent, often bluish sheen.

Streak The color a mineral makes when it is finely powdered, such as when it is rubbed across a ceramic plate. This color remains consistent for each mineral no matter what color it might appear to be on a larger scale. For example, hematite can be brown, red, or metallic silver in color, but its streak will always be a brick red.

Other physical and chemical interactions Some iron-rich minerals will stick to a magnet, and others can be permanent magnets themselves. Other minerals may absorb water or dissolve in it, and still others may fizz when exposed to weak acids. Some can conduct electricity or create a glowing light when hit together. These are all examples of unique properties specific to certain minerals or groups of minerals, and they will be highlighted in different mineral entries as they apply.

SOMETIMES "FELDSPAR" IS THE BEST YOU CAN DO

Several mineral groups have a bevy of members. These members all share common diagnostic physical traits, like hardness and cleavage, but they differ from one another in subtle ways. In the feldspar group, for example, plagioclase feldspar crystals may have striations, while alkali feldspar crystals do not.

So if you see a feldspar crystal without striations, does that mean it must be alkali? Not necessarily—plagioclase may be striated, but also it may not. A non-striated crystal could be either type. More detailed information about plagioclase vs. alkali feldspar can give more clues to look for, but sometimes noth-ing that can help you make a distinction turns up. In that case, it's normal and reasonable to identify that crystal as "some kind of feldspar" and move on.

Other mineral groups that can be difficult to drill down include dark amphiboles, dark pyroxenes, dark tourmalines, and garnets. The entries for these mineral groups contain plenty of information about members and varieties to help you understand the relationships between these minerals and their geologic settings, but don't be discouraged if your field identifications aren't so exact.

★ Ten Most Common Minerals and Mineral Groups

Oregon and Washington are home to over 600 unique minerals. Most of these are rare, even microscopic. The majority of rocks are made of a handful of minerals or mineral groups that show up in different combinations. If you can learn just ten of these, you'll be able to identify the minerals in most rocks you find. Full entries for each mineral on this list are marked with a star.

Feldspar (plagioclase and alkali) Feldspar is usually blocky and white or grayish, and it's present in nearly every rock on Earth. It can leave a light scratch on glass or steel and doesn't fizz in acid. Feldspar cleavage can create stair-steps on a broken face (see page 43–46).

Quartz Quartz is usually clear. It has no cleavage, but breaks with a conchoidal fracture. It can easily scratch glass or steel and doesn't fizz in acid. As a component of an igneous, sedimentary, or metamorphic rock, it commonly appears as a round or amorphous gray-tinged bleb with a glassy to greasy luster (see page 48).

Pyroxene (clino- and ortho-pyroxene) Commonly black or dark brown with a squat, boxy shape and stair-step cleavage. Found mostly in igneous and high-grade metamorphic rocks (see page 74–76).

Amphibole (hornblende) Commonly black or dark brown with an elongate prismatic shape that makes a diamond in cross section. Cleavage planes also come together in a diamond shape. Found in igneous and moderate- to high-grade metamorphic rocks (see page 70).

Mica (biotite and muscovite) Shiny, bendable flakes found mostly in igneous and metamorphic rocks. Perfect crystals have a flat hexagonal shape. Biotite is dark brown to black, while muscovite is silver-white. Flakes may also be found in sand and sandstone (see page 61–62).

Calcite White or clear blocky mineral that cannot scratch glass or steel but does fizz in acid. It has a rhombohedral growth habit and rhombohedral cleavage, though it usually grows in a massive form (such as in veins) or as microscopic crystals in sedimentary rock (limestone, calcareous sandstone) (see page 102).

Hematite An iron oxide, or a mineral form of rust. Visible crystals are uncommon but many red rocks get their color from microscopic hematite. It can form in a weathering rind on an iron-rich rock, or it may color a rock all the way through, as seen in iron-rich sedimentary and volcanic rocks that formed on Earth's surface in the presence of oxygen (see page 98).

Chlorite A green, brittle mica responsible for the coloration of most green rocks. Crystals may be visible or microscopic. Chlorite is a metamorphic mineral found in iron-rich rocks (see page 62).

Clay minerals Individual crystals are microscopic, but clays are the major component of mud and therefore also of mudstone. Usually black, brown, red, tan, or white (see page 66).

Zeolites These are famous for their white, fuzzy, cotton-ball appearance, though few actually feel fuzzy. Most easily spotted as a white mineral filling in a void or cavity, often with a radial fibrous form. Other zeolite group minerals may have tabular, blocky, or rounded forms (see page 54–60).

Silicate Structures

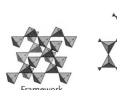
Framework

Sheet

Ring

Double Chain

Single Chain

Doublet

Isolated

SILICATES

Silicate minerals make up 92 percent of all minerals in the Earth's crust. They are by far the most diverse and scientifically important mineral class. Most rock-forming minerals—those that make up the bulk of almost every rock you'll ever see—are silicates. They are often very helpful in deciphering the history of a rock.

A silicate is any mineral that includes silicon (Si) and oxygen (O) atoms combined in a formation called a silicon tetrahedron. The tetrahedron is like a three-sided pyramid with an oxygen atom at each corner and a silicon atom nestled in the center.

The silicon tetrahedron is a silicate mineral's most important building block. It can bond with other atoms or other tetrahedra at each corner. In some minerals, the tetrahedra link up with one another to form frameworks, sheets, rings, chains,

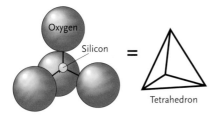

A silicon tetrahedron, the basic building block of all silicate minerals

or doublets that determine the mineral's overall shape and other properties. Many silicates also incorporate aluminum tetrahedra into critical parts of their structures; these make up a subgroup called aluminosilicates.

FRAMEWORK SILICATES

In these minerals, the tetrahedra connect to form a variety of three-dimensional frameworks or scaffolds that house other atoms—chiefly calcium, sodium, and potassium—within.

Framework

FELDSPAR GROUP

Feldspar minerals make up over half of Earth's crust. Any given rock you pick up will almost certainly have feldspar in it, usually as white, blocky chunks, though sometimes the crystals may be too small to see.

The feldspars are unified by having similar atomic frameworks, but differ in their chemical compositions. In other words, feldspars are like ice cream—one dessert that comes in many flavors. Each "flavor" of feldspar forms under different conditions.

Plagioclase Feldspar ★

(Ca,Na)(Si,Al)$_4$O$_8$

VERY COMMON

Habit Tabular euhedral crystals with rectangular cross section; lengthwise striations common; anhedral grains

Hardness 6–6.5

Luster Vitreous to pearly

Cleavage or Fracture Two cleavage planes intersect at around 93 degrees

Color White and gray most common, sometimes with a greenish cast; gem varieties are yellow, reddish, blue

Streak White

Identification A white-colored mineral in any rock you pick up, whether igneous, sedimentary, or metamorphic, is likely to be a plagioclase feldspar. Usually as tabular to blocky crystals, but also slender and elongated or as anhedral grains. Commonly has striations. Differentiated from quartz by presence of cleavage; from calcite by hardness (can scratch glass) and different angles of cleavage. White zeolite minerals that infill vugs (cavities) within basalt and andesite may at first be taken for feldspars, but closer inspection reveals that zeolite minerals are secondary growth, not a primary component of the rock. Differentiated from alkali feldspar by striations if present, sometimes color, and occurrence.

Members or Varieties Calcium-rich plagioclase is the mineral **anorthite**; the sodium-rich member is **albite**. Most plagioclase has an intermediate mix of calcium and sodium, and some of these compositions are also given names (**oligoclase, andesine, labradorite,** and **bytownite**). Some labradorite has an iridescent blue flash and is used as a lapidary (gem) material. Gem-quality labradorite in Oregon is different—the transparent yellow to red (and rarely green) variety **sunstone**.

White plagioclase crystals in porphyritic basalt. Note their overall rectangular shape.

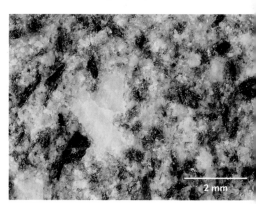

Irregular white plagioclase mass in diorite

Rectangular plagioclase with stair-step cleavage and quartz inclusion in granite

Sunstone, a yellow-pink gem plagioclase, in basalt matrix

More Info In igneous rocks, labradorite (and sunstone) is found in basalt and gabbro; andesine in andesite and diorite; and oligoclase and albite in granitic rocks and rhyolite. In most metamorphic rocks, most plagioclase has compositions closer to albite than anorthite. All types can erode into grains to make up sandstones and conglomerates. Over time, exposed feldspars will chemically decompose into clays.

Powdered plagioclase is used in the manufacture of paint, plastics, glass, and other ceramics. Bright-white albite is used as the colorant in many types of powdered nondairy coffee creamer (listed as "sodium aluminosilicate").

Notable Localities Plagioclase is practically ubiquitous; it is found in nearly every major rock type apart from chemical or biological rocks, mudstones, and most peridotites. It is much more difficult to find a rock without plagioclase than one with it.

OREGON'S STATE GEM: SUNSTONE

Just shy of 17 million years ago, enormous basalt floods erupted from the Steens Mountain area in Oregon. This was the beginning of a series of eruptions that took place over the subsequent 10 million years and created the single most distinctive and widespread stack of rock formations in Oregon and Washington—the Columbia River Basalt Group.

Those first eruptions also coughed up large, champagne-yellow to red labradorite feldspar crystals known as sunstones. These crystals grew in an underground magma chamber for thousands of years before being carried up to the surface in the rush of basalt lavas. Their slow, underground growth allowed them to attain sizes up to 2 inches long.

The yellow, orange, and red colors of most sunstones come from copper inclusions. In some stones, there is enough copper that it's visible within the crystal as tiny platelets that flash in the sun. This flash is called aventurescence or schiller. Rarely, some sunstones are also green.

Sunstone is found in southern Oregon, most notably in the Rabbit Basin and Steens Mountain areas within the BR.

Schiller from copper flecks in sunstone

Carved and faceted sunstone gems

Alkali Feldspar ★

$(K,Na)AlSi_3O_8$

COMMON

Habit Tabular euhedral crystals with rectangular cross section; anhedral grains
Hardness 6–6.5
Luster Vitreous
Cleavage or Fracture Two planes intersect at around 90 degrees
Color White, gray, pink, tan, colorless, green; some with faint lighter- and darker-banded mottling on flat faces
Streak White
Identification Tabular to blocky crystals with approximately right-angle cleavage and hardness high enough to scratch glass. Similar physical properties as plagioclase feldspar, but lacking striations. Can be difficult to differentiate white alkali from white plagioclase. Pink, tan, clear, and teal-green colorations much more common in alkali than plagioclase (though colors other than white and clear are rare in the Northwest). Some alkali feldspars may have wiggly bands of light-and-dark mottling. All feldspars are differentiated from quartz by presence of cleavage and from calcite by high hardness and angles of cleavage.
Members or Varieties Potassium-rich alkali feldspar is called (creatively) **potassium feldspar** or **K-spar**, while sodium-rich feldspar is **albite**. Yes—the same albite as plagioclase feldspar. Albite is considered

part of the plagioclase system if it has a little calcium mixed with its sodium, but part of the alkali system if it's mixed with some potassium instead. Most alkali feldspars are intermediate in composition between albite and K-spar. Some varieties include **microcline**, commonly white, pink, or teal-green with or without wiggly mottling; **orthoclase**, commonly white, gray, or pink; and **sanidine**, usually white or colorless and transparent. In practice, all these varieties are often white, only distinguishable with microscopes or X-rays.

More Info Like plagioclase, alkali feldspars occur widely in many igneous, sedimentary, and metamorphic settings. In igneous rocks, microcline occurs in rocks that cooled underground (granites), orthoclase can be found in granitic rocks but also in volcanic rock that cooled on Earth's surface, and sanidine occurs in volcanic rocks (rhyolite) and shallow dikes. In metamorphic rocks, microcline and orthoclase are found in schists and gneisses. All can erode into grains making up sandstones and conglomerates. Over time, exposed feldspars will chemically decompose into clays.

Notable Localities OR: BM, near Lime (orthoclase); distributed in HLP (sanidine in rhyolite). **WA**: NC, Washington Pass (microcline); OKH, Sherman Pass (orthoclase).

Orthoclase crystals, Lime, Oregon

QUARTZ

Quartz's simple chemical formula—made from just silicon and oxygen—belies the complexities this mineral can attain.

2 mm

Clear quartz will appear as glassy gray to black blebs in a rock due to shadows from the surrounding minerals.

Quartz ★

SiO_2

VERY COMMON

Habit Large isolated crystals are usually six-sided, elongate with pointed termination. Also, drusy (as a layer of many small crystals). In rocks, as round, gray blebs; in veins, as white masses.

Hardness 7

Luster Vitreous

Cleavage or Fracture No cleavage; conchoidal fracture

Color Colorless and gray most common; may be any color

Streak White

Identification For isolated crystals, six-sided habit with pointed top, high hardness (can scratch glass), and conchoidal fracture are diagnostic. In veins, distinguished from calcite by hardness and lack of reaction to vinegar. In rocks like diorite, granite, and sandstone, rounded gray blebs are identifiable by hardness and lack of cleavage.

Members or Varieties Quartz has an enormous number of named varieties. Individual white or clear crystals are **rock quartz**. Crystals with iron impurities can be purple (**amethyst**) and those with aluminum impurities that have also been exposed to natural radiation are black (**smoky**). Note: Smoky quartz is not radioactive itself.

More Info Large quartz crystals can grow in a variety of mirror-twinned forms, some of which are found in Washington. The large, showy crystals that form in hydrothermal veins and granite pegmatites get lots of attention, but quartz is a critical mineral in many geologic settings. In igneous rocks, it is readily found in diorite, granite, andesite, dacite, and rhyolite; in metamorphic rocks, quartzite, slate, phyllite, schist, and gneiss; and in sedimentary rocks it's a major component of sandstones and conglomerates (not to mention beach sand).

Notable Localities OR: COR, Tillamook County (amethyst). **WA**: NC, Denny Mountain, Green Ridge (amethyst), Spruce Ridge, Mt. Si (twins), Washington Pass (smoky); many other localities statewide.

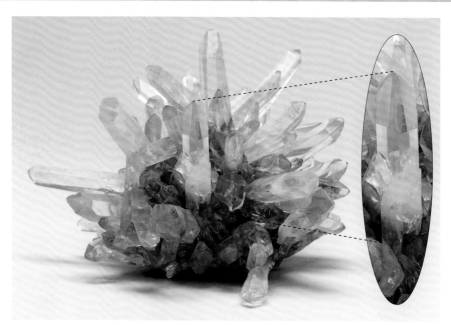

Cluster of clear quartz crystals from Spruce Ridge, Washington

Amethyst, a purple variety of quartz, from Green Ridge, Washington

Agate and Chalcedony

SiO$_2$

COMMON

Habit Microcrystalline aggregate fills cavities or coats surfaces; may be massive or banded; may contain other minerals as inclusions

Hardness 6.5–7

Luster Waxy

Cleavage or Fracture Conchoidal fracture

Color Any color; colorless, earthy reds, browns, yellows, greens, and gray-blues most common; thin pieces are translucent

Streak White; may be tinted from impurities if specimen is strongly colored

Identification Nodules, veins, or beach stones with a frosted, pitted, or waxy-looking exterior, conchoidal fracture, and high hardness (can scratch glass). Thin pieces translucent; can be mechanically polished to a high shine. See varieties for more description. Distinguished from the rocks chert and jasper by translucency; from opal by colors.

Members or Varieties Chalcedony is a massive form with no internal structures; it is usually colorless but can be any color. Agate has bands of color (**banded agate**), colorful inclusions of clay minerals (**plume** or **moss agate**), or inclusions of needle- or hair-like minerals (**sagenite agate**). Red-orange agate, whether banded or not, is called **carnelian**. Some agates retain small bubbles filled with water and gas, and the water can be seen to slosh around when the specimen is moved—these are informally called **enhydros**. Many other varieties are given local names by rockhounds in the regions where they are found.

More Info Agate and chalcedony form from silica-rich hydrothermal waters in underground veins and cavities. They are made from tiny, intergrown fibers of quartz and moganite. (Moganite has the same chemical

Agate nodule with "snakeskin" texture

Polished slab of plume agate, Homedale, Oregon

formula as quartz, but a slightly different atomic structure.) Completely pure specimens are clear like glass, but most contain microscopic impurities of other minerals like hematite. These impurities give agate and chalcedony a wide variety of beautiful colors.

Notable Localities OR: COR, near Vernonia (carnelian), beaches near river mouths; WV, near Trent (sagenite); BM, near Antelope, Maury Mountains; OWY, Leslie Gulch, Graveyard Point (plume). **WA:** OLY and COR, beaches, Salmon Creek; NC, near Ellensburg and Red Top Mountain (banded agate).

Carnelian agate geode with quartz crystals, Vernonia, Oregon

Polished "polka dot" agate with colorful iron impurities, Antelope, Oregon

Blue banded agate and drusy quartz in a cut and polished thunder egg, McDermitt, Oregon

JASPER

Jasper is a lapidary term, not a formal rock or mineral name. It's usually used to refer to colorful varieties of the rock type chert or a chalcedony with so many silica inclusions that it has been rendered opaque. The term has also been applied to other kinds of silicified rocks that can be cut and polished, including rhyolites and some sedimentary deposits.

Most jaspers are red, yellow, brown, or green, but some may contain colorful swirls, dots, circles, or other patterns. "Picture" and "fancy" jaspers have banding patterns that often resemble a landscape or another image when cut with a flat face. Jasper is also commonly found as rounded pebbles along rivers or beaches.

Notable Localities OR: COR, beaches; CB, Deschutes River; BM, near Prineville; OWY, Leslie Gulch, near McDermitt; distributed in CAS. **WA**: OLY, beaches; NC, near Liberty.

Green jasper (chert nodule with waxy broken face)

Picture jasper made from stained and silicified sediments, Antelope, Oregon

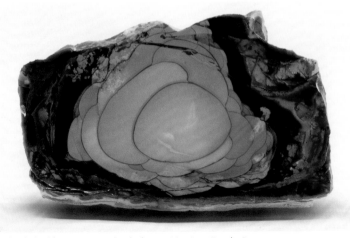

Cut and polished fancy jasper with orb shapes, Morrison Ranch, Oregon

Opal

SiO$_2$·nH$_2$O

COMMON

Habit Amorphous, fills cavities or coats surfaces
Hardness 5.5–6.5
Luster Waxy, greasy, vitreous
Cleavage or Fracture Conchoidal fracture
Color White, colorless; may be any color; may exhibit sparkly "play of color"; can be transparent or opaque
Streak White
Identification Bright white when opaque, water-clear when colorless, and tinted warm colors or rarely blue when transparent to translucent. Conchoidal fracture surface can appear jelly-like or have a wet-looking shine. In comparison, opaque chert or jasper are never bright white, and translucent colorless agate or chalcedony is usually a bit gray or has a frosted exterior. Thin layers of red-orange opal and thin layers of red-orange agate can be very difficult to tell apart.
Members or Varieties Common opal is white and opaque. **Hyalite** is clear and **fire opal** is translucent red, yellow, or orange. **Precious opal** can be any of the above colors, either clear or opaque, that also contains a play of color that flashes when the stone is turned in the light.
More Info Opal is an amorphous gel formed from stacked microscopic balls of silica bound together with water. Because it lacks a crystalline structure, it's technically not a mineral but a mineraloid. If it's made of balls of all different shapes and sizes (like pool balls, basketballs, and bouncy balls crammed into one box), it is white common opal. If the balls are all the same (like a box of ping-pong balls), the stacks cause incoming light to bend and create a play of color. Red tints in fire opal are caused by tiny iron oxide inclusions. Individual specimens can have several kinds of opal all together. Opal forms in hydrothermal systems, sometimes

Polished thunder egg with hyalite (clear), fire opal (orange), and common opal (white), Opal Butte, Oregon

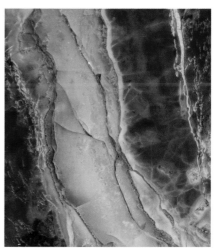

Precious opal demonstrating a play of color, Opal Butte, Oregon

associated with hot springs, and commonly interlayered with banded agate.

Notable Localities OR: BM, Opal Butte; distributed in CAS, BM, HLP, BR, OWY. **WA**: CB, near Whelan, near Spokane; distributed in CAS, CB.

ZEOLITE GROUP ★

Zeolites use their tetrahedra to build frameworks with cylindrical channels, similar to a bundle of straws. This structure allows zeolites to function as microscopic sponges and sieves. They are used by industry in myriad applications related to absorbing and filtering fluids, from odor-absorbent cat litter and fish tank filters to blood clotting powder used in treating traumatic injuries.

These widespread minerals form when water interacts with volcanic rocks, ash deposits, and other sediments at low to moderate temperatures. Over forty naturally occurring zeolite minerals exist. They commonly grow in small cavities and vugs (voids, like those created by gas bubbles) as fine-grained white aggregates that can be difficult to differentiate without microscopic study. Sometimes, though, individual crystals grow large enough to display distinct characteristics, and the more common ones are listed here.

Radiating fibrous zeolites in altered welded tuff, Haystack Reservoir, Oregon

White aggregates filling vesicles in basalt, a common way to find zeolites

Analcime

$NaAlSi_2O_6 \cdot H_2O$

COMMON

Habit Overall round form with flat crystal faces shaped like kites and squares
Hardness 5–5.5
Luster Vitreous
Cleavage or Fracture Poor cleavage
Color White, colorless; may be tinted by impurities; opaque to transparent
Streak White
Identification Analcime's crystal habit is characteristic. Differentiated from quartz, opal, and chalcedony by habit; from garnet by hardness (analcime may or may not scratch glass, and if so, only with difficulty, while garnet will scratch readily) and occurrence.

More Info Most commonly found with other zeolites in cavities within hydrothermally altered volcanic rocks and tuffs. Sometimes a primary mineral in igneous basalts.

Notable Localities OR: COR, near Kings Valley; BM, near Ritter. **WA**: PLO, near Tenino; OLY, near Porter.

Cluster of white analcime crystals with red hematite coating, Tenino, Washington

Chabazite

$(Ca,Na_2,K_2,Sr,Mg)(Al_2Si_4O_{12}) \cdot 6H_2O$

UNCOMMON

Habit Rhombohedral, distorted cubes
Hardness 3–5
Luster Vitreous
Cleavage or Fracture Imperfect cleavage planes form rhombohedral shapes
Color Colorless, white; also yellow, red, green, brown; usually opaque
Streak White
Identification Rhombohedral or distorted cubic crystals, usually opaque.

Distinguished from calcite and other carbonates by not fizzing in vinegar, even if powdered.

More Info Most commonly found with other zeolites in cavities within hydrothermally altered volcanic rocks and tuffs; also in some granitic and metamorphic rocks.

Notable Localities OR: COR, near Goble; CAS, near Springfield; BM, near Copperfield. **WA:** COR, near Oakville; distributed in CAS, NC, OKH.

White distorted cubes of chabazite, Goble, Oregon

Heulandite

$CaAl_2Si_7O_{18}·6H_2O$

COMMON

Habit Platy, coffin-shaped crystals, often curved on the large flat face; may also be pointed or blocky

Hardness 3.5–4

Luster Pearly on large flat faces, vitreous on others

Cleavage or Fracture One perfect cleavage parallel to large flat face

Color Colorless, white; also pink

Streak White

Identification Pearly luster, perfect cleavage, and flat to curved coffin-shaped crystals are characteristic. Distinguished from stilbite by careful observations of crystal habit.

More Info One of the most common zeolites, found in altered volcanic rocks, tuffs, low-temperature metamorphic rocks, and deep-sea sediments. Visible crystals usually in cavities within hydrothermally altered basalts and andesites.

Notable Localities OR: distributed in COR, WV, CAS, BM. **WA**: PLO, near Tenino; distributed in COR, OLY, CAS, especially near Mt. Saint Helens.

Group of salmon-colored, curved heulandite crystals, Dog Mountain, Washington

Mesolite

$Na_2Ca_2Al_6Si_9O_{30}·8H_2O$

COMMON

Habit Needle- to hair-like slender elongate prisms; radiating groups; compact masses
Hardness 5
Luster Vitreous, silky
Cleavage or Fracture Perfect length-parallel cleavage
Color Colorless, white; also pink, yellowish
Streak White

Identification Tufts of hair-like crystals and radiating aggregates of needles or prisms are characteristic. Crystals differentiated from natrolite by a lack of lengthwise striations. Note, however, that many zeolites not discussed in this book form in radiating fibrous or prismatic aggregates, and definitive identification is difficult without microscopic study.

More Info Most common in basaltic rocks; also found in andesites and hydrothermal veins.

Notable Localities OR: COR, near Goble; distributed in CAS, BM. **WA**: PLO, Skookumchuck Dam; distributed in OLY, COR.

Fans of prismatic mesolite, Tenino, Washington

Natrolite

$Na_2Al_2Si_3O_{10}\cdot2H_2O$

COMMON

Habit Rigid, slender needles or prisms with length-parallel striations; radiating groups
Hardness 5–5.5
Luster Vitreous, silky
Cleavage or Fracture One perfect cleavage is length-parallel
Color White, colorless, pink, gray, yellow, green, brown
Streak White
Identification Radiating aggregates of rigid needles or prisms with length-wise striations are characteristic. Prisms differentiated from mesolite by presence of striations. Note that many zeolites not discussed in this volume form in radiating needle-like or prismatic aggregates, and definitive identification is difficult without microscopic study.

More Info Found in altered volcanic rocks low in silica, especially basalt and pillow basalt. Rarely found in volcanic ash deposits.

Notable Localities OR: distributed in CAS especially near Springfield; BM, near Monument. **WA**: COR, near Doty Hills; distributed in OLY, CAS.

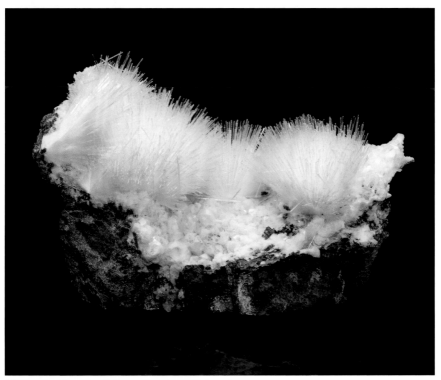

Fibrous natrolite on basalt, Dayton, Washington

Stilbite

$NaCa_4(Si_{27}Al_9)O_{72} \cdot 28H_2O$

COMMON

Habit Tabular with pointed or flat ends; crystals commonly fan in a bow-tie shape
Hardness 3.5–4
Luster Vitreous, pearly
Cleavage or Fracture Perfect length-parallel cleavage
Color White, colorless; also yellow, pink, red, green, brown, blue, black
Streak White

Identification Tabular habit, usually with a pointed termination and an end slightly wider than the base, is characteristic. Doubly terminated crystals may grow in a bow-tie shape. Distinguished from heulandite by careful observation of crystal habit.

More Info Very commonly found in cavities within altered basalts.

Notable Localities OR: COR, near Goble; CAS, near Ashland; distributed in BM. **WA**: PLO, Skookumchuck Dam; distributed in COR, OLY, NC, CAS, especially Poison Creek near Mt. Saint Helens.

Bow tie stilbite crystals, Ashland, Oregon

SHEET SILICATES

In this category, the silicon tetrahedra join together into sheets. These sheets stack on one another with layers of other atoms, for example, magnesium and potassium, sandwiched in between.

Sheet

Each sheet is strong, but the connection between the sheets is less so. This results in minerals that grow in flat, scaly, platy, or thin tabular habits, many of which stack together in books and cleave apart easily into thinner sheets.

However, as the dark micas annite, phlogopite, and others can only be distinguished through microscopic or chemical analysis, *biotite* is still a useful and widely used term.

More Info Forms in a wide variety of rocks, especially igneous granite, diorite, rhyolite, dacite, and andesite, and metamorphic schist and gneiss. Occasionally found as grains in sandstones. The potassium in biotite can be used by scientists to determine how old a rock is through the process of radiometric dating.

Notable Localities OR: distributed in KM, BM, CAS, BR, HLP, OWY. **WA**: CAS, OKH, NC, especially Gunn Peak and near Chelan (biotite gneiss).

Biotite ★

$K(Fe,Mg)_3AlSi_3O_{10}(OH)_2$

VERY COMMON

Habit Flat flakes with hexagonal or rhombic shapes; also irregular scales or stacked in large books

Hardness 2.5–3

Luster Vitreous to submetallic

Cleavage or Fracture One perfect cleavage makes flexible, elastic sheets

Color Black, dark brown, green; also light golden brown

Streak White

Identification Dark color, habit, and cleavage are diagnostic. Mica books are distinguished from other dark-colored minerals like hornblende and tourmaline by cleavage and flexibility. Shiny, light-brown flakes can sometimes resemble gold flecks, but biotite sheets will fracture or crumble if pressed with a knife blade while gold flecks will separate, indent, or bend.

Members or Varieties Technically, *biotite* is a field term for any dark mica and is no longer a formally recognized mineral name.

Mass of biotite from Washington

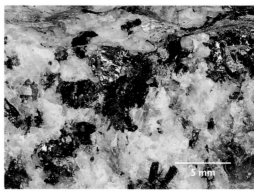

Biotite in granodiorite, Wallowa Mountains, Oregon

Muscovite ★

$KAl_3Si_3O_{10}(OH)_2$

VERY COMMON

Habit Flat flakes with hexagonal or rhombic shapes; also stacked in books or as fine aggregates

Hardness 2–3.5

Luster Vitreous, pearly, submetallic

Cleavage or Fracture One perfect cleavage makes flexible, elastic sheets

Color Silver-white, light yellow, green, pink

Streak White

Identification Light color, habit, luster, and cleavage are diagnostic. Talc is much softer, pearlier and usually found in masses. Light yellow muscovite can sometimes resemble gold flecks, but muscovite sheets will fracture or crumble if pressed with a knife blade while gold flecks will separate, indent, or bend.

Members or Varieties Very fine-grained masses of white mica are known as **sericite**. They are used to make shimmer effects in makeup products.

More Info Forms in a wide variety of rocks, especially igneous granite, diorite, rhyolite, dacite, and andesite, and

Books of muscovite from a pegmatite pocket, Leavenworth, Washington

metamorphic phyllite and schist. Occasionally found as grains in sandstones. The potassium in muscovite can be used by scientists to determine how old a rock is through the process of radiometric dating.

Notable Localities OR: distributed in KM, BM, CAS, OWY. **WA**: NC, Tunnel Creek, Gunn Peak; OKH, Sherman Creek, Mt. Mica.

Chlorite Group ★

$(Mg,Fe,Mn,Al)_6(Si,Al)_4O_{10}(OH)_8$

VERY COMMON

Habit Platy or tabular crystals; granular and massive aggregates

Hardness 2–3

Luster Adamantine, pearly

Cleavage or Fracture One perfect cleavage makes flakes or sheets that are flexible but brittle

Color Green, black; also yellow, red, brown

Streak Green, gray, white; also yellow, red, brown

Identification Visible crystals are uncommon; usually found as fine-grained aggregates that replace iron- and magnesium-rich minerals under certain metamorphic conditions (making the green color of metamorphic greenstones). Distinguished from granular epidote and nephrite by hardness and sometimes differences in green color; from massive serpentine by lack of waxy feel; from talc by lack of slippery feel.

More Info Chlorite is typical in igneous basalt, andesite, gabbro, and diorite rocks that have been metamorphosed at low-moderate pressures and temperatures, or moderate temperatures in the presence of water. In coarse-grained rocks, the chlorite may fill in the shape of the original iron- or magnesium-rich mineral it has replaced,

5 cm

Chlorite makes up the mass of this greenschist rock from Washington. Note that stacked flat crystals make a rock with an overall flat shape.

leading to green, scruffy-looking pyroxenes and amphiboles. A quick hardness test will show that the present mineral is actually chlorite. Chlorite overprinting can also occur in metamorphic rocks that form deep beneath the surface at high pressure or high temperature, then rise closer to Earth's surface and encounter water. This can turn what were once garnets soft and green, too.

Notable Localities Visible chlorite crystals are uncommon. The vast majority exist as aggregates in greenstones and greenschists. **OR:** distributed in KM, BM. **WA:** distributed in NC.

Book of chlorite crystals with partial hexagonal shape on matrix, Whatcom County, Washington

Serpentine Group

$Mg_3Si_2O_5(OH)_4$

UNCOMMON

Habit Platy, fibrous, or granular masses that are often curved and slick to the touch; visible crystals rare

Hardness 2.5–5.5 (<4 most common)

Luster Waxy, dull

Cleavage or Fracture One perfect cleavage

Color Green; also yellow, blue, brown, black

Streak White

Identification Masses are very distinctive with a waxy feel and curved platy or compact fibrous crystal shapes. Some masses may also be granular, and some may contain flexible, friable fibers. Distinguished from talc by color, waxy rather than soapy feel, and hardness (serpentine not usually scratched by fingernails); from chlorite by feel; and from nephrite jade by hardness (serpentine can't scratch glass). In some metamorphic rocks with multiple minerals including serpentine, the serpentine looks like a green-white mold on a freshly broken surface.

Members or Varieties Three types based on differences in microscopic structures. **Antigorite** and **lizardite** grow in granular, platy, or compact fibrous masses, while **chrysotile** grows in flexible, friable fibers. Chrysotile is an asbestos form of the mineral. (See amphibole section for more information about asbestos minerals.)

More Info Serpentine is a metamorphic mineral; unusually, however, it's created by rocks coming up instead of going down. It forms when olivine- and pyroxene-bearing peridotites from Earth's mantle are thrust up through the crust and onto the surface, encountering and reacting with water along the way. It signifies settings that have seen large-scale tectonic events, including rifting and collisions.

Close up of fibrous habit in a mass of serpentine, Cave Junction, Oregon

Serpentine rock (serpentinite) in outcrop, Liberty, Washington

Hazard Variety chrysotile is an asbestos. Do not inhale.

Notable Localities OR: BM, Elkhorn Range, Greenhorn Mountains; KM, Cave Junction, Gold Beach, Snow Camp, Agness. **WA**: NC, Twin Sisters area, Mt. Stuart area; distributed in OKH.

Talc

$Mg_3Si_4O_{10}(OH)_2$

UNCOMMON

Habit Fine-grained or scaly masses
Hardness 1
Luster Pearly, waxy
Cleavage or Fracture One perfect cleavage makes flexible, inelastic sheets
Color White, colorless; green, yellow, brown
Streak White
Identification Light-colored, fine-grained masses with a soapy feel that can be scratched with a fingernail. Distinguished

from serpentinite by color, hardness, and soapy rather than waxy feel; from chlorite by feel and hardness (chlorite crystals not usually scratched with a fingernail); from clays by luster, feel, and occurrence.

Members or Varieties Mixes of talc and other minerals are sometimes called **soapstone** for their slick feel.

More Info A metamorphic mineral that forms when peridotites from Earth's mantle are thrust up through the crust and onto the surface, encountering water along the way. Commonly found with serpentine, chlorite, or tremolite-actinolite in veins, along faults, or at contacts between two different rock types.

Hazard Does not pose a hazard on its own, but commonly intergrows with microscopic fibers of asbestos minerals (friable, fibrous actinolite and serpentine). Do not inhale.

Notable Localities OR: distributed in KM, especially Elliott Creek Ridge area; BM, Sumpter area. **WA**: NC, Wenatchee Ridge, Quartz Creek.

5 cm

Mass of white-gray talc with green actinolite, Wenatchee Ridge, Washington

Clay Minerals ★

Hydrous aluminosilicates with sheeted structures

VERY COMMON

Habit Crystals are irregular sheets rarely visible to the eye; usually found as aggregate masses, in layers, or as a major component of soils

Hardness <2

Luster Masses are dull, earthy

Cleavage or Fracture One perfect cleavage makes flakes or sheets

Color White, red, gray, brown, black; color may come from oxide mineral inclusions

Streak Same color as aggregate

Identification In sedimentary rocks, clays are fine-grained aggregates that make finely bedded layers of shale and slate.

Members or Varieties Dozens of clay minerals exist. Some prominent members are **kaolinite**, a powdery clay that becomes plasticky when wet; **illite**, also powdery, with little swelling or stickiness when wet; and **smectite** and **vermiculite**, which both have high swelling and stickiness when wet.

More Info Clays form from the chemical weathering of rocks, usually from air and water interacting with feldspars and micas. There are many different clay minerals with a wide variety of complex chemical formulas, but they can generally be described as sheeted silicates containing aluminum and water molecules. This structure is responsible for properties like slipperiness and ability to hold free water.

Clays are a critical component of soils, and clay types help determine soil behavior. For instance, soils high in smectite hold on to water strongly and have the classic, sticky clay feel, while soils high in illite are more granular. Soil compositions are very specific to regions, depending on the rocks the soils started from and the regional weather and plant activity. Many soil types are given names. Oregon even has a state soil, called Jory soil, renowned for its agricultural productivity (especially in vineyards).

Notable Localities Kaolinite clays have been mined from deposits in **OR**: WV, BR, and BM, and from **WA**: CAS, NC, OKH, and CB. Clays in general are found almost everywhere, either as thin surficial coatings, components of soil and sediment, or components of sedimentary rocks.

5 cm

Clays make up the tan matrix of the paleosol (fossil soil) containing this root fossil from Oregon.

Pentagonite and Cavansite

$Ca(VO)Si_4O_{10} \cdot 4H_2O$

RARE

Habit Prismatic and platy crystals in radiating aggregates
Hardness 3–4
Luster Vitreous
Cleavage or Fracture Good, length-parallel cleavage
Color Blue
Streak Light blue
Identification Blue, radiating aggregates are characteristic. Cavansite makes tighter ball forms while pentagonite aggregates are spikier with more blade-like crystals. Most aggregate clusters are less than half a centimeter across.

More Info These minerals have the same chemical formula, but have slightly different atomic structures, which accounts for the different habits. They were first discovered at the Owyhee Dam area in Oregon at an outcrop that no longer exists.
Notable Localities OR: OWY, Owyhee Dam; COR, near Goble.

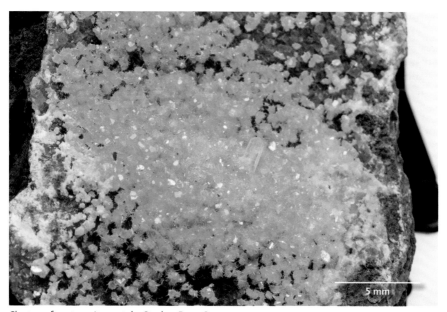

Clusters of pentagonite crystals, Owyhee Dam, Oregon

RING SILICATES

Ring

In this category, groups of silicon tetrahedra are arranged into rings that stack up on one another with unusual elements like beryllium and boron tucked away inside. Ring silicate minerals tend to grow in pegmatites, very coarse-grained granites that form from magmas rich in silicon and water, and some metamorphic rocks.

Tourmaline Group

$Na(Mg, Fe)_3Al_6(BO_3)_3Si_6O_{18}(OH)_4$

UNCOMMON

Habit Stubby to elongate prisms with rounded triangular cross sections; lengthwise striations

Hardness 7–7.5

Luster Vitreous

Cleavage or Fracture No cleavage

Dravite tourmaline crystal, Leavenworth, Washington

Fibrous luinaite tourmaline (type of schorl) showing characteristic triangular cross section, King County, Washington

Color Black, brown, dark green-blue; many other colors (see member details)

Streak Pale brown to gray or bluish-white (see member details)

Identification Habit and hardness are characteristic. Distinguished from amphiboles and pyroxenes by cross-section shape and lack of cleavage; from stibnite by luster, hardness, and streak.

Members or Varieties Tourmalines have complex chemistry and can substitute several atomic ingredients for others, leading to over ten different tourmaline minerals. The two most common are **dravite**, a magnesium-rich version that is black or brown with a pale brown to gray streak, and **schorl**, an iron-rich version that is black, brown, or dark green-blue with a gray to bluish-white streak. Other vibrant pink and green tourmaline varieties like **elbaite** exist worldwide, but virtually none are known within the Pacific Northwest.

More Info Found in igneous granite pegmatites, metamorphic phyllites, schists, gneisses, and hydrothermal quartz veins. Primarily used as a decorative stone.

Notable Localities WA: NC, near North Bend, Cannon Mountain; OKH, near Chewelah, one pocket of elbaite tourmaline reported near Sherman Pass.

Beryl

$Be_3Al_2Si_6O_{18}$

RARE

Habit Hexagonal prismatic crystals with flat terminations

Hardness 7.5–8

Luster Vitreous

Cleavage or Fracture Poor

Color Tan or cream, pale green, or blue most common; also yellow, pink, colorless; opaque to transparent

Streak White

Incomplete blue-green beryl crystal on matrix, Chewelah, Washington

Identification Hexagonal habit and high hardness (will scratch glass or steel) are characteristic. Differentiated from quartz by flat, rather than pointed, termination, although some crystals may decrease in diameter along their lengths and resemble slightly kinked, hexagonal cones.

Members or Varieties Common beryl is light-colored and opaque. The blue transparent gem variety, present but rare in Washington, is **aquamarine**; it gets its color from iron impurities. Other varieties, colored by other impurities, include **emerald**, **morganite**, **heliodor**, and **goshenite**, though none of those are known within the region.

More Info Primarily in granite pegmatites associated with quartz, feldspars, and micas; very rarely in schists or hydrothermal veins. An ore of beryllium, which is used in specialized metal alloys for aircraft and satellites.

Notable Localities WA: NC, Tunk Creek, Icicle Creek; OKH, near Chewelah, South Baldy Mountain

CHAIN SILICATES

In this category, silicon tetrahedra join together in long chains stacked together like bundled pencils, with other atoms—primarily iron, magnesium, calcium, and aluminum—placed among them. Chain silicate minerals tend to be prismatic and stubby to elongate—some as fine and long as hairs.

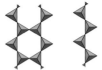
Double Chain   Single Chain

AMPHIBOLE GROUP

In amphiboles, the chains of silicon tetrahedra run together in pairs. These double chains create long crystals with a wide diamond-shaped cross section. (Sometimes the edges of the crystals are modified and the cross section looks like a squashed hexagon or octagon.)

All amphiboles have the same cleavage: two planes running parallel to the long direction of the crystal, intersecting at 56 and 124 degrees. This creates diamond-shaped cross sections on cleaved crystals.

Sometimes, instead of diamond-shaped prisms, amphiboles grow in bunches or seams of friable fibers (fibers that can be pulled apart). These are the asbestos form of the mineral group. Yes—that asbestos. Asbestiform amphiboles are safe to handle and look at, but do not inhale fibers or mineral dust from an outcrop with visible fibers.

Amphiboles are geologic thermometers. Scientists can analyze amphibole types and the specific chemistry of individual crystals to determine the temperature at which those crystals formed. This helps us understand conditions deep within the Earth, far beyond depths we are able to drill.

Hornblende ★

$Ca_2(Fe,Mg)_4(FeAl_2)(Si_7,Al)O_{22}(OH,F)_2$

VERY COMMON

Habit Elongate prism with diamond or octagonal cross section; needle-like

Hardness 5–6

Luster Vitreous

Cleavage or Fracture Two length-parallel cleavage planes at 56 and 124 degrees make diamond shapes

Color Green or brown darkening to almost black

Streak White

Identification A dark-colored, elongate mineral with a diamond-shaped cross section and diamond-shaped cleavage. Distinguished from pyroxenes by cleavage angle; from tourmalines by cross-section shape and cleavage. Distinguished from other amphiboles by color and occurrence.

Members or Varieties There are many dark-colored amphibole minerals, but they are only definitively distinguished by microscopic or chemical analysis. *Hornblende* is therefore both a mineral in its own right and a category or catch-all term for dark amphiboles. One other important dark amphibole in Washington is **arfvedsonite**, which can be found in the Golden Horn Batholith at Washington Pass.

More Info A rock-forming mineral in the full suite of igneous rocks, including basalt, andesite, dacite, rhyolite, gabbro, diorite, and granite. Most common in andesite, dacite, and diorite. Also a major component of metamorphic amphibolite schists and some gneisses, which are associated with moderate to high pressures and temperatures.

Notable Localities OR: distributed in KM, CAS, BM. **WA:** distributed in CAS, NC, OKH.

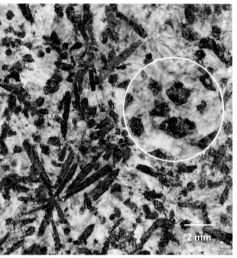

Hornblende in diorite from Oregon (note the long black crystals as well as those oriented end-on showing a modified pseudohexagonal shape)

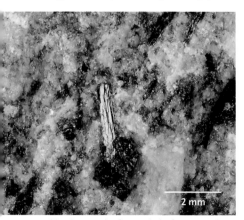

Hornblende crystal reflecting light from one of its two cleavage directions, Klamath Mountains, Oregon

Tremolite-Actinolite

$Ca_2(Mg,Fe)_5Si_8O_{22}(OH)_2$

COMMON

Habit Bladed crystals or prismatic with diamond cross section; aggregates of bundled or radiating crystals; botryoidal; also fibrous, matted

Hardness 5–6

Luster Vitreous, silky if fibrous, waxy if massive

Cleavage or Fracture Two cleavage planes at 56 and 124 degrees make diamond shapes

Color White, gray, green to dark green; also colorless, lavender; very thin pieces are translucent

Streak White

Identification A white to green elongate mineral with a diamond-shaped cross section and diamond-shaped cleavage. Distinguished from pyroxenes by cleavage angle; from tourmaline and prismatic epidote by cross-section shape and cleavage. Distinguished from other amphiboles by color and occurrence. Can also grow as brittle fibers. Botryoidal habit is possible.

Botryoidal nephrite, Darrington, Washington

2 cm

Mass of parallel, elongate actinolite crystals from Washington

Members or Varieties Nephrite jade is a mass of matted tremolite-actinolite fibers. The fibers are too small to be visible, so they present as a massive or botryoidal stone with a mottled green to white color. Friable fibrous tremolite-actinolite, called **byssolite**, is an asbestos.

More Info Tremolite and actinolite are two ends of a compositional spectrum. Tremolite is magnesium-rich and usually white or very light green, while actinolite is iron-rich and dark green. Most specimens fall somewhere between these end members—a good rule of thumb is that the darker the mineral, the higher the iron content. They are a hallmark of metamorphic rocks; actinolite can be one of the "greens" in greenschists, and tremolite is found in metamorphosed peridotites and siliceous carbonates.

Hazard Friable byssolite is an asbestos. Do not inhale.

Notable Localities OR: distributed in KM (tremolite and actinolite). **WA**: distributed in NC (tremolite), near Darrington (nephrite); distributed in OKH (tremolite), Wenatchee Ridge (actinolite); distributed in OKH (actinolite).

Glaucophane-Riebeckite

$Na_2(Mg,Fe)_3(Al,Fe)_2Si_8O_{22}(OH)_2$

UNCOMMON

Habit Elongate prismatic, bladed; fibrous, massive; may have length-parallel striations

Hardness 5–6

Luster Vitreous, silky if fibrous

Cleavage or Fracture Two cleavage planes at 56 and 124 degrees make diamond shapes

Color Gray, light blue to blue-black

Streak Gray to bluish, lavender, blue-black

Identification Crystals gray to blue, elongate with a diamond-shaped cross section and diamond-shaped cleavage. Distinguished from pyroxenes and feldspars by cleavage angle. Distinguished from other amphiboles by color and occurrence. Can also grow as brittle fibers.

Dark blue glaucophane crystals in schist, Rhoda Creek, Oregon

Members or Varieties Fibrous form, when infiltrated by silica, is polished and sold as **blue tiger's eye**.

More Info Glaucophane and riebeckite share the same chemical relationship as tremolite and actinolite. Glaucophane, the magnesium-rich member, is the blue in blueschist and a hallmark mineral of subduction-zone metamorphism. Riebeckite, the iron-rich member, is a primarily igneous mineral found in rocks with moderate to low iron content.

Hazard Friable fibrous form of glaucophane-riebeckite is an asbestos. Do not inhale.

Notable Localities Glaucophane is found in isolated blueschist blocks in **OR**: KM; BM and **WA**: NC. Riebeckite is found in **WA**: NC, at Washington Pass.

Mass of blue amphiboles with mica in blueschist, Bandon, Oregon

PYROXENE GROUP

In pyroxenes, the chains of silicon tetrahedra are single strands. This creates crystals of stubby to elongate prisms with square to rectangular cross sections.

All pyroxenes have two cleavage planes running parallel to the long direction of the crystal and intersecting at 87 and 93 degrees (almost right angles). This creates square-shaped cross sections or rectangular stair-steps on cleaved crystals.

In addition to being important components of Earth rocks, pyroxenes are also found in meteorites and rocks from the Moon.

Clinopyroxene ★

$(Ca,Mg,Fe)_2Si_2O_6$

VERY COMMON

Habit Stubby prisms, tabular crystals, rounded anhedral grains; prisms may appear to be leaning
Hardness 5.5–6.5
Luster Vitreous
Cleavage or Fracture Two cleavage planes intersecting at 87 and 93 degrees make square shapes in cross section
Color Generally green to dark green; also brown, black (see member details)
Streak Generally greenish; also pale brown, white (see member details)
Identification Usually dark, greenish, stubby prismatic to tabular crystals with square cross sections and right-angle, stair-step cleavage. Differentiated from orthopyroxenes by streak (clino usually greenish, ortho usually pale brown); from amphiboles by cleavage.
Members or Varieties Clinopyroxene is a group of several distinct minerals, but the minerals have similar physical characteristics and can be difficult to differentiate without microscopic or chemical analysis. Important group members include **augite**, which is green to brown to black with a pale brown to greenish-gray streak; **diopside**, which is pale to dark green with a green to white streak; and **hedenbergite**, which is green to brownish-green to black with a pale green to tan streak.
More Info Clinopyroxenes are important components of igneous and metamorphic rocks. Augite is a rock-forming mineral in

Single crystals of augite, Tillamook, Oregon

1 cm

Clinopyroxenes, Fidalgo Island, Washington

1 cm

Cluster of hedenbergite crystals from Washington

igneous basalts and gabbros, as well as some andesites and diorites. It may also occur in high-grade metamorphic gneisses. Diopside and hedenbergite are more commonly found in metamorphic rocks, especially skarns (zones where calcium-rich carbonates and silicates have been heated and infiltrated by water).

Notable Localities OR: COR, Cedar Butte in Tillamook County (augite). **WA**: NC, Vesper Peak (hedenbergite and diopside).

Orthopyroxene ★

$(Mg,Fe)_2Si_2O_6$

VERY COMMON

Habit Short rectangular prisms, rounded anhedral grains

Hardness 5–6

Luster Vitreous; submetallic to dull

Cleavage or Fracture Two cleavage planes at 87 and 93 degrees make square shapes in cross section

Color Pale yellow to green, brown, black, gray, colorless (see member details)

Streak Pale brown, gray, colorless (see member details)

Identification Usually dark, brownish, stubby prismatic to tabular crystals with square cross sections and right-angle, stair-step cleavage. Differentiated from clinopyroxenes by streak (ortho usually pale brown, clino usually greenish); from amphiboles by cleavage.

Members or Varieties Orthopyroxene is a group of several distinct minerals, but they have similar physical characteristics and can be difficult to differentiate without microscopic or chemical analysis. Important group members include **enstatite**, which is pale yellow-green, gray, or colorless with a pale brown, gray, or colorless streak, and **ferrosilite**, which is green or dark brown with a pale brown or gray streak.

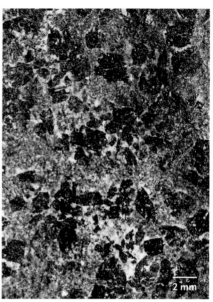

Black orthopyroxene in gabbro with white plagioclase feldspar and olivine from Washington

More Info A rock-forming mineral in igneous basalts and gabbros as well as some andesites and diorites. A major component of some peridotite rocks along with olivine. Also occurs in high-grade metamorphic gneisses. Found in meteorites and rocks from the Moon.

Notable Localities Very common rock constituent, but no notable specimen collecting localities in the area.

Omphacite

(Ca,Na)(Mg,Fe,Al)Si$_2$O$_6$

RARE

Habit Stubby prisms to aggregates of anhedral grains

Hardness 5–6

Luster Vitreous

Cleavage or Fracture Two cleavage planes intersecting at 87 and 93 degrees make square shapes in cross section

Color Green to dark green; opaque to translucent

Streak Light green, white

Identification Resembles other pyroxenes—stubby prisms with right-angle, stair-step cleavage—but is commonly a lighter/brighter green than other clinopyroxenes (though it cannot be identified through color alone). Commonly massive aggregates, individual crystals indistinct. Usually identified based on association with garnets in metamorphic eclogites.

More Info Found predominantly in eclogite, which forms from the metamorphism of basaltic rocks in subduction zones or the deep crust, greater than 25 miles beneath the surface.

Notable Localities OR: KM, near Powers and Roseburg (best-known outcrop now buried).

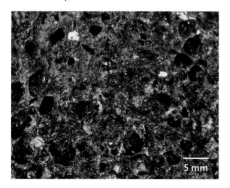

Green omphacite (individual crystals are indistinct) with red garnets in eclogite, Roseburg, Oregon

Rhodonite

MnSiO$_3$

UNCOMMON

Habit Granular, massive; rare visible crystals tabular to equant

Hardness 5.5–6.5

Luster Masses are dull; crystals vitreous

Cleavage or Fracture Two perfect cleavage planes intersecting at 92.5 degrees, uneven fracture

Color Pink or rose- to brown-red; commonly with black manganese veining

Streak White

Identification Pink masses with black manganese coating or veining are characteristic. Color is distinctive, but massive calcite and fluorite may also be pink; unlike them, rhodonite will scratch glass. It is opaque, while pink agate is translucent, and both agate and opal have conchoidal fracture instead of uneven.

More Info Forms with ores of manganese in metamorphic settings with much fluid circulation. Used primarily as a lapidary stone, cut into pendants or cabochons.

Notable Localities OR: KM, near Holland; distributed in BM. **WA**: distributed in OLY; NC, near Darrington; distributed in OKH.

Polished slab of massive rhodonite with black manganese oxide, Grants Pass, Oregon

OTHER SILICATES

In these minerals, the silicon tetrahedra are either joined in pairs or are entirely isolated from one another, with atoms of iron, magnesium, calcium, and aluminum bonding the tetrahedra together and making up more of each structure. These minerals are variable in their properties and appearance.

Doublet

Isolated

Epidote aggregate with fanned jackstraw habit, Baring, Washington

Epidote

$Ca_2Al_2FeSi_3O_{12}(OH)$

COMMON

Habit Granular masses or crusts; crystals prismatic, thick tabular, or needle-like, and may aggregate in a fan shape

Hardness 6–7

Luster Vitreous; some pearly to resinous

Cleavage or Fracture One perfect cleavage plane parallel to length

Color Green, yellow, gray, all grading to nearly black

Streak Colorless or grayish

Identification Epidote is famous for its pistachio green color, which commonly occurs when the mineral appears as granular aggregates within veins or pods. Large crystals are often dark green with striations. Distinguished from olivine and actinolite crystals by cleavage; from clino- and orthopyroxenes by cleavage and streak. Masses distinguished from nephrite by granular habit; from serpentine, chlorite, and talc by hardness (epidote can scratch glass) and habit.

More Info Associated with iron-rich rocks in both igneous (basalt) and metamorphic (greenstone) settings. Also found in veins and along fractures associated with hydrothermal alteration.

Granular epidote on basalt, Hells Canyon, Washington

Notable Localities OR: distributed in KM, BM. **WA**: distributed in NC, especially Denny Mountain and Sunset Falls; distributed in OKH.

Olivine Group

$(Mg,Fe)_2SiO_4$

UNCOMMON

Habit Rounded grains; short prismatic crystals
Hardness 6.5–7
Luster Vitreous, oily, submetallic
Cleavage or Fracture Poor cleavage, conchoidal fracture
Color Green; pale yellow-green to black
Streak White, grayish (may be darker with high iron content)
Identification Rounded green grains lacking cleavage are characteristic. Distinguished from epidote, pyroxenes, and amphiboles by lack of cleavage and exclusive occurrence in peridotite, gabbro, and basalt.
Members or Varieties The olivine group has two minerals, **forsterite** and **fayalite**. The former is magnesium-rich and usually lighter in color while the latter is iron-rich and usually darker, though both are simply called olivine in the field. The gem variety of any olivine is called **peridot**.
More Info Olivine is the most abundant mineral group *in* Earth, but it's hard to find *on* Earth. The layer below Earth's crust, the mantle, is mostly formed from olivine, and the mantle makes up over 80 percent of the Earth by volume. It's rare for mantle rocks to reach the surface, however (see peridotite rocks on page 137). Olivine also forms visible crystals in some basalts and, strikingly, in pallasite meteorites.
Notable Localities OR: KM, Chetco Lake (Josephine Ophiolite); OWY, in basalt of Diamond Craters. **WA:** NC, Twin Sisters Mountain (Twin Sisters Dunite); CAS, in basalt of Ape Caves near Mt. Saint Helens.

Garnet Group

$(Mg,Fe,Mn,Ca)_3(Fe,Al,Cr)_2(SiO_4)_3$

UNCOMMON

Habit Dodecahedral; overall round form with twelve crystal faces shaped like diamonds and kites
Hardness 7–7.5
Luster Vitreous
Cleavage or Fracture No cleavage, irregular or conchoidal fracture
Color Red, orange, brown, yellow, green, colorless
Streak White
Identification Dodecahedral habit is characteristic. In partly formed crystals, only the diamond or kite shape of a few adjacent faces may be visible. If on broken face of rock, will appear as a flat hexagon. Differentiated from analcime by hardness (garnet will scratch glass readily while analcime may or may

Round, green olivine crystal with white plagioclase in basalt from Oregon

Green uvarovite garnet from Washington

not scratch it, and if so, only with difficulty), and occurrence.

Members or Varieties Many minerals fall under the garnet umbrella, including almandine, spessartine, grossular, andradite, pyrope, and uvarovite. Usually, **almandine** (dark red-orange) is found in mica schists and gneisses; **spessartine** (dark red-orange) is rarely found in granitic rocks and rhyolite; **grossular** (any color), **andradite** (any color) and **uvarovite** (bright green) are associated with metamorphic skarns; and **pyrope** (dark red-orange) is found in eclogites and rarely in peridotites and serpentinite.

More Info The garnet varieties come from mixing and matching different amounts of the group's atomic ingredients. For example, pure almandine is only iron, aluminum, and a silicate group, while pure spessartine has manganese instead of iron. But many crystals grow with both iron and manganese, and so are a mix of almandine and spessartine. Many other combinations exist.

Garnets generally grow in extreme geological environments. For example, metamorphic garnets in schists have been buried beneath mountains and heated to temperatures over 1300°F, while those in eclogites have reached depths of over 25 miles below Earth's surface.

Notable Localities OR: KM, in blueschists near Bandon and other locations. **WA**: NC, in skarn at Vesper Peak, in skarn at Denny Mountain, uvarovite in chromite bands at Twin Sisters Mountain.

Grossular garnet cluster from a skarn, Vesper Peak, Washington

Red garnets in Skagit Gneiss from Washington

Staurolite

$Fe_2Al_9Si_4O_{23}(OH)$

RARE

Habit Stubby to elongate prisms sometimes twinned to form a cross shape

Hardness 7–7.5

Luster Vitreous to resinous

Cleavage or Fracture Fair cleavage is length-parallel

Color Brown, red-brown, colorless

Streak Gray, but may not streak due to high hardness

Identification Habit, color, and streak are characteristic. Twinned cross shape is diagnostic if present. Differentiated from amphiboles by cleavage and streak; from pyroxenes by cleavage and occurrence; from tourmalines by habit, lack of striations, and streak.

More Info Forms predominantly in metamorphic rocks, usually occurring as large individual crystals standing out within a mica schist. Grows from mudstones that were buried beneath mountains.

Notable Localities WA: distributed in NC; OKH, Wauconda Summit.

Brown prismatic staurolite crystals in a brown schist, Skykomish, Washington

NON-SILICATES

Though they comprise only 8 percent of the minerals in Earth's crust, many non-silicate minerals are economically valuable and useful for modern technology and society. Non-silicates, including calcite, pyrite, and gold, are any mineral that lacks the silicon tetrahedron building block that characterizes silicates.

NATIVE ELEMENTS

Gold, silver, copper—these are the minerals that form in nature from only a single atomic element. Many native elements are metals. Metallic minerals may grow as crystals with sharp edges and defined faces or as sheets, blebs, or branching wires, and it's common for them to blend together. For instance, all gold has some silver alloyed with it. Non-metallic native elements each have their own unique properties.

ORES

While metallic native-element crystals may grow large enough to see, they are more commonly disseminated as microscopic flecks within a rock body called an ore. An ore is simply any rock or mineral that is mined to extract a substance of interest. Ores can be recognized based on the minerals they contain. For instance, copper ores are generally associated with more complex copper-bearing minerals like chalcopyrite. The metal content of an ore is determined by a scientific test called an assay.

While significant industrial mining for metal ores in Oregon and Washington has largely ceased due to a combination of environmental regulations and global economics, the region still hosts notable reserves of copper, molybdenum, zinc, lead, mercury, uranium, gold, and silver in mineable ores.

Gold

Au

RARE

Habit Octahedral and dodecahedral crystals; also branching, foil, or wire forms; round or platy grains—and the rare wires or crystals—in rivers

Hardness 2.5–3

Luster Metallic

Cleavage or Fracture No cleavage; hackly fracture; also malleable and ductile

Color Golden yellow; whiter when mixed with silver and redder when mixed with copper

Streak Same as color

Identification Gold is always a golden yellow color and does not tarnish or rust. It is ductile and malleable, meaning that, if pressed by a pocket knife, it will bend and dent rather than crumble or flake. Gold is also extremely dense (very heavy for its size). Its streak is the same as its color, while the streak of pyrite, or "fool's gold," is green-black.

More Info There are two basic types of gold deposits: lode and placer. **Lode gold** is found in bedrock with sulfide deposits, often in hydrothermal quartz or calcite veins, as crystals, wires, foils, or disseminated flecks. **Placer gold** occurs when deposits of lode gold naturally weather and erode into rivers. Because gold is very heavy and doesn't rust away, the eroded gold pieces collect along the bottom of the river and can be retrieved with panning techniques. Placer gold can also be found in sedimentary rocks formed by old rivers.

Notable Localities OR: Gold has been found in almost every area of the state, excepting the COR and WV; the areas around Jacksonville and Baker City have been the most prosperous and continue to support small-time workings. **WA:** Occurrences statewide; Swauk Creek near Liberty in the NC is the most famous locality and still produces alluvial (river) wire gold specimens today.

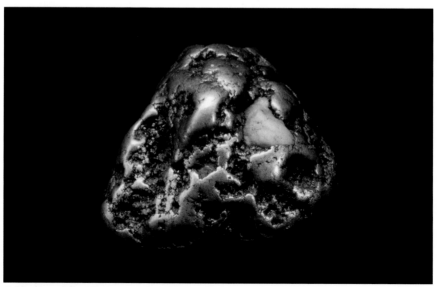

Gold nugget, Galice, Oregon

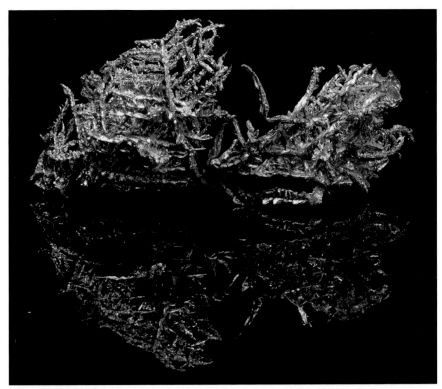

Wire gold, Liberty, Washington

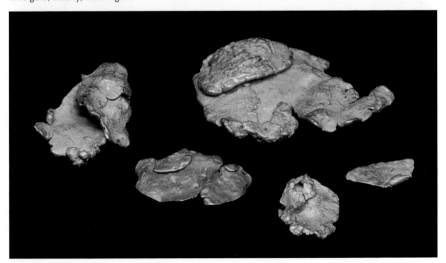

Gold flakes, Baker City, Oregon

GOLD RUSH!

Gold fever swept through the Pacific Northwest on the heels of California's nineteenth-century gold rush. In 1851, placer gold turned up along Josephine Creek in the Klamath Mountains of Oregon, attracting scores of hopeful prospectors who began to settle the land. Other finds in the Blue Mountains and Washington's Yakima Valley followed similar patterns.

Of course, the few who actually did strike it rich were not the men with pans and picks, but those who sold them supplies and provided them with transportation. When larger gold fields opened in Canada and Alaska, Seattle's ports became the gateway to the North. The economic influx helped the city rebuild after the Great Fire of 1889 and prosper into the twentieth century.

Gold drew many immigrants to the Northwest, including a sizable number of Chinese immigrants. As the gold played out, however, white settlers enacted a series of discriminatory laws and practices that limited the areas Chinese workers could mine, taxed Chinese businesses unfairly, and depressed Chinese workers' wages. Eventually, virtually all Chinese residents returned to their homeland, taking with them even the bones and bodies of their dead.

Silver

Ag

RARE

Habit Branching and wire forms; masses; also cubic and octahedral crystals

Hardness 2.5–3

Luster Metallic

Cleavage or Fracture No cleavage; hackly fracture; also malleable and ductile

Color Silver-white; gray to black when tarnished

Streak Same as color

Identification Metallic attributes, commonly wiry form, and black tarnish are characteristic. Malleable and ductile. Black manganese oxides coating other minerals may be confused for silver tarnish, but those minerals will not be malleable and ductile.

More Info Silver in Oregon and Washington is nearly always found disseminated in an ore or alloyed with gold and copper, rather than as a distinct, visible body of native silver. Here, silver production is essentially a byproduct of gold mining. However, rare instances of silver wires and flakes have been reported.

Notable Localities See localities for gold

Silver in matrix, Leadpoint, Washington

Copper

Cu

RARE

Habit Cubic and dodecahedral crystals; also branching or platy forms or large masses

Hardness 2.5–3

Luster Metallic

Cleavage or Fracture No cleavage; hackly fracture; also malleable and ductile

Color Light rose, coppery red, brown; green when oxidized

Streak Same as color

Identification Metallic attributes and color, along with green oxidation, are characteristic. Malleable and ductile.

More Info Copper in Oregon and Washington is nearly always found disseminated, bound in sulfide or carbonate ore minerals, or alloyed with gold and silver, rather than as a distinct, visible body of native copper. Rare instances of copper crystals have been reported. Copper is also associated with basalt flows and has been found as tiny inclusions in zeolites and feldspars. It's responsible for the yellow to red coloring of Oregon's state gem, sunstone.

Notable Localities OR: as inclusions, particularly in sunstone of BR and OWY. **WA**: OKH, Mt. Tolman near Keller hosts the one of the largest copper-molybdenum deposits in the United States; distributed in NC.

Copper crystals, Copper Creek, Washington

Graphite

C

UNCOMMON

Habit Platy or tabular hexagonal crystals; also granular

Hardness 1

Luster Metallic to earthy

Cleavage or Fracture One perfect plane cleaves into sheets

Color Metallic black to gray

Streak Same as color; can mark on paper

Identification Commonly metallic gray and can mark on paper. Color, hardness, and occurrence are characteristic. Silver-colored hematite has a brick red streak, and massive galena is much heavier. Silvery muscovite has elastic sheets and will not mark on paper.

More Info Found primarily in the metamorphic rocks schist, phyllite, and marble, giving those rocks a gray coloration; may be disseminated throughout a rock or collected in veinlets or lenses. Forms when organic material like plant matter is trapped in sedimentary layers that are then heated during metamorphism. Because the structural changes that create graphite occur during the purely physiochemical heating process, this all-carbon material qualifies as inorganic and therefore a true mineral. Used to make the "lead" in pencils and the dry lubricants for lock mechanisms and metal bearings.

Notable Localities WA: distributed in NC and OKH, most notably at the American Graphite Mine near Disautel.

Graphite on matrix (note that the specimen pictured is not from the Pacific Northwest)

SULFIDES

Sulfides form when one or more metallic elements bond with the element sulfur. For example, iron and sulfur combine to form iron pyrite, or "fool's gold," a common yellow mineral found in many settings. Sulfides form primarily in igneous and hydrothermal settings, and high concentrations of sulfide minerals may signify that the host rock is a mineable metal ore.

ACID MINE DRAINAGE

One of the major environmental hazards associated with metal ore mining is acid mine drainage. This phenomenon occurs because of sulfides. When a sulfide mineral encounters oxygen and water at or near the Earth's surface, it oxidizes, meaning the metallic elements break their bonds with the sulfur atoms and combine with oxygen instead. This forms oxide minerals. The leftover sulfur stays in the water and forms sulfuric acid.

This is a completely natural process that occurs in small amounts around us all the time, but mining operations expose many tons of sulfide-containing ore to oxygen and water much more quickly than occurs in nature. This can generate large quantities of acidified water, which is harmful to plant and animal life. Even after mining operations are shut down, rain and groundwater percolate through the disturbed, sulfide-bearing rock and acid drainage continues. Careful engineering is required to mitigate this problem not only for the lifetime of a mine but for many years beyond.

Pyrite

FeS_2

VERY COMMON

Habit Anhedral grains and masses; cubic, octahedral, and dodecahedral crystals, some with striations

Hardness 6–6.5

Luster Metallic

Cleavage or Fracture Indistinct cleavage

Color Yellow, light brassy yellow

Streak Greenish black to brownish black

Identification Shiny yellow color with black streak. By far the most common yellow mineral. Also known as fool's gold, it's easily distinguished from gold by its streak and brittleness. Pyrite can scratch glass or steel, while gold and chalcopyrite cannot. Chalcopyrite also has a generally warmer color.

More Info Widespread in igneous rocks and hydrothermal settings, usually as anhedral grains and masses. When present in large amounts with other sulfides, may be indicative of a copper or gold ore deposit. Can be mined itself as an iron ore.

Notable Localities OR: distributed throughout the state, most co mmonly in KM and BM. **WA**: distributed throughout the state, most commonly in NC and OKH. World-famous pyrite crystals in NC at Spruce Ridge.

Mass of pyrite in an exposed vein through sandstone from Oregon

Pyrite crystals with dodecahedral habit, Spruce Ridge, Washington

Chalcopyrite

$CuFeS_2$

COMMON

Habit Massive, granular aggregates; crystals resemble tetrahedrons, octahedrons

Hardness 3.5–4

Luster Metallic

Cleavage or Fracture Rarely perceptible in aggregates

Color Brass yellow, may have light iridescence

Streak Green-black

Identification Brass yellow color and occurrence are characteristic. Will not scratch glass, unlike pyrite, and is brittle with a black streak, unlike gold. Bornite is redder on a fresh surface and tarnishes more vividly.

More Info Primary ore mineral of copper. Found in copper ore deposits with other sulfides including bornite, pyrite, and galena.

Notable Localities OR: distributed throughout KM, CAS, and BM, most notably around Baker City. **WA**: distributed throughout CAS, OKH, and NC, most notably near Goldmyer Hot Spring.

Chalcopyrite on quartz, King County, Washington

Bornite

Cu_5FeS_4

UNCOMMON

Habit Massive, granular aggregates
Hardness 3
Luster Metallic
Cleavage or Fracture Rarely perceptible in aggregates
Color Coppery with vivid, iridescent purple-blue tarnish
Streak Gray-black
Identification Also known as peacock ore, bornite's iridescent tarnish and underlying coppery color are characteristic. It's brittle, unlike elemental copper. Chalcopyrite may have some iridescent tarnish but is yellow at baseline.
More Info In copper ore deposits with other sulfides including chalcopyrite and pyrite.
Notable Localities OR: distributed in KM and BM. **WA:** distributed in NC and OKH.

Purple-blue bornite with yellow chalcopyrite, Baring, Washington

Sphalerite

ZnS

UNCOMMON

Habit Tetrahedral crystals; also cubes and dodecahedrons, granular masses

Hardness 3.5–4

Luster Resinous to submetallic

Cleavage or Fracture Perfect dodecahedral cleavage (six cleavage planes)

Color Yellow, brown, black, green, red; translucent to opaque

Streak Brownish white to light yellow-brown with sulfurous (rotten egg) odor

Identification Resinous luster and smelly yellow streak are characteristic. Galena has a gray streak and a gray color; brown siderite has a white streak and occurs in different settings.

More Info Found in hydrothermal settings with quartz or calcite and other sulfides, including galena and pyrite. Can be mined as an ore of zinc.

Notable Localities OR: distributed in CAS, KM, BM. **WA**: NC, Middle Fork of Snoqualmie River, Washington Pass; distributed in OKH.

2 mm

Dark sphalerite with white quartz from Washington

Galena

PbS

UNCOMMON

Habit Cubic crystals, cleavable masses, fine aggregates

Hardness 2.5

Luster Metallic

Cleavage or Fracture Perfect cubic cleavage

Color Lead gray

Streak Gray

Identification Galena is very dense and therefore heavy for its size. Its gray color, perfect cubic cleavage, and gray streak are characteristic. May resemble other minerals but doesn't share these characteristics:

graphite is light and can mark on paper; specular hematite streaks brick-red; magnetite strongly attracts a magnet; and silver is malleable and ductile and tarnishes black.

More Info Found in hydrothermal settings with quartz, calcite, and sulfides like sphalerite and pyrite. Can be mined as an ore of lead.

Hazard Galena is a lead ore. Wash hands after handling and do not ingest or inhale.

Notable Localities OR: distributed in CAS, KM, BM. **WA**: NC, near Goldmyer Hot Springs; OKH, near Metaline Falls, Leadpoint.

Cleaved cube of galena, Metaline Falls, Washington

Cinnabar

HgS

UNCOMMON

Habit Massive, granular aggregates or coatings; crystals rhombohedral or short prisms

Hardness 2–2.5

Luster Adamantine to earthy

Cleavage or Fracture Perfect length-parallel cleavage

Color Red, brownish-red

Streak Vivid red

Identification Red color and scarlet streak are characteristic. Hematite's streak is more brick-red, and hematite crystals lack cleavage. Realgar is usually associated with bright yellow-orange orpiment.

More Info Forms in low-temperature hydrothermal systems associated with volcanics; found in veins and hot springs. It's the primary ore of mercury.

Hazard Cinnabar is a mercury ore. Wash hands after handling and do not ingest or inhale.

Notable Localities OR: distributed in BM, especially Horse Heaven (also native mercury); CAS, near Oak Grove; distributed in KM, BR, OWY. **WA**: distributed in NC, especially Blewett Pass area; CAS, Green River Gorge, Mashel River near Eatonville.

Cinnabar on matrix, Ashwood, Oregon

CATCHING QUICKSILVER

Mercury, or quicksilver, is a metal element that's liquid at surface temperatures in its pure state. It has been known since antiquity and used in applications ranging from thermostats to millinery to fluorescent lightbulbs.

Historically, mercury has also been important for gold mining. Elemental mercury can be used to collect microscopic gold particles from ore rocks and placer deposits. The mercury-gold amalgam is then heated, vaporizing the mercury and leaving only the gold behind. The availability of extractable mercury from cinnabar in Oregon was important to the history of mining in the region. However, because mercury vapor is toxic, it was largely phased out of industrial mining after the 1960s.

Realgar

AsS

RARE

Habit Short prisms with lengthwise striations; usually granular aggregate or encrustation

Hardness 1.5–2

Luster Resinous

Cleavage or Fracture Good length-parallel cleavage

Color Red

Streak Red to orange-red

Identification Bright red color and orange-red streak are characteristic. Exposure to light causes realgar to disintegrate into pararealgar, which has a bright yellow-orange color (not to be confused with near-identical-looking powdered orpiment). Cinnabar and hematite lack associated pararealgar and have scarlet and brick-red streaks, respectively. Hematite also lacks cleavage.

More Info Forms in hydrothermal systems with other sulfide minerals; can be associated with lead, silver, and gold ores. Realgar is an ore for arsenic, which is used as an insecticide and in the manufacture of some lasers.

Hazard Realgar is a toxic arsenic ore. Wash hands after handling and do not ingest or inhale.

Notable Localities OR: CAS, near Trent. **WA**: CAS, Green River Gorge produces world-class specimens; distributed in NC.

Realgar crystals on matrix, Black Diamond, Washington

Stibnite

Sb_2S_3

RARE

Habit Elongate prisms or needles with complex terminations

Hardness 2

Luster Metallic

Cleavage or Fracture Perfect length-parallel cleavage

Color Lead gray with bluish iridescent tarnish

Streak Gray

Identification Metallic gray prisms or needles and bluish tarnish are characteristic. Unlikely to be mistaken for other minerals; hornblende and tourmaline prisms and needles are brown-black with white and pale brown or bluish-white streaks, respectively.

More Info Forms in hydrothermal systems at low temperatures with other sulfides. Stibnite is an ore for antimony, used in the manufacture of semiconductors, ceramics, and glass, and also for the treatment of some parasitic diseases.

Hazard Stibnite is an antimony ore and can be toxic. Wash hands after handling and do not ingest or inhale.

Notable Localities OR: CAS, southeast of Cottage Grove; distributed in BM. **WA**: NC, Lucky Knock Mine near Tonasket, distributed in OKH.

Stibnite needles in matrix from Washington

OXIDES AND HYDROXIDES

Oxides form when one or two elements, usually metals, bond with the element oxygen. Hydroxides are a related group where the oxygen also has a single hydrogen atom attached. Many oxides and hydroxides form when other minerals react with water and air, usually at or near Earth's surface. In other words, oxides and hydroxides form when certain minerals rust.

They are commonly found in soils and clays, sedimentary rocks, and hydrothermally altered rocks. Some also grow as primary minerals in igneous systems. Once formed, oxides and hydroxides are generally very stable minerals because most aren't chemically affected by moisture or oxygen. They keep a strong color when powdered (streaked) and were among the first pigments used by early human artists to make paintings like those in the famous caves at Lascaux in France. Many ancient pictographs colored with these mineral pigments can be found throughout Oregon and Washington as well.

Brown and yellow iron oxides on a fracture surface, Liberty, Washington

Iron oxides coloring an altered volcanic rock, Wallowa Mountains, Oregon

Limonite

$FeO(OH)·nH_2O$

VERY COMMON

Habit Commonly massive or botryoidal; also thin crusts
Hardness 4–5.5
Luster Dull, earthy
Cleavage or Fracture None
Color Shades of yellowish to reddish brown
Streak Brownish yellow
Identification *Limonite* is a term for a mixture of iron oxides and hydroxides along with clays and other microscopic minerals.

Individual minerals within the mixture are difficult to distinguish without microscopic or X-ray study, but the mineral goethite ($FeO(OH)$) is usually a significant component. Dull luster, earthy colors and streak, and occurrence are characteristic.

More Info Forms from weathering or hydrothermal alteration of other iron-bearing minerals like pyroxenes, amphiboles, and biotite mica. May appear as a stain or crust on an igneous or metamorphic rock or as a component of soils. Also a component of "bog iron," which forms in wetlands and was once mined for ore in the Lake Oswego area of Oregon, among other places.

Notable Localities Usually a coating or alteration product found associated with iron-bearing rocks everywhere.

Hematite ★

Fe$_2$O$_3$

VERY COMMON

Habit Granular and botryoidal masses and crusts; platy or hexagonal crystals; may form rosettes

Hardness 5–6

Luster Metallic to earthy

Cleavage or Fracture No cleavage

Color Gray or steel gray; red to brick-red

Streak Brick-red

Identification A non-magnetic, gray metallic or red earthy mineral with a strong brick-red streak. Crystals are generally gray, while granular masses are generally red, and botryoidal forms may be gray or red. Distinguished from magnetite by streak and lack of magnetism, though hematite may be mixed with the weakly magnetic ilmenite (FeTiO$_3$) and therefore display some magnetism. Cinnabar has cleavage planes and a scarlet red streak, and realgar is usually associated with bright yellow-orange pararealgar. Both are much softer than hematite.

Members or Varieties Bright, metallic, gray crystals are called **specular hematite**.

More Info Forms from weathering or hydrothermal alteration of iron-bearing minerals like pyroxenes, amphiboles, or biotite mica. May appear as a stain or crust on an igneous or metamorphic rock. Red-colored sandstones and mudstones obtain their color from widely disseminated hematite grains, and hematite may stain clear or white minerals red as well.

Fan of specular hematite with amethyst, Denny Mountain, Washington

Microscopic red hematite coloring mudstone with leaf fossils from Oregon

Notable Localities The red earthy form is widespread everywhere. For specular hematite: **OR**: distributed in CAS, BM, KM. **WA**: NC, Denny Mountain, Bessemer Ridge; distributed in OLY, OKH.

Magnetite

Fe_3O_4

COMMON

Habit Octahedral or dodecahedral crystals; granular; massive
Hardness 5.5–6
Luster Metallic, submetallic
Cleavage or Fracture Poor
Color Black to dark gray with brownish tint
Streak Black
Other Strongly magnetic
Identification Black to dark gray octahedral crystals or grains that strongly attract a magnet and, if permanently magnetized, may hold up lightweight metal objects like paperclips. Specular hematite does not attract a magnet and has a brick-red streak. Galena has a higher density and is also not magnetic.
More Info Try sticking a magnet to any dark-colored, iron-rich igneous rock—magnetite crystals may be difficult to distinguish visually, but are readily found in many igneous and metamorphic rock units. Permanently magnetized magnetite was known in antiquity as lodestone and used in the first compasses, which were invented in China.
Notable Localities OR: distributed in KM, BM; also as grains in some beach sand. **WA:** NC, Green Mountain, Mt. Roosevelt; distributed in OLY, OKH.

Gray-black dodecahedral magnetite crystals with pink garnet from Washington

COUSIN CHROMITE AND THE WORLD WARS

Replacing two iron atoms in the magnetite formula (Fe_3O_4) with the element chromium gives the mineral chromite ($FeCr_2O_4$). Chromite is a rare mineral associated with igneous and metamorphic rocks derived from Earth's mantle; it looks similar to magnetite but isn't magnetic and has a more resinous luster.

Chromium is a critical component of steel alloys used to make tools, armor plating, and even stainless-steel utensils. When the United States lost access to foreign sources of chromium during the World Wars, it developed its own mines, especially in Oregon. Chromite mines in the Klamath and Blue Mountains supplied up to a quarter of the chromium used for war efforts.

Chromite pods in peridotite, Canyon Mountain, Oregon

Ice

H₂O

H_2O

VERY COMMON IN WINTER, RESTRICTED TO GLACIERS IN SUMMER

Habit Hexagonal plates (snowflakes); prismatic columns and needles; massive forms (icicles, hail)

Hardness 1.5 at 32°F, up to 5 at very low temperatures

Luster Vitreous, silky

Cleavage or Fracture One perfect cleavage plane

Color Colorless; white from included air bubbles; blue in glaciers

Streak White

Identification Ice is cold to the touch and melts at 32°F.

Members or Varieties Frost, snow, lake ice, glaciers, icicles, and more.

More Info The conditions for the occurrence of ice are widely known. One less-well-known place to find ice is in seasonal cave formations. Groundwater seeping into shallow cave systems can form spectacular curtains, stalactites, and more

Ice formations in Guler Cave, Washington

that grow throughout winter and melt away each summer.

Notable Localities At high elevations and glaciers year-round; throughout many areas, especially mountain ranges, during winter. Some well-known ice caves, which may be seasonal or year-round, include Arnold Ice Caves near Bend, OR; Guler Ice Cave near Trout Lake, WA; and Big Four Ice Caves near Silverton, WA.

Snowfield and meltwater pool at summit of South Sister, Oregon

CARBONATES

All carbonate minerals contain a carbonate molecular group in their chemical structure—a carbon atom attached to three oxygen atoms (CO_3). The carbonate group is negatively charged, so it bonds with positively charged atoms, usually metallic elements, to form minerals. Though carbon is the defining element in this group, carbonates are considered true minerals for historic reasons as well as the physiochemical processes that form them.

The vast majority of carbonate minerals form in or around oceans. Some form directly from ingredients that combine in warm ocean waters, and some make up the hard parts of shells and corals. Other carbonates make up cave formations, and still others form in hydrothermal systems and may be associated with metallic ore bodies.

SEASHELLS AND OCEAN ACIDIFICATION

Carbonate rocks will gently fizz when dropped in vinegar. This is the same reaction you get with the classic baking-soda-volcano experiment: an acid (vinegar) dissolves a base (baking soda, or sodium bicarbonate) into gas, water, and heat—cue the foamy explosion. Similar reactions happen within the ocean. As carbon dioxide gas dissolves into ocean water, it creates a weak acid. That acid slowly dissolves carbonate minerals in the ocean, most importantly those that make up the shells of many ocean animals.

As we humans burn fossil fuels, atmospheric carbon dioxide levels are rising and the oceans are becoming more acidic, weakening animal shells and making them more vulnerable to predators. This is one of many lasting problems that have developed from our dependence of fossil fuels.

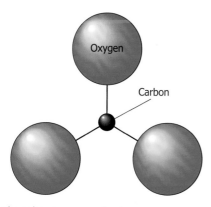

The carbonate group molecule

Calcite ★

CaCO$_3$

VERY COMMON

Habit Hundreds of forms, including rhombohedral and columnar crystals; granular aggregates and cleavable masses; stalactites (cave formations)

Hardness 3

Luster Vitreous

Cleavage or Fracture Three perfect cleavage planes, making a rhombohedron

Color Colorless, white, gray, yellow; pink, brown, green, blue; transparent to opaque

Streak White

Identification Rhombohedral cleavage and low hardness (can't scratch glass) are characteristic. Usually light in color. Distinguished from quartz by hardness. Small pieces will fizz gently if dropped in vinegar, whereas dolomite will not fizz in vinegar unless powdered. Chemically identical to aragonite, but distinguished by cleavage.

More Info Principal component of limestone. Also very common in hydrothermal settings (veins, hot springs deposits) and cave formations as both crystals and encrustations. Component of shells in marine organisms, including corals, and their fossils.

Notable Localities OR: COR, near Sheridan, Gopher Valley; WV, near Drain, Hillsboro; distributed in KM, BM, CAS, HLP, BR, OWY. **WA**: NC, near Monroe; OKH, near Metaline Falls; distributed in OLY, COR, CAS, CB.

Calcite crystals with flattened rhombohedral habit, Monroe, Washington

Cleaved chips of massive calcite

Yellow calcite with scalenohedral or "dogtooth" habit in vug, Hillsboro, Oregon

White calcite balls in vug with brown siderite, Estacada, Oregon

Aragonite

$CaCO_3$

UNCOMMON

Habit As aggregates, smooth and botryoidal masses, or stalactites (cave formations); also prismatic or needle-like crystals

Hardness 3.5–4

Luster Vitreous, resinous

Cleavage or Fracture Indistinct cleavage

Color Colorless or white; may be tinted by impurities; opaque to transparent

Streak White

Identification Light color, habit, and hardness (won't scratch glass) are characteristic. Small pieces will fizz gently if dropped in vinegar. Chemically identical to calcite, but distinguished by habit and lack of rhombohedral cleavage.

More Info Commonly forms from hydrothermal activity in near-surface environments, making cave formations or encrusting layers within and around hot springs. Component of shells in marine organisms and their fossils.

Notable Localities OR: BM, Oxbow Dam near Copperfield; distributed in KM. **WA**: COR, near Kalama; NC, near Monroe.

Botryoidal aragonite on calcite, Kalama, Washington

Sprays of aragonite needles on matrix, Kalama, Washington

Dolomite

$CaMg(CO_3)_2$

UNCOMMON

Habit Rhombohedral and columnar crystals; granular aggregates and cleavable masses

Hardness 3.5–4

Luster Vitreous, pearly

Cleavage or Fracture Three good cleavage planes make a rhombohedron

Color Colorless, white, gray; also brownish and reddish from inclusions

Streak White

Identification Similar physical properties as calcite, but doesn't fizz readily in vinegar unless powdered. Dolomite is more commonly opaque than calcite; also its crystals may have slightly curved faces and its cleavage rhombs are sometimes less perfect than calcite's.

More Info Dolomite is similar to calcite, but includes magnesium as well.

Notable Localities OR: CAS, near Williams, McGowan Creek; distributed in BM. **WA**: distributed in OKH, especially near Metaline Falls.

Rhombohedral dolomite on quartz from Washington

Siderite

$FeCO_3$

UNCOMMON

Habit Rhombohedral tabular or prismatic crystals, sometimes aggregated in balls; botryoidal masses; granular aggregates and cleavable masses

Hardness 4

Luster Vitreous, silky

Cleavage or Fracture Three perfect cleavage planes make a rhombohedron

Color Yellow- to red-brown or gray; rarely blue, colorless; may be translucent or have iridescent tarnish

Streak White

Identification Rhombohedral cleavage and brownish color are characteristic. If powdered, will fizz somewhat in vinegar. Denser (heavier for its size) than calcite and dolomite.

More Info Occurs in vugs, veins, and pockets of hydrothermal systems as well as in association with other iron-rich minerals in bedded, organic-rich continental sedimentary rocks including coal seams.

Notable Localities OR: CAS, in basalt near Estacada. **WA**: NC, Washington Pass; CB, in basalt near Pullman; OKH, near Spokane.

Ball-shaped aggregates called spherosiderite, Spokane, Washington

OTHER NON-SILICATES

This section is full of interesting minerals from less common or more obscure groups and scientific categories. They don't have any unifying chemical or physical properties, but are included here for their significance to Pacific Northwest geology.

Halite

NaCl

UNCOMMON

Habit Cubic crystals; grainy crusts or massive aggregates
Hardness 2–2.5
Luster Vitreous
Cleavage or Fracture Cubic cleavage
Color Colorless, white; may be stained with red iron oxides or other colors from impurities
Streak White

Identification Usually found as a white, grainy crust on the surface of a low-lying basin in arid environments; well-formed crystals are rare in the Northwest. Small cubes may be perceptible with magnification. Dissolves readily in water. A salty taste is diagnostic; however, other white, grainy minerals can be inadvisable to ingest, so we don't recommend extensive tasting.

More Info Halite is the scientific name for table salt. It forms when water is trapped in an enclosed basin and evaporates into the air, leaving salt minerals behind. Halite is only one kind of salt—and one of the only tasty ones. Other salt minerals formed from potassium, carbonate, and sulfate are often mixed in evaporite deposits and can be quite bitter. Salt deposits in the Northwest are found in basins around shallow lakes that represent the remnants of deep, ice-age bodies of water that have slowly been evaporating away.

Notable Localities OR: BR, the flats around Summer Lake, Lake Abert, Alkali Lake, and other lakes in the area.

Salt crystals growing on the edge of Lake Abert

Gypsum

$Ca(SO_4) \cdot 2H_2O$

UNCOMMON

Habit Many forms; tabular and prismatic crystals with or without striations; curled or twisted shapes; bedded masses

Hardness 2

Luster Subvitreous, pearly

Cleavage or Fracture Perfect and good cleavages can intersect to create mica-like sheets

Color Colorless, white, yellowish-brownish

Streak White

Identification Luster, hardness (can be scratched with a fingernail), occurrence, and light color are characteristic. Its multiple cleavages can create mica-like sheets, but gypsum is inflexible and not found in primarily igneous and metamorphic settings like muscovite and talc. Aragonite lacks good cleavage and will fizz in vinegar.

Members or Varieties Large, clear crystals are known as **selenite** and fibrous, highly striated crystals as **satin spar**. Selenite mirror twins may grow into chains of V-shapes called swallowtails, and satin spar may be curled into ram's horns. **Alabaster** refers to massive, sometimes-banded, white forms.

More Info Forms from the evaporation of seawater or saline lakes, creating bedded deposits with mudstones, salts, or carbonates. Today, these evaporite deposits are most commonly exposed in the arid eastern halves of Oregon and Washington, revealing those rock units' watery pasts. Also found in near-surface hydrothermal sulfide deposits associated with volcanic activity.

Notable Localities OR: BM, near Huntington; BR, Mud Lake area near Narrows; distributed in KM, CAS, OWY. **WA**: OKH, near Metaline; NC, near Oroville at boundary with OKH; CAS, summit of Mt. Adams.

Selenite gypsum from a volcanic vent setting in Washington

Barite

BaSO$_4$

UNCOMMON

Habit Thin bladed to thick tabular crystals; granular, massive

Hardness 2.5–3.5

Luster Vitreous to pearly

Cleavage or Fracture One perfect and one good cleavage

Color White, yellow, brown, gray, colorless, blue; opaque to transparent

Streak White

Identification Light color and unusual heaviness for its size are characteristic. Will not scratch glass. Differentiated from calcite and dolomite by density and lack of rhombohedral cleavage.

More Info Found in sulfide deposits, hydrothermal veins, and as lenses in sedimentary deposits. Pyrite, fluorite, galena, sphalerite, and carbonates are common associates. Barite is a primary ore of barium, which is mined for applications in papermaking, well drilling, and medical testing.

Notable Localities OR: KM, Silver Peak area near Agness; CAS, near Lowell; distributed in BR, BM. **WA**: NC, Spruce Ridge, Green Ridge; OKH, Flagstaff Mountain near Northport.

Cluster of large and small barite crystals, Lowell, Oregon

Fluorite

CaF_2

RARE

Habit Cubic and octahedral crystals; anhedral masses

Hardness 4

Luster Vitreous

Cleavage or Fracture Three cleavage planes intersect to make triangle shapes (faces of cleavage octahedra)

Color Blue, green, purple, yellow, brown, colorless, or white; transparent to translucent

Streak White

Identification Cubic or octahedral crystals with octahedral cleavage (creating broken faces shaped like triangles) are characteristic. When massive, distinguished from quartz by hardness (can't scratch glass) and from calcite by lack of fizz in vinegar. Fluorite is also more commonly colored than colorless or white.

More Info Forms in hydrothermal systems in veins and pockets, commonly associated with quartz, carbonates, barite, and sulfide minerals. Can be mined for the element fluorine, used to make tooth-strengthening fluoride for toothpastes and municipal water supplies as well as other compounds used in steelmaking, coatings for nonstick pans, and Gore-Tex.

Notable Localities WA: distributed in OKH, several sites along WA-20.

Mass of green fluorite (this specimen is from British Columbia, but identical in appearance to deposits in the Okanogan Highlands)

Octahedral fluorite on petrified wood, Black Butte, Oregon

Autunite and Meta-Autunite

$Ca(UO_2)_2(PO_4)_2 \cdot 10–12H_2O$

VERY RARE

Habit Thin, often square, tabular crystals in fans; granular to scaly aggregates or crusts

Hardness 1–2

Luster Pearly, waxy

Cleavage or Fracture One perfect cleavage parallel to the tabular form

Color Light to dark green or yellow

Streak Yellow

Identification Bright yellow-green color with tabular to scaly crystals arranged in fans are characteristic; also, low hardness (can be scratched with fingernail). If found as an aggregate without identifiable crystals, the distinctive coloration is diagnostic of this or related uranium minerals.

More Info Autunite and meta-autunite are two of several uranium ore minerals. Many uranium ores display distinctive bright, canary-yellow to vivid-green coloring, though some are black or brown-black. All are radioactive. The element uranium is very mobile in fluids, so uranium minerals can form in many settings, especially sedimentary and hydrothermal. In this pair, autunite forms first but, when exposed to air, loses some of its water molecules and becomes meta-autunite (first discovered in Washington State). The two are difficult to distinguish except chemically.

Hazard Contains uranium, so is radioactive. Radiation from naturally occurring minerals is generally low enough that these minerals are safe to handle and collect, but wash hands after handling and do not ingest or inhale. Hazardous radon gas is generated from the radioactive decay of uranium and builds up in enclosed spaces over time, so allow any box, cabinet or other storage enclosure to vent upon opening.

Notable Localities WA: CB, Daybreak Mine near Mount Spokane State Park, Midnite Mine on the Spokane Indian Reservation. (Note: mines are closed.)

Fans of tabular meta-autunite crystals, Daybreak Mine, Washington

Awaruite (Josephinite)

Ni_3Fe

VERY RARE

Habit Usually found as rounded pebbles in stream beds

Hardness 5

Luster Metallic

Cleavage or Fracture No cleavage, hackly fracture, malleable

Color Gray-white; may have brown or black crust; opaque

Streak Lead gray

Other Will attract a magnet

Identification Strongly magnetic and closely resembling nickel-iron meteorites, which it was initially thought to be at first discovery. Awaruite is found in only one area of Oregon, so the location helps make the identification.

More Info Most finds to date have been as small, water-worn pebbles in streambeds. Awaruite likely forms in bodies of peridotite (mantle rock) and weathers out of areas that have been altered by hydrothermal fluids, collecting in nearby streams. Also known as josephinite, it's one of Oregon's state minerals. Its extremely unusual chemical composition is similar to the composition of Earth's solid metal core.

Notable Localities OR: KM, Josephine Creek and others near Cave Junction.

Trio of awaruite pebbles

Quick List: Minerals and Varieties

Mineral Property Tables

Use these tables to help narrow down the possible identity of an unknown mineral. Then turn to the full individual entries for more information about each possibility.

Minerals by Color and Habit

The easiest things to notice about a mineral are its color and shape. These tables provide a list of minerals that can fit in each color and habit category, arranged in a slightly subjective order of most to least likely. The bolded entries are the likeliest. Recall that any crystal roughly equal in size in all dimensions, like a cube or sphere, is described as equant.

GREEN

Equant	Elongated	Flat	Massive/Globular	Branching
olivine group	**hornblende**	**chlorite group**	**chlorite group**	**copper**
epidote	tremolite-actinolite	serpentine	epidote	
clinopyroxene	**epidote**	epidote	**serpentine**	
orthopyroxene	clinopyroxene	talc	jasper	
omphacite	**orthopyroxene**	muscovite	fluorite	
fluorite	**serpentine**	biotite group	nephrite jade	
garnet group	**olivine group**	autunite	**tremolite-actinolite**	
calcite	beryl	calcite	**talc**	
alkali feldspar	calcite	copper	agate and chalcedony	
copper	natrolite	alkali feldspar	calcite	
sphalerite	tourmaline group	stilbite	copper	
chabazite	plagioclase feldspar	plagioclase feldspar		
plagioclase feldspar				

BLUE

Equant	Elongated	Flat	Massive/Globular	Branching
glaucophane-riebeckite	**glaucophane-riebeckite**	**barite**	**bornite**	[none]
bornite	pentagonite and cavansite	pentagonite and cavansite	**fluorite**	
fluorite	calcite	calcite	**agate and chalcedony**	
calcite	beryl	alkali feldspar	calcite	
barite	quartz	plagioclase feldspar	glaucophane-riebeckite	
alkali feldspar	stibnite	serpentine	barite	
plagioclase feldspar	serpentine	stilbite	serpentine	
siderite	ice	ice	siderite	
ice	tourmaline group		jasper	
			ice	

VIOLET–PINK

Equant	Elongated	Flat	Massive/Globular	Branching
rhodonite	**quartz**	**alkali feldspar**	**rhodonite**	[none]
garnet group	calcite	**rhodonite**	**calcite**	
alkali feldspar	dolomite	muscovite	**dolomite**	
calcite	beryl	heulandite	agate and chalcedony	
dolomite	tremolite-actinolite	stilbite	jasper	
fluorite	natrolite	calcite	fluorite	
bornite	mesolite		bornite	
			tremolite-actinolite	

RED

Equant	Elongated	Flat	Massive/Globular	Branching
garnet group	cinnabar	clay minerals	hematite	copper
rhodonite	realgar	rhodonite	clay minerals	
realgar	staurolite	copper	jasper	
copper		stilbite	agate and chalcedony	
cinnabar		chlorite group	rhodonite	
sphalerite		plagioclase feldspar	cinnabar	
siderite			realgar	
chabazite			opal	
fluorite			copper	
plagioclase feldspar			siderite	
			fluorite	
			chlorite group	

BROWN

Equant	Elongated	Flat	Massive/Globular	Branching
clinopyroxene	clinopyroxene	clay minerals	clay minerals	copper
orthopyroxene	orthopyroxene	biotite group	limonite	
barite	hornblende	barite	siderite	
siderite	tourmaline group	copper	jasper	
sphalerite	staurolite	gypsum	barite	
copper	gypsum	calcite	gypsum	
calcite	calcite	chlorite group	calcite	
dolomite	dolomite	serpentine	dolomite	
garnet group	natrolite	talc	agate and chalcedony	
chabazite	serpentine	stilbite	serpentine	
fluorite			talc	
			chlorite group	
			fluorite	
			copper	

ORANGE

Equant	Elongated	Flat	Massive/Globular	Branching
garnet group	quartz	**pararealgar** (see realgar)	**opal**	[none]
			agate and chalcedony	
			jasper	

YELLOW

Equant	Elongated	Flat	Massive/Globular	Branching
pyrite	**calcite**	**clay minerals**	**pyrite**	**gold**
chalcopyrite	gypsum	barite	chalcopyrite	
bornite	beryl	**gypsum**	**limonite**	
calcite	epidote	calcite	clay minerals	
gold	olivine group	**autunite**	barite	
plagioclase feldspar	orthopyroxene	**gold**	gypsum	
barite	serpentine	muscovite	**calcite**	
sphalerite	natrolite	plagioclase feldspar	**gold**	
siderite	mesolite	alkali feldspar	agate and chalcedony	
epidote		serpentine	jasper	
olivine group		talc	siderite	
garnet group		epidote	opal	
alkali feldspar		chlorite group	serpentine	
orthopyroxene		stilbite	talc	
chabazite			chlorite group	
fluorite			fluorite	

COLORLESS

Equant	Elongated	Flat	Massive/ Globular	Branching
quartz	quartz	alkali feldspar	quartz	[none]
calcite	calcite	calcite	calcite	
alkali feldspar	aragonite	barite	agate and chalcedony	
analcime	natrolite	gypsum	opal	
halite	gypsum	heulandite	gypsum	
ice	mesolite	stilbite	aragonite	
dolomite	beryl	talc	dolomite	
fluorite	orthopyroxene	ice	halite	
chabazite	staurolite		fluorite	
garnet group			ice	
barite			barite	
siderite			talc	
orthopyroxene			tremolite-actinolite	
			siderite	

WHITE–CREAM

Equant	Elongated	Flat	Massive/ Globular	Branching
plagioclase feldspar	plagioclase feldspar	plagioclase feldspar	clay minerals	[none]
alkali feldspar	alkali feldspar	alkali feldspar	quartz	
quartz	quartz	calcite	calcite	
calcite	calcite	clay minerals	dolomite	
dolomite	aragonite	muscovite	aragonite	
analcime	dolomite	barite	opal	
chabazite	natrolite	gypsum	talc	
barite	mesolite	heulandite	tremolite-actinolite	
halite	tremolite-actinolite	stilbite	barite	
fluorite	gypsum	talc	gypsum	
ice	beryl	ice	fluorite	
	ice		halite	
			ice	

GRAY

Equant	Elongated	Flat	Massive/Globular	Branching
plagioclase feldspar	plagioclase feldspar	plagioclase feldspar	quartz	silver
quartz	quartz	calcite	calcite	
calcite	calcite	muscovite	dolomite	
dolomite	hematite	clay minerals	agate and chalcedony	
barite	stibnite	hematite	hematite	
glaucophane-riebeckite	glaucophane-riebeckite	graphite	galena	
galena	dolomite	barite	graphite	
silver	orthopyroxene	epidote	barite	
epidote	epidote		glaucophane-riebeckite	
orthopyroxene	tremolite-actinolite		tremolite-actinolite	
siderite	natrolite		clay minerals	
magnetite	silver		silver	
			awaruite	
			siderite	
			magnetite	

BLACK

Equant	Elongated	Flat	Massive/Globular	Branching
clinopyroxene	clinopyroxene	biotite group	magnetite	manganese oxide*
magnetite	hornblende	chlorite group	manganese oxide*	silver
epidote	tourmaline group	clay minerals	clay minerals	
olivine group	quartz	epidote	quartz	
quartz	epidote	serpentine	silver	
silver	olivine group	stilbite	chlorite group	
orthopyroxene	serpentine	graphite	serpentine	
sphalerite	orthopyroxene		graphite	

*Manganese oxides are a group of minerals that form black crusts, masses, veins, and dendrites around and among other rocks and minerals. They are the most common reasons for black inclusions in agate or black veins in rhodonite, for example.

Minerals by Color and Hardness

Minerals don't always grow perfectly; sometimes they appear in rocks with poorly formed crystals or only a bleb of color. When that happens, the best route to identification often starts with hardness. Test if the mineral is softer or harder than your fingernail (2–2.5), a penny (3), a knife (5–6.5) or glass (5.5). Reference the hardness with color and start to narrow down on a possible ID. Bolded entries are those more commonly found in the listed color.

GREEN

Mineral	Hardness
talc	1
autunite	1–2
chlorite group	2–3
copper	2.5–3
biotite group	2.5–3
muscovite	2–3.5
serpentine	2.5–5.5 (<4 most common)
calcite	3
chabazite	3–5
sphalerite	3.5–4
stilbite	3.5–4
fluorite	4
orthopyroxene	5–6
omphacite	5–6
hornblende	5–6
tremolite-actinolite	5–6
natrolite	5–5.5
clinopyroxene	5.5–6.5
alkali feldspar	6–6.5
jasper	6.5–7
nephrite jade	6
plagioclase feldspar	6–6.5
epidote	6–7
olivine group	6.5–7
agate and chalcedony	6.5–7
garnet group	7–7.5
tourmaline group	7–7.5
beryl	7.5–8

BLUE

Mineral	Hardness
ice	1.5–5
stibnite	2
barite	2.5–3.5
serpentine	2.5–5.5 (<4 most common)
calcite	3
bornite	3
pentagonite and cavansite	3–4
stilbite	3.5–4
fluorite	4
siderite	4
glaucophane-riebeckite	5–6
mesolite	5
alkali feldspar	6–6.5
plagioclase feldspar	6–6.5
agate and chalcedony	6.5–7
jasper	6.5–7
quartz	7
beryl	7.5–8

VIOLET–PINK

Mineral	Hardness
muscovite	2–3.5
calcite	3
bornite	3
dolomite	3.5–4
heulandite	3.5–4
stilbite	3.5–4
fluorite	4
natrolite	5–5.5
tremolite-actinolite	5–6
rhodonite	5.5–6.5
alkali feldspar	6–6.5
agate and chalcedony	6.5–7
jasper	6.5–7
quartz	7
garnet group	7–7.5
beryl	7.5–8

RED

Mineral	Hardness
clay minerals	<2
realgar	1.5–2
cinnabar	2–2.5
chlorite group	2–3
copper	2.5–3
chabazite	3–5
sphalerite	3.5–4
stilbite	3.5–4
siderite	4
fluorite	4
hematite	5–6
rhodonite	5.5–6.5
opal	5.5–6.5
jasper	6.5–7
agate and chalcedony	6.5–7
garnet group	7–7.5
staurolite	7–7.5

BROWN

Mineral	Hardness
talc	1
clay minerals	<2
gypsum	2
chlorite group	2–3
copper	2.5–3
biotite group	2.5–3
barite	2.5–3.5
serpentine	2.5–5.5 (<4 most common)
calcite	3
sphalerite	3.5–4
dolomite	3.5–4
stilbite	3.5–4
siderite	4
fluorite	4
chabazite	3–5
limonite	4–5.5
natrolite	5–5.5
orthopyroxene	5–6
hornblende	5–6
clinopyroxene	5.5–6.5
jasper	6.5–7
agate and chalcedony	6.5–7
garnet group	7–7.5
tourmaline group	7–7.5
staurolite	7–7.5

ORANGE

Mineral	Hardness
orpiment (see realgar)	1.5–2
opal	5.5–6.5
agate and chalcedony	6.5–7
jasper	6.5–7
quartz	7
garnet group	7–7.5

YELLOW

Mineral	Hardness
talc	1
clay minerals	<2
autunite	1–2
gypsum	2
chlorite group	2–3
gold	2.5–3
barite	2.5–3.5
muscovite	2–3.5
serpentine	2.5–5.5 (<4 most common)
bornite	3
calcite	3
chabazite	3–5
chalcopyrite	3.5–4
sphalerite	3.5–4
stilbite	3.5–4
siderite	4
fluorite	4
limonite	4–5.5
natrolite	5–5.5
orthopyroxene	5–6
opal	5.5–6.5
pyrite	6–6.5
plagioclase feldspar	6–6.5
alkali feldspar	6–6.5
epidote	6–7
olivine group	6.5–7
agate and chalcedony	6.5–7
jasper	6.5–7
garnet group	7–7.5
beryl	7.5–8

COLORLESS

Mineral	Hardness
talc	1
gypsum	2
halite	2–2.5
barite	2.5–3.5
calcite	3
chabazite	3–5
dolomite	3.5–4
aragonite	3.5–4
heulandite	3.5–4
stilbite	3.5–4
fluorite	4
siderite	4
mesolite	5
analcime	5–5.5
natrolite	5–5.5
ice	1.5–5
orthopyroxene	5–6
tremolite-actinolite	5–6
opal	5.5–6.5
alkali feldspar	6–6.5
agate and chalcedony	6.5–7
quartz	7
garnet group	7–7.5
beryl	7.5–8

WHITE–CREAM

Mineral	Hardness
talc	1
clay minerals	<2
gypsum	2
halite	2–2.5
barite	2.5–3.5
muscovite	2–3.5
calcite	3
chabazite	3–5
dolomite	3.5–4
aragonite	3.5–4
heulandite	3.5–4
stilbite	3.5–4
fluorite	4
mesolite	5
analcime	5–5.5
natrolite	5–5.5
ice	1.5–5
tremolite-actinolite	5–6
opal	5.5–6.5
plagioclase feldspar	6–6.5
alkali feldspar	6–6.5
quartz	7
beryl	7.5–8

GRAY

Mineral	Hardness
graphite	1
clay minerals	<2
stibnite	2
galena	2.5
silver	2.5–3
barite	2.5–3.5
muscovite	2–3.5
calcite	3
dolomite	3.5–4
siderite	4
awaruite	5
natrolite	5–5.5
glaucophane-riebeckite	5–6
orthopyroxene	5–6
hematite	5–6
tremolite-actinolite	5–6
magnetite	5.5–6
plagioclase feldspar	6–6.5
epidote	6–7
agate and chalcedony	6.5–7
quartz	7

BLACK

Mineral	Hardness
graphite	1
clay minerals	<2
chlorite group	2–3
silver	2.5–3
biotite group	2.5–3
serpentine	2.5–5.5 (<4 most common)
stilbite	3.5–4
sphalerite	3.5–4
hornblende	5–6
orthopyroxene	5–6
magnetite	5.5–6
clinopyroxene	5.5–6.5
epidote	6–7
olivine group	6.5–7
quartz	7
tourmaline group	7–7.5

ROCKS

If minerals are the geological alphabet, rocks are letters formed into words. Rocks in an outcrop make a sentence, and many outcrops form a paragraph. When all a region's paragraphs are strung together, they narrate its history, sometimes repeating one theme consistently and other times hinting at tales that have mystified readers for years and generate arguments to this day.

The Rock Cycle

Where do rocks come from? Other rocks.

Earth's crust is in a constant, albeit slow, state of flux, as rocks form, break down, or are transformed into different rocks. This flux is commonly referred to as the rock cycle.

To illustrate the rock cycle, let's begin with a melt. Molten rock. Rock so hot that all its constituents are liquid. If this melt is present within Earth's interior, we call it magma; on Earth's surface, we call it lava. As melts cool, minerals crystallize and solidify into igneous rocks. Magmas that solidify in Earth's interior form *plutonic* igneous rocks, while lavas on the surface form *volcanic* igneous rocks.

Once an igneous rock has formed and become exposed at Earth's surface, it is subject to battering by wind, water, and other processes that break the rock down into smaller pieces. The physical or chemical processes that break down rocks at or near Earth's surface are called weathering, and the products of weathering are

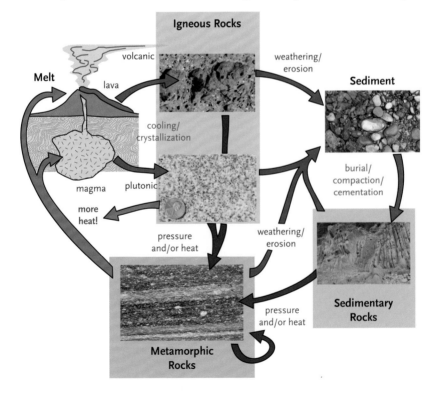

sediments. When sediment is produced, it can then be eroded and transported away from its source. If thick deposits of sediment pile up, the sediment buried at the bottom can become compacted and cemented together, forming sedimentary rocks.

When an existing sedimentary or igneous rock is subject to great pressure and temperature within the Earth's crust (deep burial at a convergent plate boundary, for example), the mineral constituents of the rock undergo a change, transforming into different minerals that are more stable at these high pressure or temperature conditions. This process of change is called metamorphism, and it produces metamorphic rocks.

Once a metamorphic rock forms, it's entirely possible that, as heat increases, parts of the rock become liquid—producing a melt! And so the rock cycle continues.

While this description makes the cycle appear as a strict progression, from igneous to sedimentary to metamorphic rocks, reality is more complex. Metamorphic rocks and existing sedimentary rocks can be weathered into sediments that produce new sedimentary rocks. Existing metamorphic rocks can be subject to more intense temperature and pressure conditions, which form different types of new metamorphic rocks without producing a melt. Some igneous and sedimentary rocks can be melted to eventually form new igneous rocks.

Now that we have a general idea of the broad rock-forming processes within Earth's crust, we can learn to use features and textures present in rocks to determine how they formed and hopefully identify them.

Identifying Rocks

Identifying and naming rocks can be tricky. Rock names are based on a combination of their textures and mineral content, but some textures are ambiguous and some minerals too small to see. Geologists in the field must learn to infer what minerals certain rocks are likely to contain based on what they observe by eye. This involves a bit of detective work, some critical thinking, and an element of personal interpretation, which is part of what makes looking at rocks so fun.

The rock entries in this guide contain information about key components, minerals, textures, and other features that define each rock type. Some terms that are used to describe individual rocks are explored in more depth in later chapters discussing large-scale rock-forming processes—don't hesitate to cross reference if you're curious. Many rocks can look superficially similar, like basalt and black sandstone, so be sure to make careful observations of all the necessary characteristics before settling on an ID. By the same token, two rocks of the same type may look very different, like red versus black basalt. The identification charts following the rock entries on page 199 can help guide your observations.

Rock Textures and Identification

Rocks tell their own stories. The shape, arrangement, and kinds of crystals or individual pieces that make up each rock record the processes that formed it. Together, these attributes decide a rock's texture. Describing a rock's texture and categorizing the process that made it is the first step toward identifying a rock.

WHAT ARE OUTCROPS, BEDROCK, AND FORMATIONS?

These terms come up frequently in geologic discussions and they are easy to mix up.

A rock outcrop is any exposure of bare bedrock. Natural outcrops often appear where the landscape has recently been eroded into or geologically built up—cliff faces are good examples, as are mountain exposures above tree line. Human-made roadcuts often create excellent outcrops.

Bedrock itself comprises the fully coherent (hard and solid) bodies of rock that make up Earth's crust. Though most of Earth's surface is covered by sediments, soils, and water, these features are a thin veneer over the foundational architecture of bedrock. Bedrock is created by the igneous, sedimentary, and metamorphic processes discussed in this chapter.

Geologists who study bedrock describe its components as formations. In this context, *formation* doesn't refer to a singular feature like a funny-looking boulder, but instead to a laterally extensive body of rock like a lava flow or a stack of layered sandstone and mudstone.

Geologic formations are often given names that refer to some region or landmark located near where they were first described in scientific literature. For example, the John Day Formation is a specific series of sedimentary and volcanic rock layers that formed between 40 and 22 million years ago and is now exposed near the Oregon town of John Day. The terms member, unit, group, supergroup, complex, and others are also often used instead of the word formation to indicate smaller and larger groupings of rock bodies. Some formations are simply named after their dominant rock type, such as the Wanapum Basalt or Nye Mudstone.

basalt flow

Deschutes Formation

~5 ft

This roadcut exposes an outcrop of an unnamed basalt flow capping tilted layers of the mixed sedimentary and volcanic Deschutes Formation. Looking at this vertical roadcut is like looking at the side of a closed book—the lines or stripes on the surface actually represent the edges of tabular layers of rock like pages that extend back into the hillside.

There are six basic ways to describe rock textures, and many rocks have a combination of two or more.

Igneous rocks may be coarse crystalline, fine crystalline, or porphyritic, and igneous units may be massive or layered. Sedimentary rocks may be either clastic or fine crystalline and massive, and most are layered (though some layers may be quite thick). Metamorphic rocks may have any combination of rock textures.

Coarse crystalline The rock is composed almost entirely of individual crystals large enough to see and the crystals fit together like puzzle pieces.

Fine crystalline The rock has few or no visible crystals and is all one color. Freshly broken faces are dull and have an irregular, rough surface.

Porphyritic Large, well-formed crystals with sharp corners and edges are scattered in a matrix of fine crystalline rock.

Clastic Broken pieces of crystals or rock fragments, called clasts, are stuck together by a matrix of naturally formed mineral cement.

Massive, homogeneous A rock with no internal structures or features. This term is usually applied to fine-grained rocks but can be used for some coarse-grained rocks as well.

Layered Rocks can develop layers for several reasons. The key to recognizing different layer types comes from examining other textures in the rock.

TYPES OF LAYERS IN ROCKS

Rock outcrops can look layered or striped for many different reasons. Look closely at what each layer is made from and how it touches the layers above and below it to determine what type it is. And if you're stuck on identifying a rock, looking at layering patterns in the outcrop may help narrow down your options.

Bedding Layers formed from sediment depositing over time, as in layers of sandstone and mudstone. Individual beds may be fine laminations (less than one millimeter) or several meters thick. This term can also be applied to successive layers of lava flows. Bedding planes may be horizontal, tilted, or folded. Found in sedimentary rocks and volcanic igneous rocks.

Flow banding Minerals are aligned by the flow of molten rock during the process of formation and cooling. Bands may be planar or swirled, and any visible mineral crystals are undeformed. Found in igneous rocks, mostly volcanic types.

Cumulate layering Light and dark banding in a coarse-grained igneous rock formed by minerals sinking to the bottom of a magma chamber. Rare. Crystals and overall rock texture are undeformed. Found in plutonic igneous rocks.

Tectonic foliation Layers formed by the alignment of flat minerals like micas that have grown or rotated to be stacked like sheets of paper forming a rock fabric. Rocks and outcrops commonly exhibit deformation features, including folding. Found in metamorphic rocks.

Compositional banding Also called gneissic banding. Light and dark banding in coarse crystalline rocks, often exhibiting folds and other features of deformation. The light minerals are usually feldspar and quartz and the dark minerals are biotite, hornblende, or orthopyroxene. Found in metamorphic rocks.

Geologic Map of the Pacific Northwest

Geologic maps show the locations of rocks at Earth's surface. This map is meant to highlight the locations of major igneous, sedimentary, and metamorphic rocks throughout the region. Each colorful blob is a unit, or a group of rocks that share defined characteristics. The rock categories are divided into groups of interest, for instance separating suites of volcanic rocks that formed from distinct phases of activity. The map key explains these groupings.

Use this map as a reference for the locations of rock types listed in the following entries. If you are reading about sandstone, for example, you can look for the units in the sedimentary rocks category to see where they are found. The units are generalized because like is often found with like—different sedimentary rocks are frequently interlayered, volcanic igneous rocks are associated with other volcanic rocks, and so on. The units designated "Mixed Lithologies" show areas with closely associated rocks from different categories like igneous and sedimentary.

Note that these units are meant to show the dominant rock type in an area, but not the exclusive rock type. Minor amounts of other rock types can be found within each unit. This is particularly true for the rocks basalt and sandstone, which can be found in minor to major amounts almost anywhere in the Northwest.

Some of the vocabulary and concepts referenced in the map key are defined or explored more fully in our final chapter, Telling the Story. Revisiting this map after reading that chapter will help you appreciate more of the information it contains.

Much of the data used to create this map is publicly available through the Oregon Department of Geology and Mineral Industries (DOGAMI) and the Washington State Department of Natural Resources. More information about data sources can be found on page 331.

Igneous Rocks

Ia Accreted volcanic and intrusive rocks, mostly associated with the Siletzia Terrane and the COR. These igneous rocks are not metamorphosed.

Ivp Volcanic and plutonic rocks geographically/geologically associated with the Cascade Range. This unit includes extrusive volcanics from Quaternary Cascades volcanism, primarily basalts and andesites. Also included are exposed plutonic rocks within the Cascade Range and the Boring Volcanic Field of northwest Oregon.

Ifb Flood basalts of eastern Washington and eastern and southeast Oregon. This unit includes the Columbia River Basalts, Steens Flood Basalts, Imnaha Flood Basalts, and others.

Ihlp Volcanic rocks of the Oregon High Lava Plains, primarily basalts and rhyolites. These rocks are associated with volcanic centers within the HLP and basaltic vents in the OWY and aren't associated with Cascades or High Cascades volcanism.

Ip Plutonic (intrusive) rocks that aren't associated with the Cascade Range or North Cascades volcanics. These rocks are mainly intrusions within the OKH, along with stitching plutons in Klamath Mountains, Blue Mountains, and Wallowa Mountains.

Generalized Geologic Map

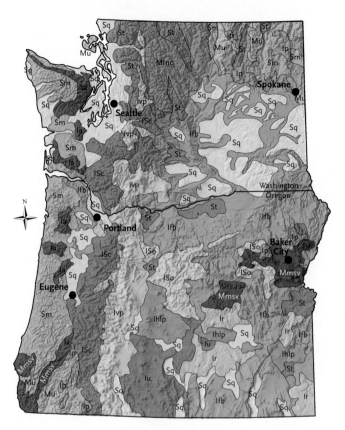

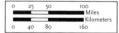

Igneous Rocks

Ia	Accreted (exotic) origin
Ivp	Volcanic and plutonic rocks of the Cascade Range
Ifb	Flood basalts
Ihlp	Volcanics associated with the High Lava Plains
Ip	Plutonic rocks of non-Cascade origin
Ir	Rhyolites, rhyolite tuffs
Iu	Undifferentiated volcanic rocks

Sediments and Sedimentary Rocks

Sq	Quaternary sediments (fluvial, glacial, aeolian, coastal origin)
Sm	Marine origin
St	Continental origin

Metamorphic Rocks

Mu	Undifferentiated

Mixed Lithologies

ISc	Volcanic, volcaniclastic, and clastic rocks of Cascade Range
ISo	Volcanic, volcaniclastic, and continental clastic rocks of eastern Oregon
MInc	Metamorphic and plutonic rocks of the North Cascades
Mmsv	Accreted (exotic) origin

`Ir` Rhyolites and rhyolite tuffs of southeast Oregon, associated with Owyhee Plateau volcanism and possible large caldera eruptions.

`Iu` Undifferentiated extrusive volcanics of southern Oregon, mostly basalts.

Sediments and Sedimentary Rocks

`Sq` Undifferentiated Quaternary sediments. These sediments have fluvial, glacial, aeolian, lacustrine, or coastal origins.

`Sm` Sedimentary rocks with a marine origin. This group includes the active margin Tyee Formation of Oregon, sedimentary rocks in the COR in Washington, and the passive margin Metaline Formation and Windermere Supergroup in the Okanogan Highlands. In places, especially the OKH, these rocks may have undergone low grades of metamorphism.

`St` Sedimentary rocks with a continental origin. Examples of this group include the Chumstick and Swauk Formations in the Washington Cascades and North Cascades, and sedimentary rocks in the Republic Graben in the Okanogan Highlands.

Metamorphic Rocks

`Mu` Undifferentiated metamorphic rocks of the Klamath Mountains, Okanogan Highlands, and the San Juan Islands of the North Cascades. This group contains a wide variety of rocks, ranging from high-grade, deep-crustal metamorphic rocks to ocean-floor ophiolite sequences to lower-grade slates and marbles, both in situ and accreted.

Mixed Lithologies

`ISc` Volcanic, mixed volcanic and clastic, and clastic sedimentary rocks of the Cascade Range. This group includes the Ohanapecosh Formation of Washington and the Western Cascades volcanics and associated rocks of Oregon.

`ISo` Volcanic, mixed volcanic and clastic, and clastic sedimentary rocks of central and eastern Oregon that are not directly related to modern Cascades volcanoes.

`MInc` Undifferentiated medium- to high-grade metamorphic rocks and felsic plutonic rocks of the North Cascades. This group includes accreted rocks, Skagit Gneiss Complex, Golden Horn and Chilliwack Batholiths, and intrusive rocks of the Chelan Complex.

`Mmsv` Accreted exotic sedimentary, metasedimentary, and metavolcanic rocks in the Klamath and Blue Mountains provinces. This group includes multiple terranes, melanges, and accreted island-arc-related rocks. Units can include ultramafic and ophiolitic rocks. Some units in this group have undergone low grades of metamorphism. Rocks in this unit are associated with (but not limited to) the Baker, Olds Ferry, and Wallowa Terranes in the Blue Mountains, and the Applegate, Yolla Bolly, and Western Klamath Terranes in the Klamath Mountains.

★ Seven Most Common Rock Types

Oregon and Washington boast an impressive array of rock types and varieties, but a handful are much more common than the rest. Learn these rocks first, and it will be easy to spot them at a glance and differentiate them from more unusual rocks. Full entries for each rock can be found at the indicated page number.

Basalt A black, fine-grained igneous rock formed from a hot lava flow that oozed across the ground. It may contain gas bubbles and visible small, white or green mineral crystals. Basalts with many gas bubbles may also be red (see page 142).

Andesite is another kind of lava rock that can have gas bubbles and small crystals. It's usually grayer than basalt and if it contains visible crystals, they are generally white or black (see page 145).

Sandstone A sedimentary rock made up of sand-sized particles of rocks and crystals deposited along a river, lake, or ocean basin, which were then buried and compacted. A close look reveals rounded particles stuck together by natural cements. Sandstones can be black, gray, tan, red, or many other colors depending on what little bits they are made of (see page 162).

Mudstone Similar to sandstone, mudstones are rocks formed from buried and compacted mud (see page 160).

Greenstone Almost all green rocks have been altered by heat, a bit of water, and a bit of pressure. These influences cause iron-rich rocks like basalt to transform, rearranging the atomic ingredients of their original minerals to grow new ones in their place. Many of those new minerals happen to be green (see page 189).

Tuff Another rock made by volcanoes, tuffs form when an eruption explodes instead of flowing over the ground. Volcanic ash, pumice, crystals, and rock fragments ejected from the volcanic vent come to rest on the ground in a layer, which can then be solidified into a new layer of rock by a few different means (see page 166).

Granitic Rock One of the few rock types made entirely of crystals all large enough to see. These rocks are usually a combination of white, black, or gray crystals that fit together like three-dimensional puzzle pieces. They form when molten rock cools slowly underground instead of erupting out of a volcano (see page 141).

IGNEOUS ROCKS

Igneous rocks are born from fire. Their name comes from the Latin word *igneus*, meaning fiery, an apt descriptor for volcanic eruptions with glowing lava or towering ash clouds. More broadly, though, igneous rocks form whenever molten rock cools and solidifies into crystals (in the same way liquid water solidifies into ice). This may happen slowly if the molten rock remains underground as magma, or rapidly if it pours onto Earth's surface as lava.

When magma cools slowly underground, crystals may have millions of years to grow. This creates a coarse crystalline texture with many well-formed crystals that usually fit together randomly with no preferred orientation. When lava instead erupts from a volcano, crystals solidify within seconds to days, and each individual crystal is much too small to see. This creates a fine crystalline texture. A porphyritic texture comes from a combination of these processes: a magma growing crystals slowly underground may erupt before it has completely solidified, and the erupting lava carries large, already-formed crystals along to the surface. As the lava cools quickly around the large crystals, it creates the crystals-in-groundmass texture.

Most igneous rocks are made of only a few different minerals: olivine, ortho- and clinopyroxenes, hornblende, biotite, muscovite, quartz, and both plagioclase and alkali feldspars. The specific minerals that grow in a solid rock depend on the chemical composition of the molten rock. Magmas high in silicon and aluminum make rocks with lots of micas, alkali feldspars, and quartz—these rocks are called felsic. Magmas with more iron and

A porphyritic igneous rock, also called a porphyry. The large white crystals formed slowly underground and were carried to the surface with erupting lava, which cooled quickly to form the fine crystalline groundmass.

A coarse crystalline igneous rock that formed in an underground magma chamber

magnesium make rocks with lots of olivine, pyroxenes, and some amphiboles—these rocks are called mafic. Those in the middle are intermediate, and some rocks with extremely high iron and magnesium contents are called ultramafic.

Some igneous rocks have distinctive features at the outcrop scale. Columnar

A fine crystalline igneous rock that formed from a surface flow, including vesicular blocks from frozen gas bubbles

Swirly flow banding in rhyolitic obsidian in the Big Obsidian Flow, Newberry National Volcanic Monument, Oregon

jointing is a classic igneous structure. As a lava flow solidifies during cooling, the flow shrinks in volume and fractures into a pervasive polygonal-shaped pattern. These cooling fractures are usually perpendicular to the margins (top, bottom, and side) of the flow. As cooling continues, the fractures grow and divide the body of the flow into polygonal columns. Columnar jointing is quite ubiquitous throughout the Pacific Northwest, and can be observed in many basalt and andesite flows.

Layering can also occur in igneous rocks. Multiple successive lava flows create bedding that stacks up in layers. In flow banding, minerals align from the flow of molten rock during the process of formation and cooling. Bands may be planar or swirled, and individual mineral crystals are undeformed. Flow banding

Columnar andesite in Mount Rainier National Park

is more commonly seen in volcanic rocks that have erupted on Earth's surface but can also be present in plutonic (magma chamber) rocks.

In coarse crystalline rocks, cumulate layering looks like light and dark banding and is formed by minerals sinking to the bottom of a magma chamber. The individual crystals and overall rock texture are undeformed. This kind of layering is rare.

Igneous rocks are therefore identified by a combination of rock textures and mineral content. The hallmark of an igneous rock is an assortment of mineral crystals with random orientations that fit together in an interlocking texture like 3D puzzle pieces. Ultimately, the mineral content and crystal size of an individual igneous rock tell the story of that rock's formation. They help us distinguish between a rock formed from an undersea volcanic eruption and one that grew at the root of a mountain system like the Cascades. The following entries detail how to identify different igneous rock types and to learn what story each can tell.

PLUTONIC ROCKS

coarse crystalline

Plutons are large bodies of rock cooled from magma underground. Crystals are randomly oriented and some display sharp corners and well-defined edges. Nearly every crystal is large enough to see with the naked eye. Individual crystals may be small (millimeters) or large (centimeters). Rocks with this texture are also known as intrusive, because they appear to have "intruded" into existing rocks. When many plutons repeatedly intrude a large area, the composite plutonic body is known as a batholith.

Most rocks will be a combination of light- and dark-colored minerals, giving a salt-and-pepper appearance. In general, rocks with mostly dark minerals are mafic, those that are half dark–half light are intermediate, and those that have mostly light minerals are felsic.

Peridotite

Ultramafic

RARE

Key Minerals Greater than 90 percent olivine, clinopyroxene, or orthopyroxene; may contain minor plagioclase feldspar

1 cm

Dark olivine in dunite, a variety of peridotite, Twin Sisters Mountain, Washington

Black peridotite outcrop with red-orange weathering, Fidalgo Island, Washington

Rock Features Coarsely crystalline and usually without rock fabric; overall black, dark green, or dark brown with a rusty orange weathering rind.

In Outcrop Peridotite's high magnesium content prevents most plants from growing over its outcrops, so they are usually lumpy and exposed or associated with unusual plant life such as the carnivorous pitcher plant.

More Info Peridotite comes from beneath Earth's crust. It's part of the mantle, Earth's solid middle layer that makes up most of our planet's volume. Despite the mantle's enormous size, mantle rocks rarely appear on Earth's surface. They must be lifted up by tectonic forces, for example when compression pushes a piece of ocean crust up onto a continent and the top part of the mantle rides along.

Notable Localities OR: BM, Aldrich Mountains (Canyon Mountain Complex); KM, south of Cave Junction (Josephine Ophiolite). **WA**: NC, Yellow Aster Butte (Yellow Aster Complex), Longs Pass south of Mt. Stuart (Ingalls Complex), Twin Sisters Mountains, Fidalgo Island (Fidalgo Ophiolite).

Gabbro

Mafic

UNCOMMON

Key Minerals Plagioclase feldspar (labradorite) and a combination of clinopyroxene, orthopyroxene, olivine, or hornblende

Rock Features Coarse crystalline rock with plagioclase feldspar and more than 35 percent dark-colored (mafic) minerals. Usually without a rock fabric, but may display cumulate layering from mineral crystals settling at the bottom of the magma chamber during formation.

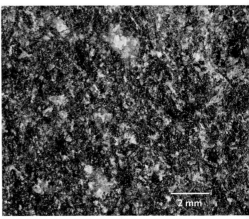

Pyroxene and plagioclase in gabbro, Klamath Mountains, Oregon

In Outcrop Irregular lumpy exposures. Layered cumulates still have coarse interlocking crystals, differentiating them from sedimentary rocks, and crystals lack a preferred orientation, differing from metamorphic rocks.

More Info Forms when peridotite from Earth's mantle partially melts and the resulting magma cools slowly underground. If that magma erupts on the surface, it forms basalt instead. Gabbro makes up the lower layer of ocean crust and the deep roots of some volcanic systems. It's usually found where ocean crust has been pushed up onto the continent by tectonic forces. This process exposes the gabbro to heat, pressure, and fluid, commonly giving the rock a green cast from low-grade metamorphism and chlorite growth.

Notable Localities OR: COR, Marys Peak; BM, Eagle Cap Wilderness (Wallowa Batholith), Aldrich Mountains (Canyon Mountain Complex); KM, south of Cave Junction (Josephine Ophiolite). **WA**: NC, Ingalls Lake (Ingalls Complex), Orcas Island (Turtleback Complex); OKH, Dishman Hills Natural Area (Priest River Complex).

Diorite

Intermediate

COMMON

Key Minerals Plagioclase feldspar (andesine, oligoclase) with hornblende, biotite, and clinopyroxene (augite)

Rock Features Coarse crystalline rock with plagioclase feldspar and less than 35 percent dark-colored (mafic) minerals. May have some alkali feldspar (orthoclase) and, rarely, minor visible quartz.

In Outcrop Irregular lumpy exposures. Also found as intrusive dikes or sills within other formations.

More Info Comes from melts with an intermediate amount of iron that cool slowly underground; if the magma erupts on the surface, it forms andesite instead. In the Northwest, diorite is usually found as small bodies associated with batholiths. It's also associated with the roots of the Cascades and similar volcanic systems.

Notable Localities OR: CAS, Mt. Hood (Laurel Hill Pluton), Shellrock Mountain; BM, Eagle Cap Wilderness (Wallowa Batholith); KM, Pearse Peak. **WA**: NC, Black Peak and Washington Pass area (Golden Horn Batholith); CAS, Wind Mountain.

Diorite from Mt. Rainier, Washington

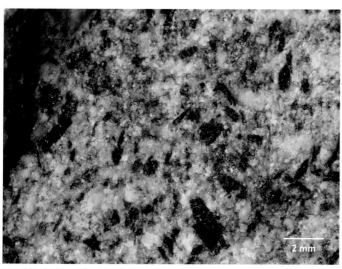

Hornblende diorite from Washington

Granite and Granitic Rocks ★

Felsic

COMMON

Key Minerals Quartz, plagioclase feldspar (albite, oligoclase), alkali feldspar (orthoclase, microcline); may contain muscovite, biotite or hornblende

Rock Features Coarse crystalline; usually light-colored overall with some dark minerals. Quartz makes up more than 20 percent of all the light-colored minerals. Rarely, the alkali feldspar is pink.

In Outcrop Irregular lumpy exposures; also found as dikes within other formations, sometimes associated with extensive veining in host rock. Large exposures of granitic rocks may weather into hemispherical shapes.

More Info True granite is rare in Oregon and Washington. Most "granitic" rocks in the Northwest don't have quite the right proportion of plagioclase and alkali feldspar to qualify for the scientific definition of granite, but they are similar enough that they are often lumped together. One common cousin is granodiorite, which has a high percentage of plagioclase feldspar. Granitic rocks form when iron-poor and silica- and aluminum-rich magma cools and crystallizes underground; if the magma erupts on the surface, it forms rhyolite or dacite. Most granitic rocks in the Northwest are found in batholiths—in our region, they formed when the landmasses that make up most of Oregon and Washington collided, burying and melting large volumes of sediment. Fluids related to granitic intrusions are often rich in rare elements, including gold, and can result in ore deposits in the rocks surrounding granitic bodies.

Notable Localities OR: BM, Eagle Cap Wilderness (Wallowa Batholith), near Cornucopia (Cornucopia Stock), Anthony Lakes (Bald Mountain Batholith); KM, Gold Hill, Mt. Ashland (true granite). **WA**: NC,

8 cm

Granodiorite from Mt. Rainier, Washington, with mafic enclaves (pieces of dark, older rock caught up by the pluton)

Quartz and feldspar in granite, Golden Horn Batholith, Washington

Washington Pass (Golden Horn Batholith), Silver Star Mountain and Liberty Bell Mountain (true granite), Deception Falls and Mt. Stuart (Mt. Stuart Batholith); OKH, Mt. Spokane (true granite).

VOLCANIC ROCKS

 fine crystalline

 porphyritic

These fine-grained igneous rocks are overall black, gray, tan, or pink and lack individual visible crystals. They break into blocky chunks with a rough, uneven, or hackly fracture surface, usually without any preferred orientation. Rocks with this texture cooled quickly from a lava on Earth's surface.

Some fine-grained rocks may include individual crystals that are large enough to stand out from the groundmass. This texture is called a porphyry. It occurs when a magma begins to grow crystals slowly underground but erupts on the surface as lava before completely solidifying. The large crystals are carried to the surface in the liquid, which solidifies around them into a fine-grained matrix. Porphyritic crystals can give us clues about the minerals present in the rest of the rock that are too small to see.

Basalt with vesicles, Newberry National Volcanic Monument, Oregon

Colorful basalt cinders near Newberry National Volcanic Monument, Oregon

Basalt ★

Mafic

VERY COMMON

Key Minerals Plagioclase feldspar, clinopyroxene and orthopyroxene; also hornblende and olivine

Rock Features Fine-grained crystalline texture with few or no visible crystals; overall black groundmass, infrequently containing porphyritic crystals of plagioclase

feldspar (greenish or grayish white), pyroxene (black), hornblende (black), or olivine (green-black). May be massive or retain vesicles from gas bubbles in the erupting lava. Very vesicular basalt may be red or other colors.

In Outcrop In thick, massive layers from large flows, basalt sometimes fractures into hexagonal columns during the cooling process. Thick flows may also contain hollow

Layers of basalt flows in Palouse River Canyon, Washington

The most common appearance for a basalt outcrop: blocky and dark brown to black, near Liberty, Washington

Surface of a basalt lava flow with ropey pahoe'hoe and rubbly a'a textures, McKenzie Pass, Oregon

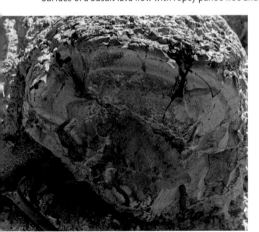

A basalt pillow near Wenatchee, Washington. These structures form when flowing basalt lava enters water. Hammer for scale.

Vesicular basalt with plagioclase feldspar porphyry, McKenzie Pass, Oregon. Feldspars in basalt are usually darker or greener than feldspars in andesite porphyry.

lava tubes. In thinner layers from smaller flows, the rock may have a smooth, ropey surface texture (called pahoe'hoe) or a rubbly and rough surface (called a'a). Mounds of loose, highly vesicular stones (called cinder) or frothy stones (called scoria) may be black or red. Also found in round, bulbous pillows that form when basalt lava erupts underwater.

More Info Forms when peridotite from Earth's mantle partially melts and the magma erupts on the surface; if the magma cools underground, it forms gabbro instead. Basalt is one of the most widespread rocks in Oregon, Washington, and around the world, covering the ocean floors as the top igneous layer of ocean crust, forming innumerable islands, and spreading over continents with extensive flows from volcanic vents.

Notable Localities Basalt can be found in every region of the Pacific Northwest, sometimes as a prominent feature, and sometimes as a minor component. The most extensive basalts are the Columbia River Basalts (CRB), which cover an area roughly the size of Kansas (164,00 square miles) within Oregon and Washington, plus a bit of Idaho. The CRBs make up such prominent landmarks as: (OR/WA) the Columbia River Gorge, including Multnomah Falls. Also, **OR**: COR, Haystack Rock near Cannon Beach; CAS, Silver Falls State Park; BM, Hells Canyon; BR, Steens Mountain. And **WA**: CB, most of the ridges and canyons of the entire Columbia Basin, including Grand Coulee and Palouse Falls. Besides the CRBs, notable basalts are found in **OR**: COR, northwest of Corvallis (Siletz Terrane); CAS, the Western Cascades; HLP, Newberry Volcanic National Monument; OWY, Diamond Craters and Jordan Craters. And **WA**: OLY, Crescent Formation; CAS, basalts of Mt. Saint Helens, including Ape Cave; distributed in NC.

Andesite ★

Intermediate

VERY COMMON

Key Minerals Plagioclase feldspar (andesine), hornblende, clinopyroxene, biotite; also small amounts of quartz

Rock Features Fine-grained crystalline texture; overall gray to pinkish groundmass with few to no visible crystals, commonly scattered with porphyritic crystals of plagioclase (white) and biotite or hornblende (black). May be massive or retain vesicles from gas bubbles in the erupting lava. Similar in appearance to dacite, but less likely to host visible quartz and more likely to have vesicles. Very dark andesite may be difficult to distinguish from basalt.

In Outcrop In thin or thick layers, usually extensive in scale. Thick layers may be fractured into hexagonal columns during the cooling process, though columnar jointing is more commonly seen in basalts.

More Info Forms when basalt or gabbro are partially melted and the magma erupts on the surface; if the magma cools

2.5 cm

Andesite with porphyritic plagioclase showing range of groundmass colors, Mt. Hood, Oregon. Feldspars in andesite are usually whiter than those in basalt porphyry.

Columnar jointing in fine crystalline andesite, Mt. Baker, Washington

Summit view from McNeil Point on Mt. Hood. The entire mountain is made largely of andesite with some dacite.

underground, it forms diorite instead. This rock type is a hallmark of Cascades-style volcanic systems—for example, it composes nearly the entirety of Oregon's Mt. Hood. Andesite can also appear in complex volcanic settings that produce several different types of volcanic rock.

Notable Localities OR: CAS, Mt. Hood, Mt. Jefferson, Crater Lake, Mt. Mazama; HLP, Frederick Butte; BR, Gearhart Mountain; BM, eastern Strawberry Mountains. **WA**: CAS, Mt. Rainier, Mt. Adams, Mt. Baker; OKH, near Republic (Sanpoil Volcanics).

Platy jointing in andesite outcrop (hammer for scale), McKenzie Pass, Oregon

Rhyolite and Dacite

Felsic

COMMON

Key Minerals Quartz, alkali feldspar (sanidine), plagioclase feldspar (andesine), biotite; also hornblende, and for dacite, clinopyroxene (augite)

Rock Features Fine-grained crystalline texture; overall pink, tan, greenish, brown, or gray groundmass, often with a sun-bleached cast to the colors, though the color has not actually been affected by the sun. Rhyolite and dacite are differentiated in the field by their porphyritic crystals, if present. Rhyolite is more likely to host significant alkali feldspar (clear sanidine) and quartz (clear or gray), while dacite is more likely to host plagioclase feldspar (white andesine), quartz, and biotite (black).

In Outcrop Both rhyolite and dacite form domes or layers with limited lateral extent and are often found together. Flow banding is common in rhyolite especially; it may be interleaved with layers of obsidian or pumice. Some rhyolite flows host thunder eggs, Oregon's state rock.

More Info Forms when sandstones or mudstones are buried and melted, or when andesite or diorite is partially melted, and the magma erupts on the surface. Rhyolite and dacite lavas are extremely viscous, readily piling and cooling into steep-sided domes. These lavas may also erupt explosively rather than flow, creating tuffs.

Notable Localities OR: CAS, South Sister, Rooster Rock near Hwy 20; HLP, Glass Buttes, near Burns; BM, Powell Butte, Grizzly Mountain; OWY, Mahogany Mountain north of Jordan Valley. **WA**: CAS, Mt. Saint Helens; NC, near Cle Elum (Naches Formation); incidental occurrences in many other areas of the state.

Glassy rhyolite with conchoidal fracture, South Sister, Oregon

Fine crystalline rhyolite, Gray Butte, Oregon

2 cm

Fine crystalline dacite with hornblende porphyry, Mt. Rainier, Washington

Rhyolite domes, South Sister, Oregon

Dacite with biotite porphyry, fresh and weathered
surfaces, Crater Lake, Oregon

Flow banding in rhyolite, South Sister, Oregon

THUNDER EGGS

The thunder egg is a beloved symbol of Oregon rockhounding, found in many deposits (and gift shops) across the state. But what is it, exactly, and where did it get its curious name?

A thunder egg is a special kind of geode that has a shell formed from volcanic rock and a jagged interior cavity usually filled with agate. Opal, jasper, calcite, barite, and other minerals have also been found in thunder egg cores. Thunder eggs look like brown, bumpy balls on the outside, but when cut open they reveal their unique and beautiful interiors.

The shells form in rhyolite lava flows, though the exact process that leads to the starburst-shaped interior cavity is still not understood. After the lava flow and thunder egg shells cool, groundwater carries and deposits minerals into these cavities over the course of millions of years. The colors that fill the centers depend on the specific mineral ingredients carried in by the water.

As for the name—many stories about its origins as an "old Indian legend" abound. In truth, the man who popularized the term was a white rockhound from the Portland area named J. Lewis Renton. He first published the name in a 1936 issue of the journal *The Mineralogist* and attributed it to an "Indian gentleman" he spoke with on what is now the Warm Springs Reservation. He surmised that the term must refer to a story about missiles hurled by the thunder gods who resided on mountaintops. Other stories claim the rocks are eggs of the giant thunder bird.

Unfortunately, no present-day sources from the Confederated Tribes of Warm Springs have confirmed the existence of any kind of ancient story or legend surrounding these rocks. While we will never know for certain what kind of conversation Renton may have had in the 1930s, it seems that his legend of the thunder egg grew in the telling.

1 cm

Whole thunder egg and cut and polished egg with opal (white), agate (gray), and amethyst (purple), Madras, Oregon

5 mm

Unfilled thunder egg "shells" in rhyolite flow

Thunder egg with blue banded and moss agate interior, Ochoco Mountains, Oregon

Thunder egg with quartz interior, Ochoco Mountains, Oregon

VOLCANIC GLASSES

A glass is a solid without any crystals. Its atoms attach to one another in an amorphous network rather than a rigid, repeating crystal lattice. Most geologic glasses form in volcanic eruptions under special circumstances, as we'll describe in specific entries.

Obsidian

Felsic

UNCOMMON

Key Components Volcanic glass with few to zero crystals or gas bubbles

Rock Features Usually black, though it may be streaked with red (variety mahogany) or iridescent colors (variety rainbow) from tiny inclusions of hematite or magnetite. Breaks in a conchoidal fracture with a razor-sharp edge.

In Outcrop Forms domes or layers with limited lateral extent, often exhibiting flow banding and interlayering with pumice or rhyolite. High-silica lava flows can cool and break apart while still in motion, resulting in a blocky, rubbly unit.

More Info Lavas that make obsidian have a low water content compared to other silica-rich lavas. This lack of water inhibits crystal growth by making the lava thicker and stickier, preventing atoms from moving into organized lattice positions. Over millions of years, however, obsidian absorbs water from the environment, and its atoms do link up into tiny crystals, causing the obsidian to devitrify. Completely devitrified obsidian is a crumbly, powdery substance called perlite.

Black obsidian with conchoidal fracture, Big Obsidian Flow, Oregon

Mahogany obsidian, Glass Buttes, Oregon

Notable Localities OR: HLP, Newberry Volcano (Big Obsidian Flow), Glass Buttes; BM, Bear Creek in Malheur National Forest; CAS, Three Sisters Wilderness (Obsidian Cliffs); many other distributed localities throughout the state, excluding COR and WV. **WA**: NC, Copper Ridge, Agnes Creek; several distributed localities in CAS and the westernmost CB.

The edge of the Big Obsidian Flow

Flow banding in an obsidian outcrop, Big Obsidian Flow, Oregon

Pumice

Felsic

UNCOMMON

Key Components Frothy volcanic glass; may include some crystals

Rock Features Overall white to gray mixture of volcanic glass and small, scattered crystals with abundant vesicles from gas bubbles.

In Outcrop Two major types: vesicular bands within obsidian flows, and pebble- to boulder-sized chunks ejected from violent volcanic eruptions (see also tuffs).

More Info Some magmas are like carbonated soda pop—they have gasses dissolved in them that bubble violently when they are shaken and pressure is released suddenly from the top. In the case of magma, this happens when it rises rapidly toward the surface within a volcano's plumbing system. Pumice is analogous to explosive soda foam that has solidified. It floats when placed in water.

Notable Localities OR: CAS, Crater Lake and Mt. Mazama; HLP, Tumalo State Park, Newberry Volcano, Burns Butte near Hines. **WA**: CAS, Mt. Saint Helens, Glacier Peak.

2 cm

Pumice, Big Obsidian Flow, Oregon

2 cm

Visibly glassy pumice, Big Obsidian Flow, Oregon

SEDIMENTARY ROCKS

Sedimentary rocks form through accumulation. Most sedimentary rocks are made of broken fragments of other rocks naturally cemented together. Water, wind, and gravity wear away at rocks on Earth's surface, eroding pieces and transporting them to oceans, lakes, or land basins where the fragments, now called clasts, come to rest. The clasts pile up in layers, and when the oldest layers are buried deeply enough, pressure from the overlying deposits can cause tiny crystals to grow from minerals in groundwater, encrusting the buried clasts and binding or cementing them all together.

Individual clasts may range from the size of a car to smaller than the eye can see. Clasts may be jagged and angular or rounded and smooth, and they may be rock fragments or individual crystals. They store a wealth of information—if a sandstone is made entirely of tiny, round quartz grains, for instance, it may have come from a sand dune deposit, which forms from particles small enough to be carried by the wind. If it's composed instead of larger, angular volcanic clasts, its source may have been deposits made by a mountain stream draining the Cascades.

Overall, the composition, size, arrangement, and roundedness of clasts record where they first came from, how they were transported, and in what environment they came to rest. This provides many clues to what the surface of the Earth looked like while the deposits were forming.

Another distinctive feature of sedimentary rocks is bedding, or the stacked layering formed by the successive deposition of sediments over time. Individual beds may be fine laminations less than one millimeter apart, or they may be several meters thick.

Some clastic sedimentary beds contain additional, distinctive features. In layers with graded bedding, the largest clasts are concentrated on the bottom of the bed and clast size gradually decreases toward the top. This texture indicates that the sediment making up the bed was carried by

Clastic texture in a rock (note the individual grains bound together by naturally formed mineral cement)

Bedding in consolidated layers of sediment

cross-bedding

bedding

Cross-bedding in sandstone near Yakima, Washington. The beds are titled to the right and the dark rock at the top of the photo is a mafic lava flow.

Graded bedding in a brown sandstone layer between two dark mudstone layers

preserved remnants of ripples or dunes. They are present across a wide range of scales, from thin layers in sandstones to meter-thick beds.

Not all sedimentary rocks are clastic—some are formed entirely by the chemical growth of minerals from water. This usually creates a fine crystalline texture that can be massive, laminated, or bedded. Mineral growth may happen in fluid-filled cavities or pore spaces underground, or it may occur when water evaporates on Earth's surface and leaves minerals behind. Other sedimentary rocks have a significant biological component, as when plant leaves are compressed into coal.

water that experienced a change in fluid flow over time. Initially, the water was moving quickly enough to transport the larger clasts, but as its speed decreased, it dropped the largest clasts to the bottom of the bed first, followed by smaller and smaller particles as the flow got slower.

Sediments transported by water or wind may also display cross-bedding—the layering of sand or gravel particles at an angle to the top and bottom of a single sedimentary bed. Cross-beds are the

While igneous and metamorphic rocks record forces acting deep within Earth, sedimentary rocks tell the story of Earth's surface. More information about surficial processes can be found in the chapter on Landscapes and Geomorphology. Records of climate, topography, and ancient, long-eroded mountains come from sedimentary rocks.

PEBBLES, SAND, AND MUD

The terms pebble, sand, and mud all refer to specific sizes of sediments—loose fragments of rock that have broken off larger outcrops and been transported by gravity, wind, or water until they accumulate and come to rest. Each individual particle is called a clast. A muddy riverbank; sand dunes on a beach; a recent landslide—these are all examples of accumulated sediment deposits.

If you picture a pebble in your head or a grain of sand, you probably have an idea of about how large each is. That's because the terms used to describe particle sizes have specific definitions based on particle diameter:

Boulder >250 mm

Cobble 64–250 mm

Pebble 2–64 mm

Sand 0.05–2 mm

Silt 0.004–0.05 mm

Clay <0.004 mm

Mud This term is generally used for sediments with a mixture of silt- and clay-sized particles

These size categories can help us understand the systems that move sediment around. For example, it's intuitive ▶

Rounded sand and pebbles on a beach, Olympic Peninsula

PEBBLES, SAND, AND MUD *(cont.)*

that a river in roaring flood is able to move larger particles than a light breeze on the beach is able to. Studying particle sizes in a sedimentary deposit can tell us a lot about the energy of the system that put it there.

Because tiny silt and clay particles can remain suspended even in still water for long periods of time, we know mud deposits form in quiet environments like isolated ponds, the very deep ocean, or at the end of a flood as the waters slowly retreat. Very fine sand and silt can be blown and deposited by wind. Coarser-grained sands require a bit more energy to shift, so they appear along riverbeds and beaches—this kind of deposit, or any sediment worked by a river, is known as alluvium. Pebbles can be carried by high-energy river systems or smaller systems experiencing a flood event. Even larger particles, cobble- or boulder-sized rocks, are moved by gravity in events like debris flows and landslides.

This correlation helps us "see" events and transport systems even if they aren't active anymore. Looking for some land near the mountains to build a new house? Before you buy, have an engineering geologist check the area for boulders or other evidence of landslide deposits so you don't build on unstable ground.

Sediments can exist as deposits that are still being worked by modern forces like rivers and oceans as well as those left behind by glaciers or ancient water-

Beach sand made of multicolored clasts, Newport, Oregon

Desiccation cracks in mud, Liberty, Washington

Compacted layer of pebbles, Olympic Peninsula

ways that have long since disappeared. They may be loose and easy to dig into with hands or hand tools, or compacted and semi-consolidated (cohesive but not firmly cemented together). Most sediments are draped relatively thinly over Earth's surface, covering up areas of bedrock. Thick deposits may eventually be buried deeply enough to become sedimentary rocks.

Every beach, lake, and active waterway contains sediments. In Oregon, notable young sediment deposits include extensive sand dunes at Oregon Dunes National Recreation Area, the area around shrinking ice-age lakes Abert and Hart, and playa lakes in the Alvord Desert that fill and evaporate seasonally. In Washington, the entire Puget Lowlands are virtually covered in glacial till and outwash, and the Palouse Hills are composed of very small quartz and clay fragments known as loess that were ground down by glaciers and blown by the wind into large mounds.

CLASTIC ROCKS

 clastic

 massive, homogeneous

 layered

These are rocks made from broken pieces of other rocks that have been naturally cemented together. Clastic sedimentary rocks cover most of Earth's surface and represent an enormous variety of different Earth processes and environments.

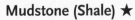

Layers of black mudstone from a freshwater lake, Randle, Washington

Mudstone (Shale) ★

VERY COMMON

Key Components Clays and silt-size grains, usually quartz

Rock Features Black, gray, tan to brown, red, or green rocks with no visible clasts that break into thin layers. Mudstone is a mix of clay minerals and silt-sized quartz grains, and its tactile texture ranges from very smooth to slightly gritty.

In Outcrop Makes finely laminated layers that can form as a thick, individual unit. If the unit has thin layering that breaks easily, it is called fissile layering. Mudstones are also found as thin horizons between other sedimentary rocks like sandstone or limestone. If the mud hosted many plant roots or animal burrows before burial and compaction, the mudstone layers may be disrupted and the unit more massive.

Fissile layering in mudstone, Mt. Baker, Washington

Typical crumbling mudstone outcrop, Liberty, Washington

More Info Mudstone forms from clay particles that fall to the bottom of large, quiet bodies of water, such as large lakes or ocean basins. Its fine layers can preserve excellent body impressions of plant and animal fossils.

Notable Localities OR: COR, near Eugene (Lorane Shale), near Newport (Nye Mudstone). **WA**: PLO, southern end of Bainbridge Island, southwestern King County (Puget Group); COR, near Humptulips. Also as thin layers interbedded with many sandstone and limestone units across both states.

Sandstone ★

VERY COMMON

Key Components Quartz, feldspar, rock fragments, clays; also calcite

Rock Features Clastic texture, with grains up to 2 millimeters in size bound by natural cements. Individual grains are pieces of quartz, feldspar, or rock fragments (usually volcanic) that show slight to extensive rounding; cement may be microcrystalline quartz or calcite.

In Outcrop Units may be a few inches or hundreds of feet thick. Layering of multiple sandstone beds and other sedimentary units is usually apparent. Sandstone layers can display many internal features, including grading and reverse grading, cross-bedding, ripple marks, and channel structures.

2 mm

Close-up of clastic texture in sandstone

Tilted beds of sandstone and shale, Riddle, Oregon

Thinly bedded sandstone and shale outcrop (pencil for scale), Sunset Bay, Oregon

More Info Sandstones can represent deposits from oceans, beaches, lakes, rivers, and sand dunes. Sandstone clasts may be made up of minerals and rock fragments from mountain ranges that have long since eroded away, and sandstone beds often represent former valleys or basins that have filled and closed. When the clasts that make up a sandstone are poorly sorted and surrounded by a high percentage of cement matrix, it is known as a wacke-type sandstone.

Notable Localities OR, COR, marine sandstone is visible in many roadcuts from Drain to Reedsport, Florence to Eugene, and Newport to Corvallis (Tyee Formation); KM, marine sandstone at Bandon Beach (Otter Point Formation); BM, river-channel sandstones at Haystack Valley (John Day Formation). **WA:** NC, floodplain sandstones in Lookout Mountain area near Bellingham and Larrabee State Park (Chuckanut Formation); OKH, volcanic clast-rich sandstones near Republic (Klondike Mountain Formation).

A wacke-type sandstone, Deception Pass, Washington

Conglomerate

VERY COMMON

Key Components Rock fragments, quartz, feldspar, clays; also calcite

Rock Features Clastic texture with particles greater than 2 millimeters in size bound by natural cements. Most clasts are rounded. Individual clasts are usually rock fragments, though large individual grains of quartz or feldspar may occur.

In Outcrop Layers from a few inches to hundreds of feet in thickness. Layering of multiple conglomerate beds and other sedimentary units is usually apparent. Conglomerate layers can display many internal features, including grading and reverse grading, cross-bedding, and channel structures.

More Info Conglomerate clasts can range from smaller than a pencil eraser to the size of a car or larger. These sizes are so large, the clasts can only have been moved by tumbling down steep slopes or being carried by high volumes of energetic water. Conglomerates may therefore represent deposits from alluvial fans, fast-moving rivers, and debris flows, including underwater landslides.

Notable Localities OR: KM, Humbug Mountain and nearby beach (Humbug Mountain Conglomerate); WV, consolidated gravels along the Willamette River (Missoula Flood deposits, Troutdale Gravels); BM, Haystack Valley (John Day Formation). **WA**: OLY, Taylor Point (Hoh Assemblage); NC, near Ellensburg (Ellensburg Formation); OKH, near Republic (O'Brien Creek Formation).

Outcrop of conglomerate rock

Conglomerate with many different clasts, including limestone and volcanic rock

Breccia

VERY COMMON

Key Components Rock fragments of any composition

Rock Features Clastic texture with particles greater than 2 millimeters in size bound by natural cement. Most clasts are angular and jagged. Individual clasts may be recognizable as fragments of igneous, metamorphic, or other sedimentary rocks. (If all clasts are only fragments of volcanic rocks, see entry for volcanic breccia under volcaniclastic rocks.)

In Outcrop Most breccias are not laterally extensive. They may be found along certain fault surfaces or in other settings where rocks were broken or crushed but not transported long distances.

More Info Many breccias are formed from the motion of a fault grinding and breaking rocks at its interface during earthquakes, while others form below steep slopes or cliffs as a result of rockfalls or landslides. Whatever the means of formation, breccias come from broken rocks that have not moved far from their origin—they're composed of angular clasts with sharp edges and corners. Clasts that spend more time bouncing and rolling along become smoother and rounder over time—these deposits become conglomerates. The major difference between a breccia and a conglomerate is the degree of rounding in the clasts.

Notable Localities Breccias are not usually extensive enough to create mappable rock formations, but they can be found in many settings that have experienced fault movement or significant rock-fall events.

Breccia, Madras, Oregon

VOLCANICLASTIC ROCKS

 clastic

 massive, homogeneous

 layered

A volcaniclastic rock is a clastic sedimentary rock in which all the clasts are volcanic. Even though they may form during events like volcanic eruptions, volcaniclastic rocks are not rocks that form directly from cooling lava, so they get their own special category within sedimentary rocks.

Tuff ★

COMMON

Key Components Volcanic ash, rock fragments, pumice, some crystals (feldspar, mica, quartz)

Rock Features Deposits of volcanic ash, rock fragments, individual crystals, and clasts of pumice that collect after an explosive volcanic eruption. Wide range of compositions, from all ash to all pumice and everything in between. Distinguished from fine-grained volcanic rocks by clastic rather than interlocking crystalline texture. Welded tuffs form when ash and other material collects while still hot and the particles "weld" together, obscuring original particle boundaries or even appearing glassy; the presence of pumice clasts helps distinguish welded tuffs from volcanic flows. Lithic tuffs are made largely of preexisting rock fragments.

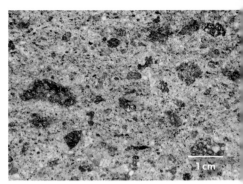

Lithic tuff, Mt. Rainier, Washington

Airfall tuff with pumice

Welded tuff with glassy fragments

Columnar jointing in the Rattlesnake Ash-Flow Tuff

Tuff spires at Smith Rock State Park, Oregon

In Outcrop Large eruptions can create units that cover hundreds of square miles. Units vary in thickness depending on proximity to the vent source and underlying topography (thicker in valleys closer to the source, thinner on ridgelines or in deposits that fall far away). Rock fragments and pumice usually fall to rest within a few miles of the source, but volcanic ash—actually tiny particles of volcanic glass—can travel around the world on high atmospheric currents and settle hundreds or thousands of miles away. Ashfall deposits can get reworked by streams before they are compacted and solidified, so some clasts in tuffs may exhibit water-worn rounding, and some deposits show structures like ripple marks and channels.

More Info Like igneous rocks, tuffs start out as lavas. They are classified as sedimentary rocks, however, because when the lavas erupt explosively, their particles solidify in the air before accumulating like sediments on the ground. Tuff names are based on their lava composition, for example, rhyolite tuff, andesitic tuff, basaltic tuff. Rhyolite tuffs are the most common.

The explosive processes that make tuffs are called pyroclastic ("fire particle") eruptions. The most formidable of these eruptions can generate clouds of volcanic gas, ash, and rock so hot they glow red and are heavy enough to rush down a slope at over 60 miles per hour, obliterating everything in the way. Tuffs are reminders of Earth's capacity for sudden violence.

Notable Localities OR: CAS, the Pinnacles at Crater Lake (Wineglass Welded Tuff) and widespread deposits of Mazama Ash; HLP, Fort Rock and Table Rock; BR, Trout Creek Mountains near McDermitt; BM, John Day River Valley (Rattlesnake Ash-Flow Tuff). **WA**: CAS, Mt. Rainier, Mt. Saint Helens; minor components of other igneous and sedimentary sequences across the state.

Volcanic Breccia

COMMON

Key Components Jagged, angular volcanic rock fragments

Rock Features Broken, jagged, and angular to somewhat rounded pieces of volcanic rock, usually basalt or andesite, bound together with natural cements. By comparison, rock fragments in tuffs are usually andesite, dacite, or rhyolite, and are also mixed with ash and pumice.

In Outcrop Layers may be internally chaotic or may display graded or reverse graded bedding.

More Info Young volcanic slopes can be very steep and unstable, and flows can break apart soon after cooling. The broken chunks fall down the sides of the volcano and collect into deposits that are later buried, compacted, and bound by the growth of natural cements from groundwater. (Non-volcanic breccias will contain clasts of any composition.)

Notable Localities Volcanic breccias may be found in association with any sequence of volcanic rocks.

Mafic volcanic breccia in outcrop, Cape Perpetua, Oregon

Volcanic breccia altered to greenstone

Lahar Deposits

UNCOMMON

Key Components Volcanic rock fragments, ash, mud, organic debris

Rock Features Particle sizes may range from tiny (ash) to enormous (car-sized).

In Outcrop Rounded volcanic clasts of widely varying sizes in thick deposits with an overall texture resembling concrete, usually displaying fluvial sedimentary structures on some scale.

More Info Lahars are muddy debris flows that originate on the snow-capped peaks of tall volcanoes. They can originate from an increase in volcanic activity heating up

10 cm

Outcrop of lahar deposit showing textures consistent with high-volume fluid transport

A lahar from the May 18, 1980, eruption of Mt. Saint Helens overwhelmed the Toutle River and carried this steel bridge structure over a quarter mile down the valley on a fast-moving slurry of rock debris and water that eventually settled into a material resembling concrete.

and melting snow and ice on tall volcanoes, through intense rainfall on a volcano, or by a partial collapse of the volcano. The flows combine a slurry of rock, mud, ash, and trees into a mixture like wet concrete that can flow at speeds greater than 60 miles per hour. River drainages coming off the volcano can funnel lahars, swamping valleys with sediment and sweeping away anything in their path.

Notable Localities Predominantly surrounding the volcanoes of both the Oregon and Washington Cascades. The lahar runout from Mt. Saint Helens's 1980 eruption is strikingly visible along the North Fork of the Toutle River where it destroyed hundreds of homes and structures. The Sandy River near Mt. Hood was named the Quicksand River by Lewis and Clark, who encountered it clogged with sediments from a lahar likely related to the mountain's 1781 eruptions. Many communities southeast of Seattle are built on deposits from geologically recent (Holocene, younger than 10,000 years) lahars from Mt. Rainier.

CHEMICAL AND BIOLOGICAL ROCKS

 clastic

 layered

 massive, homogeneous

Technically, all rocks are made from chemical processes. But the term *chemical rock* is used in a stricter sense to refer to rocks formed in two dominant ways. One, accumulated from minerals that grow directly from water. This may happen in ocean water, groundwater, or water that "sweats" off magma intrusions in fissures underground. Two, alteration of existing rocks at or near Earth's surface. In this case, oxygen and water react with rocks similar to how they cause metal to rust.

Biological rocks contain a significant amount of organic material, usually animal shells or plant matter.

Paleosols (Old Soils)

UNCOMMON

Key Components Plant matter, clays, iron oxides and hydroxides, and other oxides or hydroxides

Rock Features Baked or consolidated soils; may contain plant roots or other elements. May resemble red brick in color and texture or may be very clayey or rich in calcium carbonate; can also be yellow, brown, or purple.

In Outcrop Forms often-colorful, easily eroded layers on the scale of centimeters to about a meter in thickness.

More Info Soils are thin surface coatings of clays, other mineral grains, and organic matter (plants, bacteria, and fungus). Paleosols are soils that have been preserved in the rock record. This can happen through

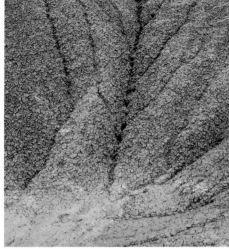

Cracks in a clay-rich paleosol, Painted Hills, John Day Fossil Beds National Monument, Oregon

Paleosols make the colorful layers of the Painted Hills.

ordinary sedimentary burial and compaction or, for instance, when a large basaltic eruption flows over a forested landscape, burning and consuming the plant life but baking the soil into a brick-like layer beneath it.

Notable Localities OR: BM, Painted Hills (John Day Formation), and many other localities within the Clarno and Mascall Formations; also found as red horizons between flows of the Columbia River Basalt Group. **WA**: CB, within the Ringold Formation; predominantly found as horizons between basalt flows.

Coal

UNCOMMON

Key Components Compressed plant matter

Rock Features Brown to black, low hardness, and very light for its size; blocky when broken. Lower grades of coal may contain recognizable plant material (peat), while higher grades of coal are strongly black, uniform, and may be shiny.

In Outcrop Forms in layers called seams from centimeters to meters in thickness.

More Info Coal forms when plant material built up in swamps or bogs is buried, compressed, and heated, driving off fluids and gasses and causing the carbon atoms from the plant materials to rearrange their bonds. Less compression or heating creates lower grades of coal, while more heating makes higher grades. In the Northwest, higher grades of coal are closer to volcanic centers than lower grades.

Notable Localities OR: COR, near Newport and along Nehalem River, also other scattered localities; KM, Coos Bay area; BM, John Day Basin (Clarno Formation, Mascall Formation). **WA**: CAS, near Carbonado, Ashford, Black Diamond; PLO, near Mt. Vernon, Bellingham (Chuckanut Formation).

Seam of lignite (low-grade coal) near Newport, Oregon

Limestone and Dolostone

UNCOMMON

Key Components Microcrystalline calcite or dolomite

Rock Features Whitish to gray, usually massive with no visible crystals and few internal features. May contain fossils like coral fragments or crinoid (sea lily) stems or collections of round to elongate blebs smaller than a pencil eraser. Some limestones may be clastic, where clasts are mostly limestone fragments bound with calcite cement.

In Outcrop Massive deposits or thin layers associated with mudstones and chert. Exposed surfaces may look smooth but feel rough and are often pockmarked from dissolution by the slight acidity of rainwater (a feature evocatively termed *tear-pants weathering*).

More Info Limestone forms from a combination of shells, corals, and other calcium-rich animal parts bound together by a calcite mud that forms in sea water. It's indicative of warm, shallow seas that did not receive much muddy or sandy runoff from land. Sometimes, seawater circulation can replace some of the calcium in limestone with magnesium, changing the calcite to dolomite. These dolostones resemble limestones in every way, though they do not fizz readily in acid unless powdered.

Notable Localities OR: KM, small bodies between Medford and Grants Pass and along the Applegate River; BM, Eagle Cap Wilderness and Hells Canyon (Martin Bridge Formation), Elkhorn Range (Baker Terrane), Greenhorn Mountains. **WA**: NC, Black Mountain (Chilliwack Group), thin layers or bodies associated with sequences of clastic sedimentary rocks; OKH, near Metaline Falls, Limestone Hill (Metaline Formation).

Paleozoic invertebrate fossils in limestone, Blue Mountains, Oregon

Microcrystalline limestone (micrite), Hells Canyon, Oregon

Clastic limestone

Coquina

UNCOMMON

Key Components Calcite, aragonite (as shells)

Rock Features A rock composed almost entirely from recognizable animal shells and shell fragments cemented together.

In Outcrop In thin layers or lenses, often associated with sandstones.

More Info Heavy wave action on a beach can create collections of broken shells, a feature easily found on modern beaches. Once buried and cemented, these collections become coquina.

Notable Localities Coquinas are usually thin bodies that are often too small to appear on geologic maps. Look for them in areas with shallow-water marine sedimentary rocks, like uplifted sedimentary beds at the coast and in the Coast Ranges.

Shell fragments and volcanic clasts in coquina

Chert

UNCOMMON

Key Components Silica (as opal or quartz)

Rock Features No visible crystals; rock has a waxy luster with a conchoidal fracture and a hardness of about 7. May be any color: earthy reds, browns, yellows, greens, grays, and blacks most common. Opaque. May have interior banding or spots.

In Outcrop Thin layers or nodules in sedimentary rock sequences, especially with mudstone or limestone. May also be found between volcanic flows or in gaps between pillow basalts.

More Info Chert forms in deep, calm waters, most commonly in the ocean but sometimes in lakes. Most chert layers form from the accumulation of silica-rich skeletons grown by microscopic aquatic organisms like radiolaria and diatoms (algae), or from the spines of animals like sea sponges. These organisms make their skeletons from opal—with burial, pressure, and time, the opal may change to granular, microscopic quartz. Nodular cherts are not biological in origin—they come from the cycling of rock silica through marine sediments under certain chemical conditions.

Notable Localities OR: BM, Elkhorn Range (Elkhorn Ridge Argillite), Greenhorn Mountains (Greenhorn Melange); KM, Rainbow Rock near Brookings (Yolla Bolly Terrane). **WA**: NC, Eagle Cove on San Juan Island (Orcas Chert), Rosario Head on Fidalgo Island (Lopez Complex); also as sedimentary clasts and gap infill associated with marine basalts in distributed CAS and OKH localities.

Fresh and weathered faces in chert samples

Ribbon chert in outcrop, Fidalgo Island, Washington

Diatomite

UNCOMMON

Key Components Accumulated diatom (algae) shells made from hydrated silica (opal)

Rock Features White, sometimes powdery; may exhibit fine laminations. Individual diatoms are microscopic, so diatomite is fairly uniform in appearance and has an overall earthy luster.

In Outcrop May be interbedded with other sedimentary rocks like tuff or mudstone or found as a surficial feature in a local topographical depression like a dry lakebed. Many deposits have been mined, and mining operations may leave behind diatomite piles or cliffs.

More Info Throughout the past 20 million years, large lakes periodically covered parts of Oregon and Washington and were home to algae called diatoms that made their microscopic shells from silica. Diatom shells accumulated on the lake bottoms for thousands to millions of years—some diatomite deposits contain fish, leaf, and insect fossils from lake dwellers throughout this time. Diatomite, also called diatomaceous earth, is mined for use in filters, paints, and insect control. Active and defunct mines can appear on aerial photographs as large white patches.

Notable Localities OR: BR, near Table Rock Airport, near Upper Klamath Lake; OWY, Trout Creek area south of Whitehorse Ranch; BM, near Beulah, near Baker City. **WA**: CB, north of Frenchman Coulee.

White, powdery diatomite, Trout Lake, Oregon

CHEMICAL ROCK FORMATIONS

Active chemical processes can create unique, localized geologic features at Earth's surface and just below it. These formations are usually limited in extent and thickness and may be ephemeral on the scale of geologic time.

Salt Flats (Playas)

UNCOMMON

Key Components Halite and other salt minerals

Rock Features A white crust of minerals, often covering a layer of mud, found in some desert valleys.

In Outcrop Salt playas are a surficial feature and not, strictly speaking, part of any outcrop.

More Info In arid climates like eastern Oregon, winter rains can create temporary lakes in topographic depressions. When the rains stop and summer comes again, the lake water evaporates away, leaving salt minerals behind. Many salt flats form on the margins of pluvial lakes, shrunken remnants of once-great bodies of water that filled basins during the last ice age.

Notable Localities OR: BR, the Alvord Desert and the flats around Summer Lake, Abert Lake, Alkali Lake, and others in the area.

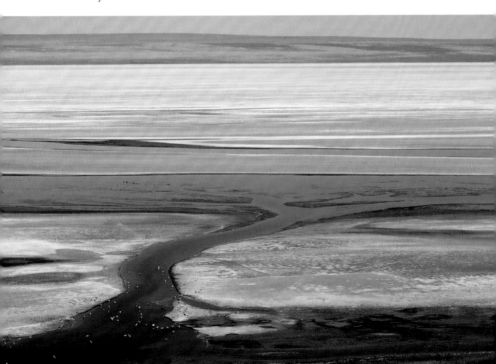

View over Lake Abert, Oregon

Hot Springs Deposits

RARE

Key Components Calcite (travertine), quartz (in sinter), or borax (a white, sodium borate mineral)

Rock Features Bulbous or tabular edifice with light-colored, often bleached appearance; interior has fine laminations that may be smooth and compact or wavy with many gaps.

In Outcrop Easily identified if the hot spring source is still active or present. Deposits from inactive springs are localized, surficial features. The "plumbing" systems of old hot springs can be recognized as fissures or breccia zones welded together by laminated travertine or sinter cements.

More Info Hot springs form when heated groundwater bubbles out onto Earth's surface. In the Pacific Northwest, much of this heating is theorized to come from the hot magma feeding our active Cascades volcanoes. Hot groundwater near these magma bodies is driven up through underground joints and cracks until it reaches the surface, where it cools and allows minerals to precipitate and grow.

Notable Localities OR: CAS, Umpqua Hot Springs (travertine); OWY, Borax Lake Hot Springs (sinter), Mickey Hot Springs (sinter, also has a geyser). **WA**: CB, Ohanapecosh Hot Springs (travertine). Note: many other active hot springs exist in the Northwest, but few have visibly deposited minerals.

Travertine deposits around a hot spring, Mt. Rainier, Washington

Cave Formations

RARE

Key Components Ice or microcrystalline aragonite or calcite

Rock Features Stalactites, stalagmites, pillars, ribbons, straws, flowstones, and other features formed by dripping water inside caves.

In Outcrop Ice formations are most commonly found within lava-tube caves, while aragonite and calcite formations are found inside limestone or marble caves.

More Info Most ice cave formations are seasonal. They occur in winter when cold temperatures freeze groundwater seeping into shallow lava tubes or other underground rock cavities and may look different every year. In contrast, limestone caves take thousands to millions of years to form. Calcium carbonate, as limestone, calcite, or aragonite, is mobilized by groundwater. The water can either dissolve it away (creating cavities) or deposit it (creating new formations inside the cave) depending on the water's acidity, pressure, and temperature.

Notable Localities OR: KM, Oregon Caves National Monument and Preserve (marble cave); HLP, Arnold Ice Cave. **WA**: CB, Guler Ice Cave; OKH, Gardner Cave (limestone cave). Note: there are many other caves in both OR and WA, many of which were formed by lava tubes, but most caves lack the interesting formations of those listed here.

Limestone formations in Oregon Caves National Monument and Preserve

METAMORPHIC ROCKS

Metamorphic rocks are complex. The Greek roots of the word *metamorphic* mean "to change form," and metamorphic rocks are igneous or sedimentary rocks that have been changed by heat and pressure. Metamorphism is similar to the process of baking—the original rock is like cookie dough, and heat transforms the metamorphic rock into a baked cookie.

But the baking analogy falls short in one important way. Metamorphic rocks are solid rocks that change into other solid rocks by growing new minerals at the expense of old ones. In the kitchen, this would be like putting a cookie dough with raisins in the oven and finding the raisins transformed into chocolate chips when you take them out. One geologic example is the clay minerals in mudstones—under a moderate amount of heat and pressure they transform into micas, and at higher levels they contribute to the growth of garnets.

Metamorphism cannot make something from nothing. It takes the elements that make up minerals in the parent rock and recombines them to form new minerals that are more stable at higher pressures and temperatures. This means that an iron-rich igneous rock that undergoes metamorphism will generate an iron-rich metamorphic rock—for example, basalt changing to greenschist. Metamorphosed igneous rocks and some meta-sedimentary rocks are therefore commonly described as mafic (rich in iron and magnesium) or felsic (rich in silicon and aluminum) to indicate the rocks' general chemistry. A few rocks, such as limestone and its metamorphosed counterpart, marble, do not contain significant quantities of iron, magnesium, silicon, or aluminum and cannot be described on the mafic-felsic spectrum.

The geologic ovens that make metamorphic rocks are the same tectonic processes that lead to mountain building. Tectonic plates coming together can push rocks from Earth's surface as much as 50 miles below it, where they are changed by heat and pressure. Plate convergence can also create the conditions necessary for rocks to melt, forming hot magma bodies that bake the rocks around them even at shallow depths.

Metamorphosed rocks that only experienced low levels of heat and pressure may look very similar to their original igneous or sedimentary forms. The clues are in the details—fine-grained minerals like white micas or green chlorite may appear to have grown over or replaced the original, primary crystals. In metamorphosed sedimentary rocks that appear to have a clastic texture when viewed from afar, close examination reveals that the minerals in the clasts or the cement have recrystallized and formed an interlocking texture resembling a fine- to medium-grained igneous rock.

With an increase in pressure, many metamorphic rocks develop the fabric called tectonic foliation. This is one of the best indicators that a rock has been metamorphosed. The new metamorphic minerals grow in alignment—for example, flat minerals like micas stack on top of one another like sheaves of paper, and it's often easy to break the rock parallel

What once were plagioclase crystals in basalt, have been altered to a fine mix of green and white micas.

A metamorphic rock displaying compositional banding of black hornblende and white plagioclase crystals. Note how the rocks don't simply have surface stripes—the broken surfaces of the outcrop show us the bands are actually layers of aligned minerals that go all the way through the body of rock.

to these sheets. This results in broken rocks that are relatively flat. At very high pressures and temperatures, even blocky minerals grow or rotate into alignment, creating alternating light and dark stripes called compositional or gneissic banding.

But not all moderate- to high-grade metamorphic rocks exhibit tectonic foliation. Some metamorphic rocks lack micas or other flat minerals and the blocky minerals don't align, which results in an interlocking fine- or coarse crystalline texture similar to igneous rocks. The key difference is the minerals that form in the end result; minerals like staurolite, omphacite, and glaucophane only grow under metamorphic conditions.

Metamorphic rock names are based on a combination of rock fabrics and mineral content. Both fabrics and minerals record each rock's tectonic pathway and give us insight into conditions deep within the Earth.

ROCKS WITH FOLIATION

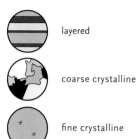

layered

coarse crystalline

fine crystalline

porphyritic

These rocks are defined by their rock fabric; their exact mineral makeup is of secondary importance. One thing that does matter, though, is their minerals' shape; the flat clays and micas that make up these rocks create the overall flat rock texture and internal layering. Some rocks also contain porphyritic minerals that can pop up like polka dots or make the layering wavy. These minerals disrupt the foliation by virtue of their chunky habits.

Rocks that have experienced very high heat and pressure can also make blocky minerals stack up in layers, and these rocks are included here too.

Slate

Felsic

UNCOMMON

Key Components Clays, zeolites, chlorite, muscovite, albite (individual crystals not visible, even with magnification)

Rock Features Commonly black or gray with a dull sheen; no visible mineral crystals or sparkle. Rocks cleave into thin layers.

In Outcrop Finely layered to massive in outcrop. Slate deforms easily and commonly hosts folds and shear zones. Eroded outcrops produce piles of chips, plates, or shards.

More Info Slate forms from mudstones metamorphosed at low pressures and temperatures. In the Northwest, it's usually found as a component within larger formations of metamorphosed limestones, sandstones, or conglomerates. It may also occur where a mudstone unit was heated by a local igneous flow or intrusion. Slate can be difficult to differentiate from mudstone—it

The Ledbetter Slate, Washington

The McHale Slate, Washington

sometimes makes a pinging sound when
struck, but is more reliably identified
by its occurrence with other metamorphosed rocks.

Notable Localities OR: BM, Greenhorn
Mountains; KM, minor occurrences. **WA**:
OKH, near Metaline Falls (Ledbetter Slate);
NC, minor occurrences; OLY, western pen-
insula (Hoh Assemblage).

Phyllite

Felsic

UNCOMMON

Key Minerals Muscovite, biotite, chlorite,
albite (individual crystals not visible, even
with magnification)

Rock Features Commonly black or gray
with a shimmery sheen from tiny micas.
Rocks cleave into layers.

In Outcrop Layers in outcrop are defined
by rock cleavage along mica planes. Phyllite
deforms easily and commonly hosts folds
and shear zones.

More Info Phyllite forms from mudstones metamorphosed at low to moderate pressures and temperatures by burial
or tectonic compression. It's intermedi-
ary between slate, which has no shimmer
or sheen, and mica-bearing schists, which
have mica flakes large enough to see with
the naked eye. It's sometimes found as small
zones associated with slates or schists.

Notable Localities OR: BM, near Durkee
(Burnt River Schist); KM, minor occur-
rences. **WA**: NC, near Darrington and Mt.
Shuksan (Darrington Phyllite); OKH, near
Huckleberry Mountain (Maitlen Phyllite).

Tight, wavy folds called crenulations in phyllite
outcrop, North Cascades, Washington

Specimen of phyllite showing reflective sheen on
an undulating foliation surface

Schist

Felsic to Mafic

UNCOMMON

Key Minerals Includes at least one of the following: muscovite, biotite, chlorite, plagioclase feldspar; may also have amphiboles or garnets

Rock Features Foliated. Visible mica flakes arranged in flat to slightly wavy layers with feldspar and sometimes quartz. Commonly includes large individual crystals of one or more accessory minerals such as amphiboles, garnets, or staurolite.

In Outcrop Foliation in outcrop is defined by rock cleavage along mica planes. Bodies of schist are usually meters to tens of meters or more. Folds and shear zones are common.

More Info Schists form under moderate to high pressures and temperatures resulting from tectonic compression. They have several subcategories. Schists dominated by muscovite and biotite mostly form from mudstones and muddy sandstones, while schists with a high proportion of chlorite or amphiboles come from rocks with a higher iron and magnesium content, like basalt, gabbro, andesite, or diorite. See also entries for greenschist and blueschist.

Notable Localities Muscovite and biotite schists. **OR**: BM, near Mitchell; KM, Rogue River and Humbug Mountain (Colebrooke Schist), Condrey Mountain (Condrey Mountain Schist). **WA**: NC, Chelan Mountains (Napeequa Schist, Cascade River Schist), Mt. Shuksan (Darrington Phyllite).

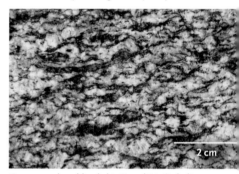

Very coarse hornblende biotite schist, Stehekin, Washington

Mica schist with garnets and deformed feldspars

Gneiss

Felsic to Mafic

UNCOMMON

Key Minerals Plagioclase feldspar, alkali feldspar (orthoclase), with or without quartz; also orthopyroxene, hornblende, biotite, muscovite

Rock Features Foliated. Classic banded gneiss has light and dark stripes defined by layers of feldspar or quartz alternating with biotite, hornblende, or pyroxene. May contain individual crystals of minerals like garnets. If a gneiss has many more light-colored minerals than dark-colored ones, the dark stripes may appear thready or incomplete, and vice versa if the gneiss is predominantly dark in color.

In Outcrop Layers in outcrop are defined by alternating bands of light and dark minerals. Bodies of gneiss are usually meters to tens of meters or more. Folds and shear zones are common.

More Info Gneisses form under high pressure and temperature conditions caused by tectonic compression. Some are metamorphosed sediments, while others are metamorphosed igneous rocks. Scientific analysis is required to tell the two types apart, but one rule of thumb is that metasedimentary gneisses tend to be finer-grained and more likely to include minerals like garnet, while metaigneous gneisses tend to be coarser and more likely to have incomplete banding.

Notable Localities OR: KM, minor occurrences (Western Klamath Terrane). **WA**: NC, Diablo Dam and Sourdough Mountain (Skagit Gneiss), Yellow Aster Butte (Yellow Aster Complex), Lake Chelan area (Swakane Biotite Gneiss); OKH, Okanogan Range, Kettle Range.

Folded compositional banding in gneiss, Wenatchee, Washington

Migmatite

Felsic to Mafic

RARE

Key Minerals Plagioclase feldspar, alkali feldspar (orthoclase), with or without quartz; also orthopyroxene, hornblende, biotite, muscovite

Rock Features Resembles a gneiss or schist but has extensive bands or pockets of igneous textures with granitic compositions. Commonly very deformed.

In Outcrop Layers in outcrop commonly goopy-looking and highly deformed. Bodies usually meters to tens of meters in size; frequently cross-cut by coarse-grained igneous dikes. Often zones within larger units.

More Info Migmatites are rocks subjected to such high pressures and temperatures they began to melt but cooled before melting was complete. They are a combination of high-grade metamorphic rock (usually gneiss) and granitic rocks.

Notable Localities Migmatites are usually associated with gneisses. An outstanding migmatite outcrop can be found southwest of Chelan, Washington, on WA-971, just off US-97.

Extensively deformed migmatite, Wenatchee, Washington

Migmatite showing foliation and zones of coarse crystalline igneous texture, Wenatchee, Washington

ROCKS WITH UNIQUE MINERALS, WITH OR WITHOUT FOLIATION

 coarse crystalline

 fine crystalline

 porphyritic

 massive, homogeneous

 layered

Some rocks only perform under pressure. Those in this section all contain minerals or textures that can only form under certain metamorphic conditions, when igneous or sedimentary rocks at or near Earth's surface are compressed and buried by the convergence of tectonic plates. For some metamorphic rocks, exposure to water and heat is also part of their mineral recipe.

Greenstone and Greenschist ★

Mafic

COMMON

Key Minerals Chlorite, feldspar (albite); also white mica, actinolite, epidote

Rock Features Overall green color from fine-grained chlorite that replaces iron-rich minerals such as pyroxene, hornblende, and biotite. Undeformed rocks are called greenstone and may retain primary igneous traits (like vesicles in basalt), while deformed rocks have a foliation fabric and are called greenschists.

In Outcrop Undeformed outcrops may retain primary igneous features such as flow layers or pillows. Deformed outcrops have a schistose foliation that cleaves into slabs, which may be wavy or flat.

More Info Greenstone and geenschist form when iron- and magnesium-rich igneous rocks such as basalt or gabbro encounter low to moderate geothermal heat. In static areas at or near Earth's surface, high heat can metamorphose the minerals without changing the rock texture, creating greenstone. This can occur near bodies of hot magma or hot hydrothermal fluids. In other settings such as a tectonic collision or the upper part of a subduction zone, pressure

5 cm

Sample of greenschist with foliation surface

from plate motions creates a foliation fabric, making greenschist.

Notable Localities OR: distributed in BM, especially Hells Canyon (Wild Sheep Creek Formation), Greenhorn Mountains (Greenhorn Melange); KM, Rogue River, Red Mountain, Galesville Reservoir, Condrey Mountain (Condrey Mountain Schist). **WA**: distributed in NC, especially Mt. Shuksan (Shuksan Greenschist), San Juan Island (Garrison Schist, Deadman Bay Volcanics).

Greenschist in weathered outcrop looking down on foliation surface, Carleton, Washington

Fine crystalline basalt altered to greenstone

Greenstone preserving an original igneous structure, a mafic dike with chilled margins (see structure chapter for more about dikes)

Amphibolite

Mafic

RARE

Key Minerals Hornblende or other dark amphibole, plagioclase feldspar; may also have epidote, garnet, biotite, pyroxene

Rock Features The classic amphibolite is greater than 90 percent black or dark brown hornblende with some light-colored plagioclase feldspar. Hornblende crystals may be aligned like a bundle of pencils or may grow in radiating groups or random clusters. Rocks made predominantly of amphiboles other than hornblende are usually called schists (actinolite schist/greenschist, glaucophane schist/blueschist).

In Outcrop Usually found as a crystalline body that is meters to tens of meters thick. Outcrop fabric is informed by the rock fabric.

More Info Amphibolite forms when iron- and magnesium-rich rocks such as basalt and gabbro experience moderate to high

heat and pressure in a tectonic collision or the middle part of a subduction zone. Some sedimentary rocks also have enough iron and magnesium to transform into amphibolite under these conditions.

Notable Localities OR: KM, Iron Mountain, Red Mountain. **WA**: NC, Lake Chelan area (Swakane Biotite Gneiss); OKH, Kettle Falls.

Foliation in an outcrop of fine-grained amphibolite, Barney's Junction, Washington

Amphibolite with visible hornblende crystals (small black lines) undulating on foliation surface

Eclogite

Mafic

VERY RARE

Key Minerals Omphacite, garnet
Rock Features Formed entirely of vivid green omphacite and red garnet crystals. Texture is massive crystalline.

In Outcrop Commonly found as a broken block within a melange zone (see page 303) ranging in size from meters to tens of meters. The rock's massive crystalline fabric can make it more resistant to weathering and erosion than the melange's matrix, causing the eclogite to form a knob sticking out of the landscape.

More Info Eclogite forms when iron- and magnesium-rich rocks such as basalt and gabbro experience high temperatures and very high pressures. This can occur in the lower reaches of the continental crust or the deepest parts of a subduction zone.

Notable Localities OR: KM, near Roseburg (best-known outcrop now buried).

Eclogite with characteristic green and red minerals, Roseburg, Oregon

Blueschist

Mafic

VERY RARE

Key Minerals Glaucophane, muscovite; also garnet and epidote

Rock Features Gray-blue overall due to glaucophane (blue amphibole); white mica, green epidote, and red garnet may also be present. May be massive or foliated.

In Outcrop Commonly found as a broken block within a melange zone (see page 303) ranging in size from meters to tens of meters. The block's resistance to weathering and erosion can make it stand out as a knob in the landscape.

More Info Blueschist forms when iron- and magnesium-rich rocks such as basalt, gabbro, and some sandstones are subjected to very high pressures but remain at low temperatures. These conditions only occur in the interiors of subduction zones.

Notable Localities OR: BM, Meyers Canyon near Mitchell (Baker Terrane); KM, Port Orford, Signal Buttes, Bandon, Winston Bridge south of Roseburg. **WA**: NC, Mt. Shuksan, Bell Point on San Juan Island (Garrison Schist).

2 cm

Deformed blueschist specimen with glaucophane and epidote, Klamath Mountains

Serpentinite

Ultramafic

UNCOMMON

Key Minerals Serpentine with or without talc, chlorite

Rock Features A mass of compact fibrous minerals that breaks into waxy, lens- or dish-shaped hand samples.

In Outcrop Outcrops can look scaly and are almost always highly deformed, sometimes presenting an overall fabric but usually appearing chaotic.

More Info Serpentinite forms when mantle peridotites encounter water as they are pushed up to Earth's surface by tectonic movements. They are often associated with suites of rock from ocean crust or zones between landmasses that have been pushed together. Serpentinite is commonly one of the rock types found jumbled among others in a melange (see page 303), often as a matrix.

Notable Localities OR: BM, Elkhorn Range (Baker Terrane Melange), Greenhorn Mountains (Greenhorn Melange); KM, Iron Mountain, Gold Beach, Snow Camp, Agness. **WA**: NC, Twin Sisters area, Mt. Stuart area (Ingalls Complex), San Juan Islands (Fidalgo Complex); distributed in OKH.

Mottled, green, scaly outcrop of serpentinite, Liberty, Washington

Outcrop breaking into characteristic lens shapes, Liberty, Washington

Large lens shapes in outcrop, Liberty, Washington

Quartzite

Felsic

UNCOMMON

Key Minerals Quartz; may have minor muscovite

Rock Features Made of more than 90 percent quartz grains with recrystallized boundaries that are irregular and interlocking rather than rounded.

In Outcrop Light-colored, blocky outcrops without layering. If enough mica is present there may be foliation.

More Info Quartzite forms when very pure quartz sandstone or chert experiences moderate to high pressures and temperatures. The quartz grains are squeezed, removing all air pockets and causing the edges of the grains to grow into one another, creating a recrystallized texture. Small amounts of mud in the original sandstone are metamorphosed to micas.

Notable Localities OR: minor occurrences in KM, BM. **WA**: NC, Yellow Aster Butte (Yellow Aster Complex); OKH, Selkirk Mountains (Addy Quartzite); CB, Steptoe Butte.

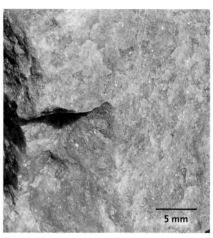

Quartzite's sugary, recrystallized texture, Steptoe Butte, Washington

Foliated quartzite outcrop near Barney's Junction, Washington

Marble

Carbonate

UNCOMMON

Key Minerals Calcite, sometimes dolomite; may have minor quartz, graphite

Rock Features Usually gray; rarely white. Made of more than 90 percent calcite with visible crystals demonstrating recrystallization (interlocking boundaries in a sugary to coarse texture). Dolomite marbles appear similar.

In Outcrop Massive or thickly bedded; may be associated with slates. Rainwater slowly dissolving the carbonate minerals often creates surfaces that appear softly rounded, but remain rough to the touch.

More Info Marble forms when limestone is metamorphosed at any range of pressures and temperatures. This may occur during a tectonic collision or where a limestone body has been heated by a nearby magma source. The recrystallized texture differentiates it from limestone. Take care when making your ID, as many Northwest marbles have been only minimally recrystallized and still resemble limestones to the naked eye.

Notable Localities OR: BM, Eagle Cap Wilderness and Hells Canyon (Martin Bridge Formation). **WA**: NC, Yellow Aster Butte (Yellow Aster Complex); OKH, near Metaline Falls (Metaline Formation).

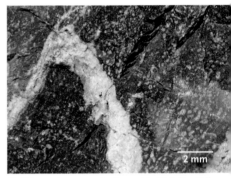

Mottling and overgrowths in marble, Metaline Falls, Washington

Marble outcrop (lens cap for scale), Metaline Falls, Washington

Skarn

Felsic

RARE

Key Minerals Calcite; also quartz, garnets, epidote, tremolite, and other calcium- and silica-bearing minerals

Rock Features White calcite is the most useful indicator. Usually lacks a rock fabric.

In Outcrop A horizon or tabular layer of fine-grained calcite with accessory minerals near a contact between limestone or marble and an igneous body like granodiorite.

More Info Skarns form when magma intrudes a body of limestone, causing calcium, silica, and hot fluids to mix. This can also create many unusual minerals appealing to collectors.

Notable Localities WA: OLY, Buckhorn Mountain; NC, Denny Creek, Vesper Peak. Skarns are usually thin bodies and often too small to appear on large-scale geologic maps. Look for them in regions where limestone or marble bodies and granitic bodies are both present, like the Blue Mountains (also in OR), North Cascades, or Okanogan Highlands.

Skarn with green epidote, pink garnet, and white calcite

Calcite from a skarn

Quick List: Rocks

Rock Identification Flow Charts

These flow charts can help you narrow down a rock ID. They focus on pathways that help readily identify common rocks or rocks with consistent, distinctive features—they don't cover every rock included in this book.

The charts work best when you're trying to identify a rock that's "in place," or at the outcrop where it originally formed. Outcrop context is very helpful for making IDs. You can also use the charts for identifying random, isolated stones like those found loose along a river or on a beach, but sometimes those rocks will remain mysterious.

To use the charts, start with determining the rock texture. Decide whether your rock is coarse crystalline, fine crystalline, porphyritic, clastic, massive, or layered, and follow the chart for whichever you select. Some rocks may fit into more than one category—simply choose the texture you feel defines the rock best.

Coarse Crystalline: Visible, Interlocking Crystals

1. Is the rock almost entirely a combination of black or dark brown, gray, or white minerals?
    → Yes (go to 2)   → No (go to 6)

2. Are two or more of the following minerals present (or, if both quartz and muscovite are present, three or more minerals)?
    feldspar, quartz, muscovite, biotite, hornblende, clino- or orthopyroxene, olivine
    → Yes (go to 3)   → No (go to 8)

3. Are the crystals randomly oriented or foliated (aligned)?
    → random (go to 4)   → foliated (go to 5)

4. This is probably a plutonic igneous rock. See entries for granite and granitic rocks, diorite, gabbro, and peridotite. [END]

5. This is probably a metamorphic rock. See entries for amphibolite, schist, gneiss, and migmatite. [END]

6. If the rock is mostly green, it's likely a greenstone or eclogite. If not, continue to 7.

7. If the rock has blue amphibole (glaucophane), it's a blueschist. If not, continue to 8.

8. If more than 90 percent of the rock is quartz, this is quartzite. If more than 90 percent of the rock is calcite or dolomite, this is marble. [END]

Fine Crystalline: Few or No Visible Crystals, Usually All One Color

1. Does the rock have a conchoidal fracture?
   → Yes (go to 2)   → No (go to 5)

2. Are very thin edges or shards of the material translucent?
   → Yes (go to 3)   → No (go to 4)

3. If the material is black or black and red and the broken face is very shiny, this is obsidian. If the material is any other color, including colorless, and the luster is more waxy than glassy, this is agate or chalcedony. [END]

4. If the material is found in nodules or thin layers, this is probably chert or lapidary jasper. Broken faces will have a dull or waxy luster and the material will readily scratch steel or glass. If it's found in thick deposits, layers, breccia piles, or domes, it's probably rhyolite or a welded tuff. The deposits may display features like flow banding. [END]

5. Is the rock green?   → Yes (go to 6)   → No (go to 7)

6. If the rock feels slippery or waxy and some broken faces are curved, it's probably serpentinite. If it's granular, it's probably greenstone. Note that green tuffs and green mudstones also exist—these rocks have a clastic texture, not a fine crystalline one, but if they are very fine-grained it can be difficult to differentiate. [END]

7. If the rock is made of more than 90 percent calcite or dolomite, it's a limestone or a fine-grained marble. If not, continue to 8.

8. Is the rock dark-colored and does it readily break into fine layers? The flat surfaces of the layers may have a perceptible shine.
   → Yes (go to 9)   → No (go to 10)

9. This rock is sedimentary mudstone or metamorphic slate or phyllite. Note: if the rock has fine layers but doesn't readily break along those layers, it may be a volcanic igneous rock with flow banding. [END]

10. This is probably a volcanic igneous rock. It may have features like vesicles or outcrop-scale columnar jointing. In some outcrops, layers of flows may be visible. The most likely rock types are basalt, andesite, or rhyolite/dacite. [END]

Porphyritic: Large Visible Crystals Scattered in a Fine Crystalline Matrix

1. Are the visible mineral crystals randomly oriented, or are they aligned with each other or with layering in the surrounding rock?
   → random (go to 2)   → aligned (go to 5)

2. Is the matrix black, gray, tan, or reddish to pink?
   → yes (go to 3)   → no (go to 4)

3. This is probably a volcanic igneous rock. See entries for basalt, andesite, rhyolite/dacite. See also the entry for sedimentary volcaniclastic tuff. [END]

4. If the matrix is green from microscopic chlorite, this is greenstone or greenschist. If it's blue from microscopic glaucophane, it's blueschist. [END]

5. Are the visible crystals...

   → feldspar, hornblende, biotite, muscovite, or quartz? This may be a flow-banded igneous volcanic rock or a sedimentary volcaniclastic tuff. See entries for rhyolite/dacite and tuff. [END]

   → staurolite or garnet? This may be a metamorphic phyllite or schist, greenschist, or blueschist. [END]

Clastic: Broken Pieces of Other Rocks That Have Been Naturally Cemented Together

Note: Mudstone, while a clastic rock, does not appear to have a clastic texture because its clay minerals are too small to see. If a rock looks like solid mud or solid mud with fine layers, it may be a mudstone.

1. Are the clasts almost all (more than 90 percent) made from calcite or dolomite fragments? Vinegar and hardness tests can help distinguish this.
   → Yes (go to 2)   → No (go to 3)

2. If the calcite fragments are almost all pieces of shells, this is a coquina. If they are simply black, gray, or white calcite clasts, this is a limestone. Limestones may have some shell fragments or other fossils, too. [END]

3. Are almost all clasts less than 2 millimeters in size?
   → Yes (go to 4)   → No (go to 5)

4. This is a sandstone. The clasts may be made of many different rock and mineral fragments and they may be very rounded or very angular. In some sandstones, the cement matrix is hard to see, but in others it's very visible. Sandstones that are more than 15 percent matrix are known as wackes. Note that some sandstones with few or no calcite clasts may be bound by calcite cement, and the cement may fizz in vinegar. [END]

5. Some or all of the clasts are greater than 2 millimeters in size. Are most of the clasts angular and jagged, or are they more rounded?
    → angular and jagged (go to 6)   → rounded (go to 7)

6. If the clasts are almost all fragments of volcanic rock, this is a volcanic breccia. If the clasts include pumice or individual unbroken, undeformed crystals, it may be a tuff. If the clasts have a mix of origins, including sedimentary or metamorphic rocks, this is a simple breccia. [END]

7. The clasts are mostly rounded. Are the largest clasts scattered randomly throughout the deposit with large amounts of smaller clasts or clay-sized matrix separating them?   → Yes (go to 8)   → No (go to 9)

8. This may be a debris flow or lahar deposit. In some areas it may almost resemble cement. Look around the outcrop for sedimentary structures that indicate flow, such as cross-bedding, ripple marks, or channel structures. Organic material like wood may also be trapped in the deposit. It's important to confirm other sedimentary structures because some tuff deposits are worked by streams before they are fully lithified, which can give them rounded instead of angular clasts as well. [END]

9. This is a conglomerate. The rock is probably clast supported, meaning the largest clasts touch one another and the smaller clasts make up the matrix that fills in the gaps. When viewed in outcrop, the clasts are likely to have some kind of organization. For example, the largest clasts may be arranged together at the bottom of a bedding layer with the smallest clasts at the top (or vice versa). [END]

Massive, Homogeneous: No Internal Structures or Patterns

1. If the rock is almost all quartz, it may be a quartzite. Look for quartz grains that have recrystallized so they fit together in an interlocking crystalline texture. If the rock is not all quartz, proceed to 2.

2. Is the rock almost all calcite or dolomite? Vinegar and hardness tests can help distinguish this.　→ Yes (go to 3)　→ No (go to 4)

3. If the rock is tan, gray, or black and has no visible crystals, or if it has a clastic texture with calcite-only clasts, it's a limestone—it may contain shells or other fossils. If the rock is white, gray, or black, and it's made of visible interlocking crystals that show flashes of light on broken rock faces, it's a marble. Low-grade marbles may retain some fossils, while high-grade marbles will have none. [END]

4. Does the rock have a conchoidal fracture?　→ Yes (go to 5)　→ No (go to 8)

5. Are very thin edges or shards of the material translucent?
→ Yes (go to 6)　→ No (go to 7)

6. If the material is black or black and red, and the broken face is very shiny, this is obsidian. If the material is any other color, including colorless, and the luster is more waxy, this is agate or chalcedony. [END]

7. If the material is found in nodules or thin layers, it's probably chert or lapidary jasper. Broken faces will have a dull or waxy luster and the material will readily scratch steel or glass. If it's found in thick deposits, layers, breccia piles, or domes, it's probably rhyolite or a welded tuff. [END]

8. Is the rock green?　→ Yes (go to 9)　→ No (go to 10)

9. If the rock feels slippery or waxy and some broken faces are curved, it's probably serpentinite. If it's granular, it's probably greenstone. Note that green tuffs and green mudstones also exist, though those are less likely to have a massive homogeneous texture than greenstone. [END]

10. This is probably a volcanic igneous rock. It may have features like vesicles or outcrop-scale columnar jointing. In some outcrops, layers of flows may be visible. The most likely rock types are basalt, andesite, or rhyolite/dacite. If you're not convinced your rock is volcanic, continue to 11.

11. Some sedimentary mudstones don't have visible layers and don't break into layers. This occurs if the mud, before burial, was churned up by animals digging and making burrows, disrupting the layering made by deposition. Here's a fun test to be sure: nibble on a tiny piece of rock. A mudstone will "melt" and feel mostly smooth in the mouth (it may also have a bit of graininess from microscopic quartz particles). [END]

Layered: Internal Layers

1. Does the rock have sedimentary bedding; i.e. is it a clastic rock either with layers defined by different grain sizes or with a single layer that has gradations in grain size from large grains on the bottom to smaller grains at the top or vice versa?   → Yes (go to 2)   → No (go to 3)

2. Go to the clastic flow chart to identify your rock. [END]

3. Is the rock fine crystalline in texture with gray or black coloration and made almost entirely from calcite or dolomite? Shell fragments or other fossils may or may not be present. This is sedimentary bedding in a limestone. If not, continue to 4.

4. Is the rock fine crystalline in texture with a conchoidal fracture?
   → Yes (go to 5) → No (go to 7)

5. Does the rock have finely spaced layers that possibly bend or swirl? This may be flow banding in an igneous volcanic rock like rhyolite/dacite or obsidian. If not, continue to 6.

6. Is the rock found in thin layers among other sedimentary rocks like limestone and mudstone? This may be chert. If not, continue to 7.

7. Does the rock have a fine crystalline or porphyritic texture with volcanic features like vesicles, outcrops with columnar joints, or chilled margins? These are layered volcanic flows, another kind of depositional layering.
   → Yes (go to 8)   → No (go to 9)

8. This is probably an igneous volcanic rock, most likely basalt, andesite, or rhyolite/dacite. It could also be a sedimentary, volcaniclastic tuff, especially a welded ash-flow tuff. [END]

9. Are the layers defined by the alignment of platy minerals, such as clays or micas (chlorite or muscovite) stacked like sheets of paper?
   → Yes (go to 10)   → No (go to 12)

10. If the rock is finely layered and made of clays, it's a sedimentary mudstone or a metamorphic slate. If not, continue to 11.

11. If the layers are defined by micas, this is a metamorphic rock. See entries for phyllite, schist, greenschist, blueschist, gneiss, and quartzite. See also serpentinite, which is made of the sheet silicate serpentine (not a mica but has a similar overall flat structure). If not, continue to 12.

12. Are the layers defined by stripes of blocky light and dark minerals, like quartz or feldspar (light) and hornblende or pyroxene (dark)? This is gneissic banding, and this rock is probably a metamorphic gneiss. Micas like biotite and muscovite may or may not be present. Look around, however, to see if there are layers or pockets of coarse crystalline igneous texture (granitic rock) within the rock. If so, it may be a migmatite. [END]

Did I Find a Meteorite?

Meteorites are rocks from outer space that have traveled through Earth's atmosphere and collided with the ground. They can be pieces of asteroids, moons, planets, or even comets. Meteorites range in size from microscopic flecks to enormous masses. New meteorites fall to Earth every day.

Because meteorites come from many different celestial objects, they can have a variety of compositions and appearances.

5 cm

The Morrow County meteorite, a 40-pound stony meteorite showcasing regmaglypts from atmospheric heating. It was collected in 1999 from a roadside ditch in central Oregon but not recognized as a meteorite until a decade years later.

A cut and polished slab of the Klamath Falls iron meteorite, discovered in Oregon in 1952. Long crystals of nickel and iron are intergrown in a distinctive texture that forms only when molten metal cools slowly within a planetary core.

5 cm

The Salem meteorite struck a house in Oregon in 1981. It is an uncommon type of light-colored stony meteorite with an exceptional dark fusion crust formed by atmospheric heating.

5 cm

Despite this, almost all meteorites have some important features in common. Your rock may be a meteorite if:

1. A magnet sticks to it. Meteorites come in three major types—iron, stony-iron, and stony—but nearly all contain enough iron to attract a magnet. Some ordinary Earth rocks can also stick to magnets, so this test is important but not definitive.
2. It's heavy for its size. Meteorites are usually very dense, also due to high iron content.
3. The interior is completely steel-colored, dark with metallic, red, or round light flecks, or (very rarely) light-colored. You may have to sand and polish a surface to see these features.

4. The exterior shows sign of alteration by heating. When meteors enter Earth's atmosphere, they heat up as they pass through the air they compress along their trajectory. This is the phenomenon that makes shooting stars and fireballs appear in the night sky, and it produces one or both of the following characteristics: a dark outer crust or depressions that resemble thumb prints (called regmaglypts).

Your rock is not a meteorite if it has bubbles or holes. These signify that the rock is either an Earthly volcanic rock or a piece of industrial slag.

If you've found a rock with at least three of the four common features of meteorites, it's worth having it examined by an expert. In the Pacific Northwest, our best resource is the Cascadia Meteorite Laboratory at Portland State University.

North America's Largest Meteorite

Only twelve confirmed meteorites have been recovered from Oregon and Washington, in part because heavy, dark meteorites can be difficult to notice among the heavy, dark volcanic rocks that are so abundant in our area. But that only makes them and their stories more exciting!

The Willamette meteorite is the largest and most famous meteorite found in North America. Weighing in at 15.5 tons, it's a fragment of metallic planetary core from an early formed planet that was smashed apart by collisions in our young, chaotic Solar System. After orbiting the sun for billions of years, the fragment ended up on a collision course with Earth.

Though it was discovered near today's town of West Linn, Oregon, there's no impact crater at the site where it was found—because it didn't initially land in Oregon. A complicated and fascinating journey moved this massive iron meteorite, an unlikely candidate for travel, hundreds of miles across the North American continent.

It probably landed on a thick Canadian ice sheet during an ice age between 13,000 and 15,000 years ago. The ice sheet then carried the meteorite south to the Montana or Idaho area. When the sheet broke up into icebergs on a huge glacial lake near Missoula, one of the icebergs carried the meteorite. In what we would come to call the Missoula Floods, the ice dam holding this glacial lake would burst periodically, allowing the lake to drain catastrophically, sending unimaginable volumes of water rushing across Washington, down the Columbia River, into the Willamette Valley, and eventually out to sea. One of these floods carried the iceberg with the meteorite into the Willamette Valley, where the iceberg melted and ultimately dropped its load. As the floodwaters receded, the meteorite came to rest in Oregon. While this ice-raft journey may sound improbable, many ordinary glacier-carried rocks also experienced this trip. Collectively they are called dropstones—read more about dropstones and the Missoula Floods on page 284.

The Willamette meteorite at the American Museum of Natural History

After arriving in western Oregon, the region's persistently wet weather caused the sulfides in the meteorite's iron body to break down into an acidic solution. This acid etched large crevices into the meteorite's surface, which are a unique and distinctive feature of the meteorite today. The indigenous Clackamas people call the meteorite Tomanowos and believe it brought unity and healing as an emissary of the Sky People. When the meteorite was still in nature, they performed ceremonies with the rainwater that collected in its crevices.

In 1902, a white settler named Ellis Hughes came upon the meteorite on land owned by the Oregon Iron and Steel Company and worked for three months with his son and his horse to drag it three quarters of a mile until it was on his own property. He built a shack around the meteorite and charged visitors to see it—until a representative of Oregon Iron and Steel discovered the scheme and the long drag marks that clearly led back to company land. A legal battle ensued, in which the company eventually triumphed and displayed the specimen at the 1905 Lewis and Clark Centennial Exposition. Oregon Iron and Steel then sold the meteorite to a private collector, who in turn sold it to the American Museum of Natural History in New York, where it remains to this day.

The descendants of the Clackamas people are now part of the Confederated Tribes of the Grand Ronde. In 2000, they reached an agreement with the museum to be able to visit the meteorite and perform private ceremonies annually, allowing the museum to retain the meteorite so long as it is kept on display.

Did I Find a Fossil?

Fossils are preserved remnants of ancient life. Familiar fossils include petrified wood and bones encased in rock. This section will help you identify whether or not an object you found could be a fossil. If you wish to identify your finds more exactly, many excellent reference works for specific fossil identification are available.

Shells

Shells make excellent fossils. When a shelled animal dies and its soft body decomposes, it leaves a hard shell behind. If it is buried in mud, sand, or gravel, and that sediment is buried further and becomes sedimentary rock, the shell can be preserved.

Preservation happens in a few different ways. The original shell material could remain encased in the rock, largely unchanged. These types of fossils can look almost identical to modern shells you find on the beach. The only way you can tell they're millions of years old is by the rocks in which they're bound.

Often, though, the heat and pressure that transform sediments into sedimentary rock cause the buried shell to partially or completely dissolve away. Several things can happen after that. For one, the space where the shell used to be could remain empty, leaving only an impression of the inside or outside of the shell in the surrounding rock. Another possibility is for minerals circulating in the groundwater to fill in that empty space, replacing the original shell material with something different. Shells that have been replaced by agate are a striking example of this process, but many variations of the general mold-and-cast idea also occur.

Some shell fossils look very familiar, because animals similar to clams, scallops, and snails have lived on Earth for over 500 million years. But some ancient shelled animals are very different from those we see commonly today. Two notable types include crinoids, ancient sea lilies with stems that look like tall stacks of (teeny tiny) tires, and ammonites, predatory animals with flat spiral shells that ranged from a few inches across to up to 6 feet in diameter.

Petrified Wood

Petrified wood is wood that has been turned to stone. The scientific name for this process is permineralization, and it occurs when wood is buried in sand or mud mixed with volcanic ash. Groundwater circulating through the sediment grows minerals within the pore spaces of

Bivalve shells in sedimentary rock

Tree limbs replaced by pink agate (also called limb casts). Note how the surface texture of the limb is preserved, but the interior cell texture is gone, replaced by banded agate.

the wood. Eventually, the wood itself is replaced entirely with minerals.

Very complete permineralization can preserve structural details within the wood, from annual growth rings down to the level of individual wood cells. Some-

times, though, the wood will partly or completely rot away before it is replaced, and the minerals simply fill in the space left behind. In this case, the outside surface of the fossil may retain the textures of bark and wood knots, but the interior doesn't

A scaly conifer fossil

look like wood at all. This kind of fossil is called a limb cast.

The material that most commonly replaces wood is agate, but quartz, calcite, barite, and other minerals are also fairly common. The colors in petrified wood come from the replacement minerals, not the original wood.

Leaves and Other Plant Debris

When a falling leaf comes to rest on a muddy lake bottom, it will eventually be buried. Over millions of years, it may be buried deeply enough for the mud around it to be compressed, lightly heated, and turned into mudstone. The original leaf is often baked away during this process, but the leaf's impression is hardened into place between the layers of mud. The baking process can also stain the impression with the leaf's chemical compounds, coloring the impressions black, brown, or red. In some circumstances, actual organic material may be preserved.

Most plant material can be preserved in this way, from woody bark or root balls

A fossilized broadleaf pile

to delicate flowers, and the process is capable of recording exquisitely fine details in surface texture. Small insects are sometimes captured in these fossils, too.

Some of the best leaf and insect fossils in Oregon can be found at Woodburn High School near Portland and in the Clarno and John Day Formations near Fossil. The best dig site in Washington is at the Stonerose Interpretive Center and Eocene Fossil Site in Republic.

Broken bone with visible spongy interior texture

Bones and Teeth

Like shells, bones and teeth may retain their original material unchanged during burial and sediment compaction. Like wood, they may also be permineralized, or petrified. In both cases, fossil bones and teeth are often a dark brown or black color from staining or new mineral growth. Teeth generally look like teeth, with a root and a crown, and many bones have a spongy interior texture from the voids that held marrow when the animal was alive. If a bone is still porous like this, it may stick to your tongue! This is a fun test to distinguish bone from random shards of rock. In some permineralized bones, the voids may be filled in by minerals.

This smooth brown specimen preserved in sandstone is a fossilized porpoise skull.

Hard bones and teeth are the most common kinds of vertebrate animal fossils. Soft tissues—skin, fur, feathers, muscle, fat, and organs—are nearly always eaten or rotted away before they can be preserved. Even mud impressions of skin or hair are rare. Bones and teeth are much more durable and much easier to fossilize. Mummified animal fossils with soft tissues do exist, but not only are they extremely rare, they are almost always found in unique environments like bogs, caves, or glaciers.

Unlike most other fossils in this list, it is illegal to collect bones and teeth from any public land, even those that allow other kinds of collecting. Vertebrate fossils—fossils of animals with backbones, including reptiles, mammals, birds, and fish—are prohibited from private collection by federal law. Bones and teeth are fun to look at, but do not disturb them or take them home. They may only be removed with a federal permit granted to scientific investigations.

Mammoths, ancient bison, fish, extinct mammals called oreodonts, and aquatic reptiles like ichthyosaurs are just some examples of vertebrate bones found in the Pacific Northwest. Fossils in the rock layers of the John Day Fossil Beds National Monument in Oregon create an astonishingly complete record of mammalian evolution from the end of the age of the dinosaurs through today, including many ancestors of the modern horse.

Fossil tracks of a worm-like animal

Tracks, Burrows, and Traces

Animals don't have to die to leave behind fossils. Wherever animals hop, scurry, or dig, they leave impressions in the ground that can be buried and preserved between layers of rock. This may take the form of footprints or the furrow of a dragging belly imprinted in muddy ground, or it could be a burrow that disturbed layers of sediment and left behind a long, filled-in tube. It could also take the form of things animals leave behind: *coprolite* is the scientific term for fossil poop.

What About Dinosaurs?

During the dinosaurs' heyday, from about 200 million to 65 million years ago, most of the rocks that make up Oregon and Washington were either under water or existed as islands off the coast of the ancestral North American continent. Dinosaurs were

A fossil burrow that has been filled in with light-colored minerals

cut off from these lands, and no dinosaurs means no dinosaur fossils.

To date, however, three dinosaur fossils have been recovered here. In order of discovery, they are: a hadrosaur bone from Cape Sebastian near Gold Beach, Oregon; a theropod thigh bone from the San Juan Islands in Washington; and an ornithopod toe bone near Mitchell, Oregon. The Cape Sebastian hadrosaur and the Washington theropod were found in rocks that originally formed somewhere down in California or Mexico; those rocks shifted slowly northward along fault lines, moved by tectonic forces until they reached their position in the present day. The ornithopod near Mitchell is a bit different—it was found in some of the few regional, dino-aged marine rocks that formed close to shore, capturing the bones of an animal that died on the coast and washed out to sea.

Are there more dinosaur bones out there? Very likely. But they would only exist in a few small areas within the Northwest, and aren't abundant.

Bones from sea creatures that also lived during the dinosaurs' time are much more likely to turn up. Crocodiles, ichthyosaurs, plesiosaurs, and other marine reptiles that swam Mesozoic seas have been found preserved in the Klamath Mountains and Blue Mountains of Oregon.

STRUCTURES AND DEFORMED ROCKS

Rock units have dimension; they are layers, bodies, and blobs that together make up Earth's crust. The architecture, or structure, of these units is a record of how the crust was built and what tectonic processes affected it over time. Structures reveal the history of a rising mountain, for example, or the opening of a basin.

Some structures are a result of rock formation, while others come from deformation. They come in all types and sizes, from microscopic to mountain-range.

Sometimes structures are very obvious in outcrop, while others you have to look for carefully. This chapter is a guide to some outcrop- or smaller-scale structures you may come across, how these structures form, and what sort of history you can interpret from them.

Primary Structures: Rock Formation and Relationships

A body or unit of rock forms through a process or series of events; a lava flow

Highly deformed amphibolite gneiss along US-395 in the Okanogan Highlands, Washington

represents a volcanic eruption, for example, while a sedimentary bed may represent the sediment washed down a river in a storm, and a coarse-grained metamorphic rock is the culmination of millions of years of pressure and heat. As geologic processes proceed over time, new rock units form on top of, under, and even within existing rocks.

Primary structures are those associated with the formation of a rock body. Contacts are places where two different units of rock touch—they are one of the easiest-to-spot types of primary structures. Careful observation of a contact can reveal the relationship between units of rock.

Depositional contacts form from layers of sedimentary rocks or lava flows—anything where one rock unit was deposited on top of another at Earth's surface.

These contacts tend to be planar and form horizontally, though in places they can be undulatory if the underlying rock had some sort of topography (for example a river channel). They are found among sedimentary and volcanic rock units.

Depositional contact between older sandstone and overlying younger conglomerate

Contacts separating successive lava flows in the Columbia River Basalt Group near Grand Coulee, Washington

Intrusive contacts occur when a body of molten rock is forced into existing rock units of any kind. The hallmark of an intrusive contact is a chilled margin, in which hot magma was literally chilled by touching the existing, surrounding rock, causing the margins to cool quickly. This manifests as the rock's largest crystals in the center of the rock body with their size decreasing markedly at the margins near the contact. If the intruding magma body, or pluton, is large and irregular in shape, the contact surface will often have an irregular or wavy edge. Additionally, some plutons send out thinner, tabular bodies of magma called dikes or sills. Dikes cut across preexisting features like bedding, while sills intrude parallel to those existing planes. These bodies can be planar, like a lava flow, but unlike a lava flow, they'll display symmetrical chilled margins on both the top and bottom where the magma touched the surrounding rock.

A chilled margin at an intrusive contact between an intrusive quartz diorite (top of photo) and older andesite (bottom of photo). Note how the crystal size in the diorite becomes smaller closer to the andesite, indicating that the diorite intruded into the andesite.

Once you have identified contacts between different bodies of rock, you can study the rocks' relative positions and geometry to learn more about their history. This is called the study of stratigraphy.

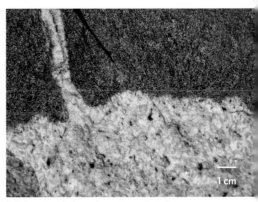

A light-colored pluton intruding a dark, finer-grained crystalline rock. The pluton's chilled margin is almost imperceptible, perhaps because it formed at a great enough depth within the Earth that the surrounding rock's temperature was itself rather high. However, the wavy nature of the contact and the small finger of igneous material poking out into the host rock reveal the intrusive relationship.

Stratigraphic Relationships

Principles of rock stratigraphy, which have to do with the deposition of layered rocks and relative age relationships between different rock units, are a useful tool when analyzing outcrops. Here, we have outlined a few of the major principles, but it should be pointed out that there are always exceptions—you are encouraged to see the following as guidelines rather than rules.

Flat-lying, undeformed sedimentary rocks in the Oregon Coast Ranges illustrate both the principle of original horizontality (these rocks are undeformed and in their original horizontal orientation) and the principle of superposition (the oldest rocks in the outcrop are on the bottom and youngest are at the top).

A vertical basalt dike cutting across preexisting sedimentary rocks along US-97 in the Washington Cascade Range

Principle of Original Horizontality

In general, layered rocks that are deposited or flow into place form horizontally (think of sand or dust settling into layers). The orientation of a layered rock is defined by the top surface of an individual sediment layer, lava flow, or ash-fall tuff, or the contact between separate rock units. In most cases, the top surface of layered rocks is originally horizontal. If we see rocks where the top surface of a layer, or contacts between layered rock units, aren't horizontal, we know some sort of deformation had to have tilted the rocks.

Principle of Superposition

Simply stated, in a vertical stack of undeformed rocks the oldest rocks are at the bottom of the stack and the youngest at the top. This principle holds for sedimentary rocks, air-fall ash or tuffs, and lava flows.

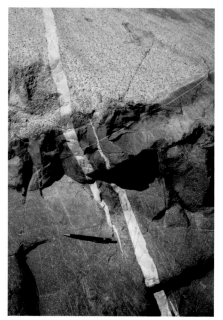

A light-colored felsic dike cutting across pre-existing bodies of diorite and andesite (see following page), Cascade Range, Washington

A dark, mafic sill within the Ohanapecosh Formation near Mt. Rainier, Washington. The younger sill is parallel to layering within the older formation.

Principle of Cross-Cutting Relationships

Any structure or other feature that cuts across preexisting rock layers must be younger than the rocks it's cutting. Some of the best examples of cross-cutting relationships are intrusions of igneous rocks. Dikes are intrusions that cut across preexisting rock layers, and sills intrude roughly parallel to preexisting layers (see page 219). For a non-igneous example, any sort of fracture cutting a rock must be younger than the rock itself.

Unconformities

An unconformity is a surface representing a gap in time between two rock units. It generally indicates a period of erosion and removal of rock material rather than rocks forming. For example, if a sandstone is deposited over a granitic rock, the contact between them is an unconformity—because the granitic rock formed deep underground, lots of overlying rock must have eroded away to expose it at Earth's surface before it could be covered by the sand that became the sandstone.

Any sort of discontinuity within a stack of rock layers can be considered an unconformity.

Nonconformity is a contact between an underlying crystalline layer, which must be igneous or metamorphic, and sedimentary layers or lava flows deposited or formed on top of the crystalline rock.

Disconformity is when there was a large gap in time between the deposition or formation of vertically successive layers.

Angular unconformity is when flat-lying rock layers are present on top of older, tilted rocks. This type of unconformity

An angular unconformity between the flat-lying sediments above and the tilted sedimentary rocks below, at Sunset Bay State Park, Oregon

represents a sequence of events starting with older, previously horizontal rocks becoming tilted, eroded, and having new rocks deposited horizontally on top.

Processes that Deform Rocks

We usually think of rocks as strong, solid objects. Try to deform or break a rock in half with your hands—it's probably close to impossible, and even with a sledgehammer it takes a lot of effort. How then do rocks break and become deformed?

Within Earth, it comes down to two things: pressure, called *stress* in geologic terms, and rock strength. We can mathematically define stress as force applied over a given surface area (pounds per square inch, for example), or we can think of stress qualitatively as how hard something is being squeezed or stretched. As for rock strength, this characteristic basically describes how much stress a rock can withstand before it begins to break or deform. Rock strength varies widely based on a given rock's composition, any preexisting weaknesses within it, its temperature, and how fast stress is being applied to it. For example, a solid granitic outcrop can withstand much more stress before deforming than a heavily fractured and weathered piece of granite. However, that same solid granite heated to high temperatures and subjected to stress deep within the crust will deform quite readily.

There are two main sources of stress that rocks can experience: burial and regional. Burial refers to stress that is equal in all directions. A cube of rock subjected to burial decreases in volume but remains a cube with sides of equal length. A good analogy is hydrostatic stress, which you feel when you dive to

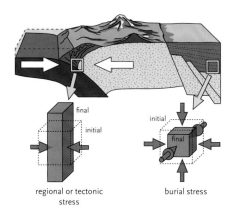

Regional or tectonic stress is associated with plate boundaries, in this example, a convergent subduction zone. Burial stress is associated with deep burial, for example, in a sedimentary basin.

the bottom of a swimming pool. The deeper you dive, the more pressure you feel on your head—likewise, burial stress increases the deeper a rock gets buried within the Earth. In contrast, regional, or tectonic, stress is applied more strongly in one direction than in others. This distorts our imaginary cube.

Regional stress has three subtypes, depending on the direction in which the stress is applied: compression occurs when a rock is squeezed horizontally; extension, also called tensile stress, when the rock is "stretched" horizontally; and shear, when one side is moving or sliding relative to the other side. Regional stress is typical of plate boundaries.

No matter which type of stress is applied to a rock, once the amount of stress exceeds the rock strength, deformation will begin. This can involve the rocks breaking, bending, or flowing into a new shape. Deformation is categorized as one of three types:

Types of Regional Stress

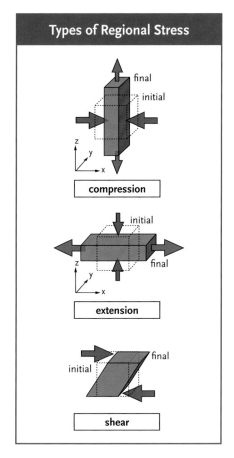

compression

extension

shear

Brittle deformation occurs when rocks fracture or break. This type of deformation is permanent (the rocks are "forever" broken) and happens in low-temperature conditions within the upper crust.

Ductile, or plastic, deformation occurs when a solid rock flows like putty. This is accomplished by shifting individual atoms within crystals to permanently change a rock's shape without breaking it. It generally occurs under higher temperatures and pressures within the crust.

Elastic deformation happens when rocks under stress bend and change shape without breaking, then "bounce" back to their original shape when stress is released. Any elastic deformation is impermanent or recoverable.

Deformation takes the form of fractures, faults, folds, and more. These features are known as secondary structures, and they are the record of a rock's history of stress—and the history of the tectonic movements that caused them.

Secondary Structures Resulting from Brittle Deformation

Deformation in the cold upper crust is usually brittle, taking the form of fractures and faults.

Fractures or Joints

Fractures, also known as joints, are cracks in rocks that result from regional or tectonic stress or from the removal of stress. Generally, fractures are the first structures to form when a rock is undergoing brittle deformation, and they form roughly parallel to the direction the rock is being squeezed or perpendicular to the direction the rock is being stretched. When a fracture is filled by a secondary mineral, it is referred to as a vein.

Foliation in low-grade metamorphic rocks such as slate is actually a system of pervasive fractures all oriented in the same direction. Sometimes referred to as rock cleavage, foliation can intersect with planes of weakness inherited from the unmetamorphosed parent rock to produce long, thin pieces. This is an example of pencil cleavage, and the individual pieces are creatively named pencils.

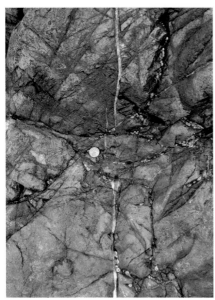

Fractured greenstone with a calcite-filled vein near Deception Pass, Washington

Pencil cleavage in slate near Hurricane Ridge in Olympic National Park, Washington

Faults

Once a rock has fractured, the broken blocks can move and slide relative to one another. When this occurs the fracture has become a fault. To determine if motion has taken place across a fracture, look for matching rock types, or marker beds, on either side and judge if the markers have been offset. If the marker beds don't match across a fracture, then there has been motion, and you are looking at a fault.

Faults are classified according to the type of stress—compressive, tensile, or shear—that caused them. They can range in size from small features with only inches or millimeters of displacement to giant features that break through the entire crust. Regardless of size, we use the same observations and criteria to identify them.

The fault itself is the fracture surface across which the rocks on either side have moved relative to one another. In cases where the fault surface is not vertical but at an angle, the block of rock vertically above the fault is called the hanging wall, and the block below the fault the footwall. To remember which is which, imagine a tunnel dug right along the fault. It's probably dark, so to see you would hang a lantern on the wall above you (the hanging wall), and your feet would be on the block below the fault (the footwall). Certain fault types are defined based on the relative motion of the hanging wall and footwall blocks, so when observing a fault, it's a good idea to first identify the

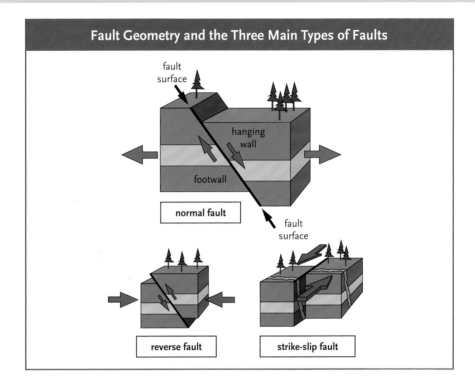

Fault Geometry and the Three Main Types of Faults

fault surface

hanging wall

footwall

normal fault

fault surface

reverse fault

strike-slip fault

hanging wall and footwall, then look for any markers or rock layers that may have been offset.

Normal faults are produced by horizontal extension or tensile stress and involve the hanging wall moving down relative to the footwall. Today's Basin and Range province has many normal faults as a result of extension. In the past, even bigger normal faults brought rocks formed over 13 miles beneath the crust to the surface at the Okanogan Highlands. Much smaller normal faults can be found upon close examination of outcrops that have undergone even small amounts of extension—look for fractured rock layers that appear to have been dropped down or thinned out across a small break.

Thrust and reverse faults are formed from horizontal compression or shortening of the crust. When rocks are compressed across a fault, the hanging wall will move up with respect to the footwall. The difference between the two is how steeply the fault is inclined from horizontal. If the fault is shallow (less than 45 degrees), it's a thrust fault. If the fault is steep (greater than 45 degrees), then it's a reverse fault. Thrust or reverse faults with a lot of offset can sometimes be difficult to identify in the field, though looking for regions where older rocks have been moved on top of younger rocks can help narrow down the geographic locations of large faults. Smaller thrust or reverse faults can be identified in outcrop when individual rock layers have been broken

Normal fault in the John Day Formation, Blue Mountains, Oregon. The thick, dark brown layer can be used as a marker, indicating that the left side (hanging wall) has been displaced down with respect to the right side (footwall).

and stacked on top of themselves. Any region in the Northwest that has experienced compression in the geologic past, or is currently being compressed, is likely to contain outcrop-scale thrust or reverse faults. Small thrust faults are common in the Coast Ranges on the Olympic Peninsula, as this area is being squeezed in an east-west direction on top of the Cascadia Subduction Zone.

Faults that involve horizontal, rather than vertical, motion are classified as strike-slip faults. These faults are produced from shear stress, and the fault plane is vertical, so the blocks slide side-by-side. Transform boundaries such as the Blanco Fracture Zone and San Andreas Fault are examples of large crustal-scale strike-slip faults.

Fault Motion Indicators

Figuring out which way a fault has moved requires a couple steps. First, identify the fault's hanging wall and footwall. Next, locate a marker rock layer, or other feature such as a dike, sill, or offset fracture, on either side of the fault. Finally, use the marker to gauge whether the hanging wall has been moved up or down with respect to the footwall (strike-slip faults can be identified in a similar fashion, by looking for lateral displacement of markers across the fault).

In some cases, it may not be possible to identify offset markers and we must look for other features determine fault motion. Straight grooves on a fault surface are called fault lineations, or slickenlines, and form during fault motion. Fault surfaces

A small thrust fault in sedimentary rocks along the Olympic Peninsula coastline. The fault trace is parallel to the pencil. Note the thick bed acting as a marker, showing the hanging wall pushed up relative to the footwall.

can be rougher than coarse-grit sandpaper. As the blocks of rock on either side of a fault move, the rough surfaces will grind and scratch the opposite side. This grinding process produces lineations along the fault parallel to the direction of motion. Although slickenlines can help us figure out if the fault motion was up-down, strike-slip, or a combination of the two, determining the exact sense of motion and type of fault requires more information.

Slickenfibers are mineral growths on fault surfaces that can help us identify a precise direction of motion. Think about the idea of faults with rough surfaces. As one side of a fault moves relative to the other, any bumps or steps along the fault could lead to small void spaces forming between the two sides. Since faults are cracks in a body of rock, any fluids present (for example, water) will preferentially flow along the fault surface. Fluids flowing along a fault can also contain minerals dissolved out of the local rock—for example, dissolved calcite, silica (quartz), or serpentinite.

These minerals can precipitate out of the liquid, filling in the small spaces along a fault. As fault motion continues, minerals can continue to precipitate in the extending voids, leaving behind linear mineral fibers that have grown parallel to the motion.

WHERE DO EARTHQUAKES COME FROM?

Earthquakes make the ground shake. They are the release of stored elastic energy that takes place when crustal rocks under stress break. In much of the Earth's crust, rocks are brittle but have a small amount of elasticity, meaning the rocks can bend to absorb some amount of energy before breaking. Imagine bending a small wooden stick with your hands. When you first start to bend the stick, the stick changes shape. If you don't bend the stick too much, when you let go, the elastic energy stored in the bent stick causes it to bounce back or rebound to its original shape. But bend the stick too much, and the change in shape goes beyond the stick's "breaking point," and soon enough. . . you have two sticks!

A very similar process takes place within the Earth's crust, especially along and near active faults. Tectonic stresses squeeze, stretch, or shear rocks across a fault, pushing or pulling the rocks on either side in opposite directions. Since rock bodies are rough, there's a significant amount of friction between them, which causes the rocks to resist motion and "stick" along the fault. This allows elastic energy to build up, which causes the rocks to bend. Energy continues building until either (a) the elastic energy exceeds the friction on the fault, or (b) the elastic energy becomes greater than the rocks can sustain. Once this happens, the bodies of rock slip along the fault or the rocks themselves break, releasing the elastic energy into the surrounding crust as a series of waves. This is the earthquake. When the waves reach ▶

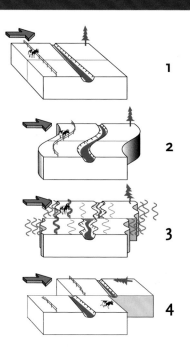

Block diagrams illustrating the Elastic Rebound Theory. (1) An undeformed block of crust is cut by a fault, represented as a red line extending horizontally across the block. A stream channel flows across the fault. Tectonic stresses are shearing the block, and pushing the upper half toward the right relative to the lower half. (2) As applied stress continues, the rocks deform elastically, bending across the fault. This bending and buildup of elastic energy continues until . . . (3) EARTHQUAKE! The stresses bending the rocks become greater than the rocks can sustain, and the fault slips. (4) The rocks on either side of the fault rebound back to their original shape, but are now in a new position. This change in position produces an offset across the fault.

WHERE DO EARTHQUAKES COME FROM? *(cont.)*

Photo of small offsets along a set of normal faults outside of Sisters, Oregon. Faults are highlighted in red, and marker layers and contacts used to indicate offset are in white. Blocks to the right of the faults have been displaced down relative to the left side. The magnitude of offset across the faults is less than 2 feet, which would be typical of a single small earthquake.

the Earth's surface, the vibrations cause the ground to shake.

After the rocks slip or break they rebound back to their original shape but have been moved to a new position. This can produce a measurable offset across a fault. Depending on the size of the earthquake, fault offsets or displacements can range from fractions of an inch for small earthquakes to tens of feet for extremely large earthquakes.

The Pacific Northwest is no stranger to earthquakes. Our plate tectonic setting squeezes and stretches North American crust to the point of produc-

ing notable earthquakes every 30 to 50 years, on average. A few recent examples include the 2001 Nisqually earthquake located outside of Olympia, Washington; the 1993 Scotts Mills earthquake (a.k.a. The "Spring Break Quake") in Oregon's Willamette Valley; 1965 and 1949 earthquakes in the Puget Sound region; and of course the 26 January 1700 Cascadia earthquake along the Cascadia Subduction Zone. In addition to these large, infrequent temblors, tiny earthquakes only detectable by sensitive instruments shake the ground every day.

Slickenfibers in serpentinite along US-97 in the Washington Cascades

How Slickenfibers Grow

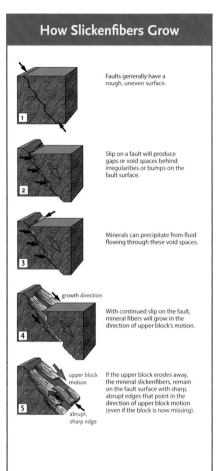

1 Faults generally have a rough, uneven surface.

2 Slip on a fault will produce gaps or void spaces behind irregularities or bumps on the fault surface.

3 Minerals can precipitate from fluid flowing through these void spaces.

4 growth direction — With continued slip on the fault, mineral fibers will grow in the direction of upper block's motion.

5 upper block motion / abrupt, sharp edge — If the upper block erodes away, the mineral slickenfibers, remain on the fault surface with sharp, abrupt edges that point in the direction of upper block motion (even if the block is now missing).

However, since slickenfibers develop along the fault surface itself, we can't observe them unless one side of the fault has been removed or eroded away. Where this has happened, the linear slickenfibers have one smooth end and the other end is abrupt or sharp. Determine the smooth versus abrupt ends by running your finger along a single slickenfiber or set of them. The abrupt or sharp ends will all face in the direction that the missing block moved.

Secondary Structures Resulting from Ductile Deformation

When rocks undergo ductile deformation, they can either fold or flow. This usually occurs at depth in the lower crust, where rocks are subjected to high heat and pressure. Some rock types, however, such as shales and some sandstones, can deform ductilely at low temperatures in the shallow crust.

Folded Rocks

One of the most prevalent and easily identifiable ductile structures, folds occur when rocks buckle or bend under applied stress. This produces rocks that are tilted, sometimes into zig-zag or S-shaped patterns. Using the principle of original horizontality, we can infer that rocks tilted into these patterns have undergone a describable deformation.

Fold Geometry

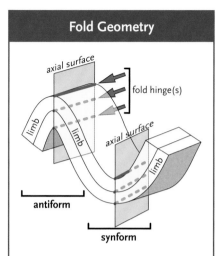

The fold hinge is the location where a single fold is tightest or has maximum curvature. Hinges for multiple layers define a three-dimensional axial surface. The fold limbs are on either side of the fold hinge, in between axial surfaces.

Understanding a bit of terminology used to describe fold geometry is useful when discussing different types of folds. The fold hinge is the point of maximum curvature, generally where the bending of a folded layer is the tightest. The fold hinges for multiple folded layers combine to make an axial surface, an imaginary plane that defines the maximum curvature in three dimensions. On either side of the fold hinge or axial surface are the fold limbs. The axial surface basically bisects the angle made by the fold limbs. Fold types are defined according to how the fold limbs are oriented with respect to the fold hinge or axial surface.

Monoclines are folds that have a single tilted limb in between horizontal segments (*mono* = one, *cline* = tilted layer).

Synforms are folds whose limbs are tilted toward the hinge. They look like

a smile. A specific type of synform is a syncline, where the youngest rocks are located in the center of the fold, and the rock layers get older moving away from the fold hinge. It is important to note that to classify a fold as a syncline, you need some information about the relative ages of the rocks involved. This is simple for folded sedimentary rocks, thanks to the principles of original horizontality and superposition, but many highly deformed metamorphic rocks obscure age relationships between their layers.

The opposite of synforms, antiforms are folds with limbs that are tilted away from the fold hinge. They look like a frown. Anticlines are a specific type of antiform where the oldest rocks are in the center of the fold, and the folded layers become younger moving away from the axial surface. Again, you'll need information about the ages of the folded layers to determine anticline versus antiform.

We can add more detail to our fold descriptions based on the orientation of the fold limbs, fold hinge, and axial surface. If its hinge is horizontal, a fold is considered horizontal. A plunging fold has a tilted hinge. Symmetric folds have limbs tilted evenly on either side of an axial surface. Asymmetric fold limbs have different amounts of tilt on either side of the axial surface, usually one steeply tilted limb and one shallow. An upright fold has a vertical axial surface, while inclined folds have a tilted axial surface. If the axial surface has been tilted to the point where it is horizontal, the fold is recumbent. In the case of inclined folds, if one limb has been tilted to the point of being upside-down the fold is overturned. Recumbent folds are always overturned.

A small monocline in Pleistocene beach cobbles along the Olympic Peninsula coastline. The monocline itself is the steeply tilted part in between the horizontal segments.

A synform in folded chert on Fidalgo Island, Washington

Close-up of an anticline in folded marine sedimentary rocks near Sutherlin in the Oregon Coast Ranges

An anticline-syncline pair in folded marine sedimentary rocks near Sutherlin in the Oregon Coast Ranges

An overturned, recumbent antiform-synform pair in highly deformed gneiss along US-395 in the Okanogan Highlands

Shear Zones

While brittle deformation involves the breaking of rocks under applied stress in colder, shallower conditions in the crust, and ductile deformation is generally associated with stress in warmer conditions deeper within the crust, between these regions there is a transition zone where deformation changes from localized faulting to ductile flow in wide shear zones. Where this transition takes place within the crust depends on crustal composition

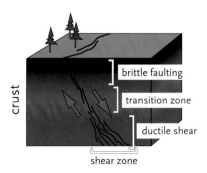

The transition from brittle deformation and faulting in the upper crust to ductile deformation and shear zones in the warmer lower crust

and local temperature structure, but in general it occurs at depths between 7.5 and 11 miles, or at temperatures greater than 600°F. Though these ductile shear zones form at depth, crustal extension or compression can uplift and expose them at Earth's surface. Rocks and structures that form in shear zones are fairly unique, and they contain clues as to the type of shear that shaped them as well as the processes that brought them to the surface.

Mylonites

Mylonites are metamorphic rocks that form within ductile shear zones. Any rock subject to ductile shear can become a mylonite through dynamic recrystallization, a process where the mineral components of a rock recrystallize under extreme pressures and differential stress. This recrystallization reduces mineral grain sizes, making individual crystals very small, and also produces a foliation aligned parallel to the direction of shear. At first glance, a mylonite may appear similar to a banded gneiss, but the small grain size and other deformation features like sigma clasts (see below) distinguish it.

Many mylonitic rocks can be found in regions of the Pacific Northwest where deep crustal rocks have been brought to the surface, such as the North Cascades and Okanogan Highlands.

Lineations

Lineations are linear arrangements of minerals that form or realign during deformation to be parallel to the direction of shear. Common in mylonites, lineations are best exposed on foliation planes and can be identified by the preferred orientation of recrystallized minerals or

Mylonitic gneiss in the Okanogan Highlands, Washington

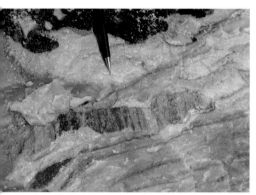

Lineations present in a mylonitic quartzite along US-395 in the Okanogan Highlands, Washington. The lineations are present on the exposed foliation plane and oriented in a direction parallel to the pencil.

elongate minerals such as members of the pyroxene or amphibole groups. Like slickenlines on fault surfaces, lineations in mylonitic rocks can help determine the general direction of motion, but you'll need more detail to determine the specific type of shear.

Sigma Clasts

Sigma clasts are asymmetric crystals of quartz or feldspar in a gneiss that are larger than the surrounding grains. If a gneiss is undergoing ductile shear during metamorphism of recrystallization, these larger crystals will grow and develop asymmetric tails parallel to foliation that point in the direction of shear. These tails are similar in shape to the Greek letter σ (sigma) and are called sigma clasts. Even though sigma clasts may be small (anywhere from millimeters to centimeters across), their asymmetry describes the overall motion across the rock's entire shear zone.

You can use sigma clast tails to determine which direction the rocks above the sigma clast were being transported relative to the rocks below the clast. Think of sigma clasts as ball bearings sandwiched between two sheets of metal that are being moved in opposite directions. As the sheets move (shear), the bearings rotate. Now imagine the ball bearings are a little mushy, and with rotation they smear out a bit. That smearing points in the direction that the plates above and below the bearing were moving. This motion can be described using cardinal directions (for example, top-to-the-east transport) or by including whether the top moved up or down relative to the rocks below the sigma clast via normal (upper block down with respect to lower block) or thrust/reverse motion (upper block up).

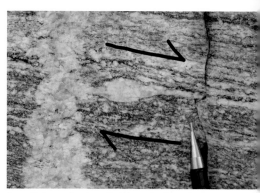

A small sigma clast in mylonitic gneiss from the Okanogan Highlands. The sigma clast and its tails are in the center of the photo, and the arrows indicate the direction of shear.

How to View Outcrops from a "Deformed Rocks" Perspective

When observing a single rock or outcrop and analyzing it for structures or deformation, there are a few things to keep in mind—sort of a thought process to follow during your observations. First, you'll want to make some observations of the entire outcrop, such as: Are there some big outcrop-scale features such as fractures or cracks present? Are different rock units or rock types in the outcrop continuous across the entire exposure, or are they disrupted somehow? Do the rock units appear to be flat-lying, or are the rocks tilted or buckled?

Once you've made these first-order observations, it's time to take a closer look. If a region has undergone deformation, you're likely to see patterns emerge the closer and more detailed you get. Are all the rock units tilted or oriented the same way? Is there a similar pattern of shapes the rocks make throughout the outcrop?

In your final stage of observations, it may be helpful to have a hand lens or other magnification device handy. If the rock is crystalline, and you can see the individual minerals that make up the rock, do any minerals have a preferred orientation? Are platy minerals such as micas aligned in a certain pattern? Are elongate minerals like hornblende or amphibole oriented in a similar direction? Do other mineral grains look like they've been smeared?

You may not need to make all of these observations—you may even be able to stop after a first glance at an outcrop. Regardless, use these suggestions as your first tools to help identify any evidence of past deformation.

LANDSCAPES AND GEOMORPHOLOGY

As you travel around the Pacific Northwest looking at all the amazing rocks and minerals, you'll also notice the incredibly wide variety of landscapes. The processes involved in shaping these landscapes take place on a variety of scales, from small features observable in outcrops to entire valleys and volcanoes. In this chapter, we'll walk through a number of major processes responsible for shaping landscapes and geomorphic features in the Pacific Northwest.

Geomorphology is the study of processes that shape Earth's surface and the landforms or topography these processes create. It can be described within the context of three major concepts. First is the production of material at Earth's surface. This includes new volcanic rocks, but also sediment and soil from the breakdown of older preexisting rocks. Second is the whole suite of processes responsible for the erosion of material and subsequent transport across Earth's surface. After erosion, the initial removal of material, transport is primarily driven by gravity but can be aided by running water, wind, waves, and glaciers. Third is deposition, which takes place once the transport process ends. In this chapter, we will help you identify and interpret the processes

and landforms associated with the creation, removal, transport, and deposition of material.

To fully observe processes that are shaping the Pacific Northwest, we first need to adjust our geomorphology goggles, the lenses with which we view the landscape. As when observing an outcrop of rock for the first time, there are certain clues we can look for that tell us about the processes taking place. These clues come at all different scales, from tiny features or color changes on the side of a rock to the shapes of entire valleys. The great thing about geomorphology is that a lot of these clues will point to similar stories. When observing the landscape, it can be helpful to start small, formulate ideas and correlate observations, and work toward bigger features. Or you could start by looking at the bigger features then move to progressively smaller ones to see if the same story emerges. No matter which direction you go, look for patterns.

Production of Material

In geomorphology, the term *material* broadly describes rocks, rock fragments (also called sediment), and soil found at Earth's surface. Many of the processes that produce material can be observed

A patch of loose sand, rocks of all shapes and sizes, and fractured marine shells—also called a deposit of sediment

in outcrop and categorized as the physical breakdown of rocks, the chemical alteration of rocks, or the generation of volcanic rocks and features. The processes that cause physical or chemical breakdown are called weathering, because they require exposing preexisting rocks to the atmosphere.

Physical Weathering

When a rock breaks down into smaller pieces that maintain the same composition as their source, this is physical weathering. In other words, sediments, the products of physical weathering, are chemically identical to the original rock. Smashing a rock into small bits with a hammer could be considered an example of human-caused physical weathering.

Here are a few of the readily observable products of physical weathering and their associated processes, which are common in the Pacific Northwest.

Fractured Outcrops

Many fractures form through a process of unloading, or the removal of pressure. Intrusive igneous rocks, sedimentary rocks, and metamorphic rocks form at varying depths within the Earth's crust. Here, these rocks are subject to pressure and compression from being buried underneath miles of other rock. As the overlying rocks are eroded away over time, rocks that form at depth are brought toward the Earth's surface, lessening compression and allowing them to expand. Because the rocks are solid and brittle

A heavily fractured and weathered outcrop of granodiorite in the Blue Mountains near Baker City, Oregon

Exfoliation sheets on the Early Winters Spires in the North Cascades of Washington

when the pressure is relieved, this expansion causes them to fracture. A specific type of unloading is exfoliation, in which rocks break via surface-parallel fractures called exfoliation sheets, which resemble the layers of an onion. Exfoliation sheets are commonly found in regions where

Talus pieces in the foreground with talus slopes across the valley. These angular chunks of rock were likely produced by freeze-thaw weathering, as this location near Mount Rainier National Park sees a wide range in daily and annual temperatures.

plutonic igneous rocks are exposed at the surface, such as the Golden Horn Batholith in the North Cascades, other smaller plutons in the Okanogan Highlands, or the Wallowas within the Blue Mountains.

Talus and Freeze-Thaw Weathering

Throughout Oregon and Washington, you'll find cone-shaped piles of angular rocks at the base of steep slopes and cliffs. These piles are known as talus slopes, and the individual rocks are called talus. Talus slopes can form through a process of freeze-thaw weathering, where water, via precipitation or snowmelt, seeps into fractures in an outcrop and freezes. As it freezes, it expands, enlarging the fracture a small amount. The ice melts and is replaced with new water, which then freezes and enlarges the fracture a tiny bit more. This freeze-thaw process repeats until the rock breaks into smaller, angular shaped pieces.

Root Wedging

The freeze-thaw cycle isn't the only process to widen fractures in a rock. Plants and trees can help too. As roots grow downward, they take advantage of fractures present in the underlying rock. During growth the roots widen in addition to increasing in length. This essentially creates a wedge that drives itself ever so slowly into the fracture. Over time, root wedging will expand fractures to the point of breaking an outcrop into smaller pieces. Sometimes root wedging can be hard to spot, but any forested region with bedrock outcrops is a good place to find evidence of the process.

Example of root wedging near Deception Pass, Washington

Spheroidal Weathering

Some outcrops you'll find will have large angular pieces, while other pieces will appear much more rounded. If these rounded pieces are still part of the main outcrop (not loose blocks that have fallen off), their shape is the result of spheroidal weathering, the rounding of in situ blocks within an outcrop. It can occur in heavily fractured areas where multiple fracture orientations are present.

This weathering essentially rounds sharp corners. Sharp corners form where two or more planar features in an outcrop intersect. They become a focus for physical and chemical weathering processes because they have more surface area than a flat rock face and are more exposed to the atmosphere.

It's important to point out that spheroidal weathering applies only to rocks that are a part of an outcrop. There are many other processes associated with rivers that can produce sediment with a round shape that is not part of an outcrop.

Honeycomb Weathering

In regions near the Pacific Ocean or Puget Sound, saltwater spray from waves produces a unique type of physical weathering that has the appearance and texture of a honeycomb. First, saltwater enters

Varying degrees of spheroidal weathering in an outcrop of tuff near Mt. Saint Helens

fractures or small void spaces between clasts on the surface of these rocks. Then, as the water evaporates, any salt in the water precipitates out as small crystals. If enough salt precipitates within a fracture it can cause the rock to break apart grain-by-grain, creating more voids for the salt to fill and repeat the process.

Honeycomb weathering is prevalent where rocks are within the spray zone, all along the shorelines of the Coast Ranges and Olympic Peninsula. It is best observed in sedimentary rocks. Some excellent examples can be found near Cape Arago, Oregon, and in the coastal portions of Olympic National Park.

Chemical Weathering

In contrast to physical weathering, which produces sediment of the same composition as the original rock, chemical weathering involves a chemical or compositional change. This can be accomplished through a number of different processes—here, we'll describe some that are common in the Pacific Northwest.

Oxidation

A distinct reddish stain on the surface of a rock indicates that iron-rich minerals within the rock were exposed to oxygen. Iron can react with oxygen to form new iron oxide minerals like hematite or

Honeycomb weathering on the surface of Miocene Hoh Assemblage sandstones along the coastline of the Olympic Peninsula

Reddish-brown coloring on the surface of an andesite near Mt. Rainier indicates that iron-rich minerals in the andesite reacted with oxygen in the atmosphere or in water to form an iron oxide stain.

limonite. For example magnetite ($4Fe_3O_4$) plus oxygen (O_2) oxidizes into hematite ($6Fe_2O_3$). These iron oxides have a reddish-brown color.

Reduction

Reduction reactions are the opposite of oxidation and involve a mineral losing oxygen to its environment. These reactions turn sediments a blue-gray to green color and take place in anoxic environments, which have little to no ambient oxygen, such as deep lakes or overly saturated clays or other sediments. Commonly produced through the weathering of clay minerals, reduction reactions look something like this:

$$2Fe_2O_3 \text{ (hematite)} - O_2 \rightarrow 4FeO$$
(ferrous oxide)

A classic example of rocks that have undergone reduction are the sediments in Blue Basin, Oregon, part of the John Day Formation. The sediments here began as clays and volcanic ash, and were previously buried in an anoxic lake environment where the iron-rich minerals became reduced and altered to a blue-gray color.

Dissolution

Rainwater is naturally mildly acidic, as water vapor in the atmosphere can react with carbon dioxide to form carbonic acid. Over time this mild acidity in precipitation will dissolve rocks at the surface, particularly rocks that contain or are composed of carbonate minerals. In

Blue Basin in the John Day Formation. Sediments here get their greenish color from reduction reactions that followed their deposition in an anoxic lake. The brown vertical strip of rock in the center of the photo is a clastic dike.

Tear-pants weathering on the surface of marble near Oregon Caves National Monument and Preserve

sedimentary rocks with carbonate cement, dissolution can remove the cement and loosen the individual clasts within the rock. In other rocks it leaves behind an etched, rough texture that's sharp to the touch, affectionately known as tear-pants weathering. An example of a dissolution reaction with carbonate minerals is:

$CaCO_3$ (calcite) + H_2CO_3 (carbonic acid) $\rightarrow$ $Ca(HCO_3)_2$ (calcium bicarbonate, dissolved in water)

Carbonate rocks within the Okanogan Highlands, Klamath Mountains, and Blue Mountains display varying degrees of dissolution weathering. An extreme example of dissolution takes place when mildly acidic groundwater flows through fractures in carbonate rocks, forming caves. The Oregon Caves in the Klamath Mountains and Gardner Cave in the Okanogan Highlands are both very accessible examples.

Differential Weathering

Different rock types and compositions react differently to physical and chemical weathering processes. Some rocks break down readily and quickly at Earth's surface, others are very resistant to weathering. When rocks that weather at different rates are present in the same outcrop, the more resistant rocks will be much more

Interior of the Oregon Caves, where large cavities have been produced through dissolution weathering of carbonate rock

prominent than the less resistant rocks. Differential weathering is especially noticeable in outcrops of sedimentary rock with alternating beds of sandstone and siltstone or mudstone. Due to their larger grain size and usually higher degree of cementation, sandstones are more resistant to weathering than the finer-grained siltstone or mudstone. This will lead to the sandstones being prominent in outcrop, with the silt or mudstones being recessive. Another common example of differential weathering occurs in outcrops containing lava flows that cooled on top of sedimentary rocks. The crystalline lava is much more resistant to weathering and will stand out more than the clastic rocks.

Marys Peak in the Oregon Coast Ranges is a large-scale example of differential weathering. The mountain has a crest elevation of 4100 feet, roughly 1000 feet above its neighboring ridges. This is because the high part of Marys Peak is composed of a gabbro sill, which is much more resistant to weathering than the sandstones and marine sediments of the surrounding Tyee Formation.

Production of Volcanic Material

Perhaps the most striking and recognizable landscape features of the Pacific Northwest are the volcanoes of the High Lava Plains and Cascade Range. Volcanoes come in all shapes and sizes, and the differences between them can be explained by the properties of the magma that feeds or fed the volcano. Once volcanic material is produced, it's subject to physical and chemical weathering processes and can be broken down into sediment. Here we will look at common volcano types in Oregon and Washington, how they form, and where examples can be found.

Shield Volcanoes

Shield volcanoes are volcanoes with broad, gently sloping flanks, similar to a medieval knight's shield laid on its side. The Hawaiian Islands are classic examples of shield volcanoes. Many smaller examples exist in the Pacific Northwest, most in Oregon—Belknap Crater in the central Cascades, Larch Mountain, and Mt. Sylvania in the Portland metropolitan region are a few.

The shape of a shield volcano is a result of the basalt lava that forms them. Lavas with a basaltic composition erupt at a higher temperature than lavas with a more andesitic or rhyolitic composition. This higher temperature plus a relatively low silica content creates a low viscosity lava, one that's fluid and with a low resistance to flow. These lavas can flow some distance from their vent, creating wide volcanoes with gently sloped sides.

Example of differential weathering near Mt. Saint Helens. A resistant basalt stands out above a less-resistant stack of fine-grained sedimentary rocks.

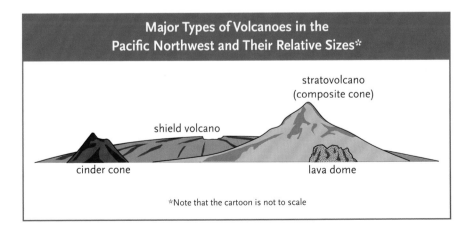

Major Types of Volcanoes in the Pacific Northwest and Their Relative Sizes*

stratovolcano (composite cone)

shield volcano

cinder cone

lava dome

*Note that the cartoon is not to scale

Belknap Crater (left) and Little Belknap Crater (right), two of the youngest shield volcanoes in the Cascade Range. These volcanoes are at McKenzie Pass in Oregon, and their most recent eruptions were between 1500 and 3000 years ago.

Stratovolcanoes

Also called composite cones, stratovolca-noes are large, steep-sided volcanoes that form the backbone of a subduction-zone related volcanic arc. All the major peaks in the CAS are stratovolcanoes, plus Mt. Baker and Glacier Peak in the NC.

Stratovolcanoes get their name from the process that forms them. Successive eruptions of a stratovolcano mix basaltic andesite or andesitic and dacitic lava flows with rocks and pyroclastic debris from explosive eruptions. These lavas and pyro-clastic materials form layers that stack up to eventually build the volcano. Since the lavas that form stratovolcanoes are much less runny than basaltic lava (andesitic

and dacitic lavas have a higher viscosity) these volcanoes can sustain steeper flanks and grow into the large, localized volcanic peaks like those in the Cascades.

Cinder Cones

Much smaller than stratovolcanoes, cinder cones are steep-sided volcanoes formed from explosive eruptions of basaltic lava. These eruptions originate from fluid basaltic magmas with a high concentration of gasses, or volatiles. While the magma is under pressure within the earth, the volatiles remain dissolved within the liquid, similar to a sealed and pressurized carbonated beverage. When the magma moves toward the surface, the confining

Stratovolcanoes Middle and North Sister (left and right respectively) in the Oregon Cascades, viewed from the summit of South Sister

pressure drops and the volatiles exsolve from the liquid to form bubbles—just as soda pop forms bubbles when you first twist off the top.

These escaping gasses can be forceful and voluminous, flinging frothy blobs of lava skyward during an eruption. The blobs cool and fall to the ground around the volcanic vent, piling up in a compact cone shape. Smaller fragments are known as volcanic cinders, while larger pieces are called volcanic bombs.

The High Lava Plains in Oregon have a wealth of cinder cones, reaching from the Jordan Craters area in the east to Lava Butte and Pilot Butte near the town of Bend. Other cinder cones can be found in the Boring Volcanic Field in the greater Portland region.

Lava Domes

Lava domes are small eruptive centers that form when incredibly thick, viscous lava with a dacitic or rhyolitic composition works its way to the surface at localized vents associated with stratovolcanoes or nearby fracture zones. Because the melt that forms lava domes is so thick, it doesn't flow far from the vent but piles up into steep-sided lobes composed of a mixture of rhyolite, dacite, pumice, and obsidian.

The most famous lava dome in the Pacific Northwest also happens to be the youngest. Since the 1980 eruption of

Lava Butte near Bend, Oregon, is a cinder cone.

Loose basalt cinders at the summit of Lava Butte, Oregon

A volcanic bomb on top of loose cinders, Lava Butte, Oregon

Lava dome of the Big Obsidian Flow in Newberry National Volcanic Monument

Mt. Saint Helens, a lava dome has been growing in its crater. Other lava domes in Oregon include the approximately 1300-year-old Big Obsidian Flow within the Newberry National Volcanic Monument and a chain of lava domes along the south flank of South Sister near Bend.

Calderas

Calderas are large circular or semicircular depressions resulting from a volcano's collapse into its own magma chamber following a massive eruption. During these eruptions the magma chamber feeding a volcano empties, leaving the mass of the volcano above unsupported. The volcano then collapses in on itself, leaving behind a large depression. Over time, calderas can fill with volcanic material from subsequent eruptions, sediment, or water.

Calderas can be enormous. The Crooked River Caldera north of Bend, Oregon, is over 20 miles across (it's also notable for erupting the tuff that makes up one of Oregon's premiere rock-climbing destinations, Smith Rock State Park). On the smaller side, the centerpiece of the Newberry National Volcanic Monument is a caldera containing cinder cones, lakes, and lava domes, and the eponymous lake of Crater Lake National Park fills a caldera formed when Mt. Mazama erupted 7700 years ago. Washington's calderas are less well known, but include the Kulshan Caldera of the North Cascades, which formed 1.5 million years ago in an eruption comparable to the one that formed Crater Lake.

Volcanic Necks

Volcanic necks are the eroded remnants of extinct stratovolcanoes or cinder cones. Magma that works its way into a

stratovolcano or cinder cone but doesn't erupt will crystallize in the volcano's interior. Since this crystallization happens more slowly than in erupted lava, the resulting rock is harder and more resistant to erosion. Over time, the outside portions of the volcano, composed of lava flows or loose pyroclastic debris, can erode away leaving behind the resistant neck.

The Oregon portion of the Cascade Range is full of volcanic necks, most remnants of stratovolcanoes associated with High Cascades volcanism. A few examples include Mt. Washington, Three-Fingered Jack, and Mt. Thielsen. Beacon Rock in the Columbia Gorge is also a volcanic neck, formed from a cinder cone that was part of the Boring Volcanic Field.

Sculpting the Landscape

Any loose material at Earth's surface can be eroded and transported. Erosion refers to the initial removal of material from its original position, and transport is what happens between erosion and the material's final deposition. If you know which clues to look for, you can use the principles of erosion, transport, and deposition to interpret the processes that shaped and are still shaping the landscape of the Pacific Northwest.

Hillslope Processes and Features

The majority of Earth's land surface that isn't covered by water can be considered a hillslope. Some slopes are incredibly steep, some are quite flat, and everything else falls in between. On steeper slopes, material (sediment, soil, loose rock) moves downward under gravity at varying speeds depending on steepness of the slope, type

Crater Lake is a water-filled caldera formed from the eruption of Mt. Mazama 7700 years ago.

Mt. Thielsen in the Oregon Cascades is a volcanic neck.

of material, and how saturated the slope is with water. The downward movement of material on a hillslope is referred to as either *mass movement* or a *landslide*. Evidence for past landslides can be found in many places around the Pacific Northwest.

While material on a hillslope might appear to be stable, and in many cases is stable, a few factors might trigger or initiate a landslide. First, if the hillslope is over-steepened, it can become unstable. Every material has an angle of repose, or the steepest slope a material can hold before it collapses. For example, a pile of dry sand has an angle of repose somewhere around 30 degrees. If a slope is steepened above its angle of repose (for example, via undercutting by a stream), it's more likely to collapse in a landslide. Second, if loose material on a slope becomes oversaturated through heavy precipitation or snowmelt, the slope can collapse. This is a very common cause of landslides in the Pacific Northwest, especially on the western side of the Cascade Range which has a distinct rainy season between November and April. Third, if the stabilizing root systems from trees and other vegetation are removed from a hillslope (via forest fire, for example), it is more susceptible to collapse. Lastly, earthquakes can shake material loose on a hillslope and initiate a landslide. While many other factors can initiate landslides around the world, these are the most common in the Pacific Northwest. Once a mass movement is initiated, we can use various clues in the landscape to identify and classify them.

Soil Creep

Ever look at a steep, tree-covered hillside and notice that many of the tree trunks are bent at the base? This is a classic sign of soil creep, a very slow type of landslide. Soil creep occurs where hillslope soil contains a significant amount of clay minerals. Clays swell when wet and shrink as they dry out. When they swell, clays within a hillslope push out the soil surface perpendicular to the slope. During drying, the clay shrinks but the surface doesn't follow the same path back, instead moving straight down under gravity. Over time, this creates a zig-zag pattern of motion, transporting material downhill. Tree roots anchor the above-ground portion of the tree into the lower, more stable layers of soil—if the upper portion of the soil is being transported downslope via creep it will push that part of the tree trunk with it, but the rest of the tree above the soil will continue to grow straight up, producing a bend at the base of the trunk.

Slides, Falls, and Flows

Slides, falls, and flows can be extremely hazardous and even deadly when they are occurring—the Oso mudslide that occurred in Washington in 2014 left forty-three fatalities. They also leave behind specific landforms useful for identifying where they've taken place in the past and could possibly occur in the future.

The steep, sometimes semicircular cut in the landscape where the movement of a slide, fall, or flow started or broke away is called a scarp. The lobe-shaped deposit of unsorted material downslope of the scarp

Trees bent at their base is an indication that soil creep is taking place. This creepy hillslope is near South Sister, Oregon.

Scarp of a flow along Newberry Road outside Portland

where the movement ended is the toe. If the slide or flow was large enough, the area between the scarp and the toe will have uneven, hummocky topography created by material from the fall. In mountainous regions, fast mass movements often leave behind a path of downed or damaged trees and other rocky debris. Deposits of material from these movements will typically consist of sediment in a wide range of sizes (very small to large, car-sized boulders) and angular shapes.

Different types of slides, falls, and flows are classified based on the material involved in the movement and whether it was saturated with water or not. Observing a scene soon after movement has occurred is the best way to know how much water was involved, but even if we only identify a scarp, toe, or both, we can still look at the materials in them and come up with a hypothesis as to what happened. Fast, dry mass movements consisting of rocks and smaller sediment that fall vertically are considered rockslides or rockfall. If the rocks and soil are saturated with a large amount of water, the movement is termed mudslide or mudflow. If organic material such as trees or vegetation are incorporated into the movement along with rocks and soil saturated with water, then it's a debris flow. A dry movement of organic debris, rocks, and soil is a debris avalanche. Lahars are a specific type of mudslide or debris flow that initiates on the slopes of a stratovolcano due to intense rainfall, collapse of a portion of the volcano itself, or rapid melting of snow or ice on the volcano.

Looking down a debris avalanche chute on the flanks of Marys Peak in the Oregon Coast Ranges

Landscapes Shaped by Rivers

With all the rain and snow that the Pacific Northwest receives, it's fitting that water running through rivers does a huge amount of work shaping the landscape. Mass movement processes transport material down off of hillslopes into rivers where it's further transported down toward the Puget Sound or Pacific Ocean. Any large or small landform produced by running water in rivers is considered a fluvial landform, formed by fluvial processes. Deposits of sediment left behind by fluvial processes are called alluvium.

V-shaped valleys carved by fluvial processes in the Klamath Mountains of southern Oregon

V-Shaped Valleys

Mountainous valleys primarily shaped by fluvial processes will have a V-shaped cross-section profile with a narrow floor where the river or stream channel itself runs. The valley walls don't have to be steep or symmetric, but they will be fairly straight and form a recognizable V. This particular shape is produced as rivers cut down into the landscape and hillslope processes shed material into the groove. The river channel could also be set into a flat floodplain where sediment is deposited during floods, but it will still be surrounded by V-shaped slopes.

Bedrock River Channels

When the amount of water in a river or the slope of the stream is high enough, it can move any loose material in the river channel along and expose the bedrock under the stream bed. These channels are typical of steep mountain streams or larger rivers that cut through areas with erosion-resistant bedrock. Bedrock channels can either have a step-pool morphology, with steep drops in between relatively flat pools, or have a continuous slope.

Circular depressions carved into bedrock channels are known as potholes. Potholes will often have smaller rocks inside them that act as "tools" when the river flow is high enough. Water will swirl around the pothole as a vortex and move the tools around, grinding away at the bedrock and increasing the depth and size of the pothole.

Knickpoints are local sections of a stream channel that are steeper than the upstream and downstream sections.

Rapids along the North Fork of the Nooksack River, Washington. The large boulders in the channel are resting on top of bedrock.

Pothole with tools in the Illinois River channel, southern Oregon

Bedrock rapids or waterfalls in a stream are both knickpoints. Large examples of knickpoints include Willamette Falls in Oregon and Snoqualmie Falls and Palouse Falls in Washington. Smaller knickpoints can be found in almost any bedrock channel.

Sediment Transported and Deposited by Rivers

Loose sediment that has been transported by rivers has a very distinct shape—round. If you spot any deposits of rounded sediment that aren't associated with an ocean beach, chances are pretty good it was left there by a past river.

The shape and size distribution of individual rocks in a deposit of alluvium can help you figure out approximately how far the sediment has been transported. When loose sediment is first produced by physical weathering processes, the size of the rocks varies widely but the shape of the individual pieces is angular and sharp (think back to talus slopes). As it's transported by mass movement processes, the sediment can be roughly bounced around, causing the pieces to break apart and rounding their sharp corners slightly. Once in a river channel, especially during high-flow or flood events, the larger sediment is pushed or rolled along the stream bed, smoothing out its corners even more and making individual pieces smaller. After a while, sediment becomes smooth and round and similar in size (small). Closer to the source, individual pieces of sediment will be angular in shape and

Bedrock gorge on the Rogue River in southern Oregon, with examples of pools, small knickpoints, and shallow potholes

The shapes of these rocks are a rough indication of how far each piece has been transported from its original location. Angular, jagged rocks (left) generally haven't traveled far from their sources—rocks get rounded (right) over time with more transport.

have a wide range of sizes. The farther away a river transports sediment from its source, the smaller, rounder, and more uniform in size its pieces will be.

Floodplains are wide, flat deposits of small sediments (gravel, sand, silt, or clay) left at the bottom of river valleys. Floodplains form when rivers have incredibly

John Day River and its wide, vegetated floodplain in central Oregon

large amounts of water in them during flood events and overflow their channel, depositing small sediments on one or both sides. Once river flow decreases and floodwaters recede, an almost-flat deposit is left behind. Most rivers in the Willamette Valley and Puget Lowlands, Coast Ranges, and Olympic Peninsula have well-developed floodplains.

Fluvial terraces are ancient floodplains preserved within a stream valley. They form when the main stream is downcutting or incising into the landscape.

Deltas are triangular or fan-shaped deposits of sediment that form when a stream or river carrying a large amount of sediment flows into a lake or ocean. A classic example is the delta forming where the Elwha River flows into the Strait of Juan de Fuca on the north side of the Olympic Peninsula. This delta has been growing rapidly since the 2014 removal of the Glines Canyon dam on the Elwha River, which released a vast amount of sediment that had been accumulating behind it.

Alluvial River Channels

Any river whose channel is full of sediment (alluvium) is considered an alluvial channel. River systems fill with sediment when the power of the river to transport material is less than the amount of material available for transport.

Terraces along the Methow River in northern Washington. The red barn sits on a wide, low-relief platform that is an old fluvial terrace—the flat surface above the barn is another, older terrace.

This often happens in young, mountain streams and in mature rivers that have well-developed floodplains.

Braided streams are alluvial mountain streams with multiple interwoven channels and islands or gravel bars. These streams are fairly steep, and contain rounded sediment in a wide range of sizes. The channels and islands shift constantly with successive high flow or flood events. If you're standing next to a braided stream during high flow you might be able to hear the clatter of clasts being transported along the stream bed. Many rivers and streams in the Cascade Range and North Cascades that drain glaciated stratovolcanoes or other high peaks are braided channels; for example, the White River near Mt. Rainier and Suiattle River near Glacier Peak in Washington, and the Sandy River near Mt. Hood in Oregon.

Streams and rivers flowing through wide valleys with a low slope will have a sinuous, windy path. Each individual loopy bend in the stream is called a meander, and the overall channel shape is meandering. Meandering channels have wide floodplains which build up over time as these rivers flood and deposit sediment.

Each individual meander bend in a stream has distinct erosional and depositional landforms. The cut bank is the outside of the bend, where the river's current is the fastest and material is removed

The White River near Mt. Rainier is a classic braided stream.

A meander bend in the Toutle River, Washington. The river is flowing from right to left across the photo. The broad deposit in the foreground is the point bar, and the steep, tree-lined bank in the background is the cut bank.

Glaciers on Mt. Rainier, Washington. The amount of ice on Mt. Rainier is greater than all the other glaciers in the Cascade Range combined.

via erosion. Here the river is cutting into its bank and widening the meander bend. Cut banks are generally quite steep, and in urban or developed areas humans often reinforce cut banks with rip rap or concrete intended to slow erosion and stabilize the slope to prevent property damage. The gravel or sand deposit on the inside of a meander bend is called a point bar—this is where the river's current slows enough to drop sediment it may be transporting.

The Willamette River between Eugene and Salem and its tributaries in the Willamette Valley, sections of the Quinault and Chehalis Rivers on the Olympic Peninsula, and portions of the Snoqualmie and Stillaguamish Rivers in the North Cascades are great examples of meandering streams.

Landscapes Shaped by Glaciers

Glaciers are large masses of ice that form in high-altitude or high-latitude regions when the amount of yearly snowfall is greater than that of snowmelt. Once enough snow has accumulated, its weight compresses it into ice, which then flows downhill. As glaciers move, they can do an incredible amount of work removing material from the landscape, transporting eroded sediment as part of the glacier, and depositing it once the glacier melts. The processes associated with glacial erosion and deposition of material create some very unique landscapes.

While very few places within the Pacific Northwest are glaciated at present, it was much different in the recent geologic past. An ice age is an extended period of cooler global temperatures that allow for the formation of massive glaciers and continental ice sheets. During the Pleistocene (approximately 2 million to 10,000 years ago), Earth's northern hemisphere, including the Pacific Northwest, went through numerous climate cycles, fluctuating between ice ages, when glaciers grew, and inter-glacial periods where the ice presence decreased. The most recent ice age, referred to as the last glacial maximum, occurred around 15–20,000 years ago. During the last glacial maximum, many places in Oregon and Washington were covered by glaciers and large sheets of ice. The provinces most affected by this major glaciation were the NC, many of the higher peaks in the CAS, high mountains in the OLY, portions of the OKH, small areas of high topography within the BM, and Steens Mountain in the BR. Obviously, the large glaciers that were once present are now only remnants of their former selves or have since melted entirely, but they left behind evidence of their presence in many features that can be readily identified in the Northwest landscape. These generally fit into two categories: features formed through erosion by glaciers, and features formed through deposition of material by glaciers or processes associated with glaciers.

U-Shaped Valleys

Valleys in mountainous or alpine regions that have primarily been carved by glaciers have a U-shaped cross-section profile. Also called glacial troughs, these valleys have a wide, flat to semi-rounded floor and steep to vertical walls. This shape is distinct from the V-shaped valleys of rivers, which cut down into

the landscape—instead glaciers pluck material from the base and sides of the valley, widening its floor and steepening its walls.

While U-shaped valleys presently occupied by glaciers are rare in the Pacific Northwest (only a couple glaciers in the North Cascades and the Emmons Glacier on Mt. Rainier are still large enough to potentially be considered valley glaciers), many valleys in the North Cascades, high alpine valleys on the Olympic Peninsula, and valleys carved into the sides of most stratovolcanoes of the Cascade Range have U-shaped profiles. One of the best examples is at Washington Pass along US-20 in the North Cascades, where a viewpoint is located at the divide between two large glacial valleys.

Erosional Features Produced by Glaciers

Glaciers are affectionately known as nature's bulldozers for their effectiveness in eroding and moving material. As glaciers move, the ice can pluck blocks of rock from underlying bedrock. Also, blocks that have already been picked up and frozen into the base of a glacier can abrade or scrape the bedrock below the glacier as it moves, grinding the rocks into fine particles called glacial flour. These processes of plucking and abrasion are responsible for most major erosional landscape features associated with glaciers.

On the sides of large U-shaped valleys, you will often find small side valleys with a similar shape, but the smaller valley floor will be much higher in elevation than the main valley—almost as if the smaller valley had been left hanging on the side of the larger trough. These hanging valleys were formed by smaller

U-shaped valleys at Washington Pass indicate that this area was once occupied and shaped by glaciers.

tributary glaciers that fed the main valley glacier. Since the tributary glaciers were much smaller, they had less erosional power, so the valleys they created weren't as deep. Now that the glaciers have melted away, the valleys formed by tributary glaciers appear to be hanging high up on the side of the larger glacial troughs. Most large glacial troughs in the North Cascades have hanging valleys, as do the high alpine regions of the Cascade Range that were once glaciated.

At the top of glacially carved valleys are numerous landforms created by the removal of bedrock by ice. Since many, many examples of these landforms can be found in regions that were covered in glaciers during the last glacial maximum, we haven't named any specific examples here, but rather describe their topographic

characteristics so that the next time you're out and about in previously glaciated regions, you'll know what to look for.

A cirque is a semicircular, amphitheater-shaped head or top of a glacial valley. The floor of a cirque is semi-rounded or flat, and surrounded on three sides by steep headwalls. Some high alpine cirques are still occupied by small glaciers or snowfields. A single small lake in the bottom of a cirque is called a tarn, and lakes linked in a chain within a single cirque or glacial trough are called paternoster lakes.

A steep, sharp ridge between two adjacent cirques is an arete. As cirque glaciers grow, they erode not only down and downslope, but also laterally and headward (toward the uphill portion of the glacier) through plucking and freeze-thaw

Erosional features from mountainous glaciers in the North Cascades. The central U-shaped valley in the photo is a glacial trough. On the side of the trough are multiple cirques, which are also located in hanging valleys. The sharp ridges separating the cirques are aretes, and the pyramid-shaped peaks surrounded by cirques are horns.

Crystal Lake near Mt. Rainier is a tarn in a cirque which is also part of a hanging valley.

Striations on a glacially polished quartz diorite in Mount Rainier National Park. Striations are roughly parallel to the pencil scale in the photo. The white stripe paralleling the striations is a felsic dike cutting across the diorite.

weathering. This lateral and headward erosion produces the steep sides of cirques and headwalls, and as two neighboring glaciers erode laterally the steep sides approach each other and create the steep, knife-edge ridge that is an arete.

A horn is a steep, multi-sided, pyramid-shaped peak surrounded by three or more cirques. Horns form when cirque glaciers on the sides of a mountain all erode headward toward the same point. As the headwalls approach each other, they produce a horn.

If you pay close attention to bedrock outcrops in previously glaciated regions, there are other clues to indicate a sheet of ice once flowed through the area. Straight, parallel scratches or grooves in a rock surface are striations, which form when large

rocks frozen in the base of a glacier scrape against underlying rocks. Striations can be used to determine the direction a glacier was flowing, as they form parallel to the direction of glacial motion. Often a rock surface with striations will be very smooth as a result of glacial polish—the process in which smaller, fine-grained rocks caught in the bottom of a glacier abrade and grind away at exposed surfaces, essentially acting as sandpaper.

Depositional Features Left Behind by Glaciers

With the number of landforms created by glacial erosion, and the large amount of sediment that glaciers can erode and transport, it makes sense that many landforms are also created when the sediment

The milky gray-blue color of the Cowlitz River in the Washington Cascades comes from the high amount of glacial flour it's transporting.

is finally deposited. In general, any sediment deposited by glaciers is called till. Till can be differentiated from alluvium (sediment deposited by rivers) by the shape and size distribution of the individual pieces. Till will have pieces of all different sizes (teeny tiny to incredibly large, even house-sized boulders) and a wide variety of shapes, ranging from very angular to very round pieces. Alluvium, on the other hand, is composed of pieces that are all fairly round to very round. This is due to the different transport mechanisms. Remember, alluvium is rolled or bounced along the bed of a river, allowing the sharp corners of individual sediment pieces to smooth with more and more transport. Till is transported by being ground up and

dragged along the base of the glacier, or frozen within the glacier itself.

Geologists sometimes joke that till is transported until it's not. As long as sediment is frozen into a glacier or being dragged along its base by glacial flow, the till will be transported. As a glacier melts, generally at its downslope end, any sediment the glacier is carrying will be deposited or carried away by meltwater rivers. Meltwater rivers have a milky or cloudy color due to the high amount of fine sediment or glacial flour they carry. The Cowlitz and White Rivers, which drain glaciers on Mt. Rainier, both carry a high amount of glacial flour, enough to completely change the color of the water and give the White River its name.

View of the Emmons Glacier and its moraine on Mt. Rainier. Emmons Glacier proper is in the background—the moraine is the ridge of till extending from left to right across the photo. The dotted line notes the moraine's crest.

The more a glacier melts, the more the volume of water in meltwater rivers increases, along with the amount of sediment they transport. This sediment gets deposited in broad, low-relief outwash plains downstream of the glacier, referred to as glacial drift. Minus a few isolated bedrock outcrops, almost the entire Puget Sound Lowland is covered in till, outwash, and glacial drift, a collection of sediments named the Vashon Till.

In previously glaciated regions, ridges of till with sharp crests are called moraines. Think back for a minute to the analogy of a glacier as nature's bulldozer. As a glacier moves in its bulldozer-like fashion across the landscape, whether through a valley or across regions of lower topography, ridges of till build up in front

of it and along its sides. When a glacier melts or recedes, the ridges left behind serve as a record of the glacier's size. Lateral moraines run parallel to glacial valleys and indicate where the sides of the glacier were. End moraines cut across valleys and show where the glacier's terminus used to be. In many cases, lateral moraines will curve to become end moraines, giving us an idea of the now-melted glacier's shape.

When a glacier flows over an area of low-relief topography that's covered in loose sediment or glacial drift, the ice can scour and reshape the till into elongate ridges. Called drumlins or fluted ridges, these long, low-lying ridges are oriented parallel to the direction the glacier was flowing. Much of the Puget Lowlands are

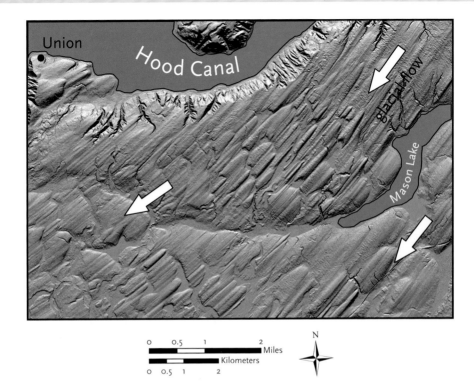

A high-resolution topographic model of the south Kitsap Peninsula in the PLO, which shows northeast-southwest oriented drumlins and fluted ridges near Hood Canal in Washington. The data used to create this image was provided by the Washington Geological Survey.

covered in fluted ridges, but they can be hard to see when they're covered with vegetation or urban development. However, high-resolution topographic data confirms their existence.

A striking landform left behind by glaciers is an erratic, a large boulder deposited on top of or included within till that is vastly different in composition to any surrounding bedrock. The term *erratic* has its roots in the Latin term *errare*, which means "to wander." Erratics can be garbage-can to house-sized boulders that were plucked by a glacier, transported

tens to hundreds of miles within the glacial ice, and dropped off when the glacier melted. These rocks often look out of place, such as a large boulder resting on top of a field of smaller-sized till.

The Puget Lowlands are home to quite a few glacial erratics. The Coupeville Erratic, affectionately named "Big Rock" by locals in Coupeville, Washington, is a house-sized boulder of greenstone that was transported south across modern-day Whidbey Island from the Deception Pass region to its present location. Wedgwood Rock, an erratic in the Wedgwood area

The large boulder near the bus stop on Highline Community College's campus is an erratic that was transported to this location during the last glacial maximum.

Landscapes Shaped by Wind

While the Pacific Northwest doesn't have the most spectacular wind-shaped landscapes in North America, there are regions along the Pacific coast and in the Columbia Basin where the topography is heavily influenced by wind-driven processes. Landforms shaped by wind are called aeolian landforms after Aeolus, the Greek god of winds. The most prevalent aeolian landforms in Oregon and Washington are produced by wind-driven movement and deposition of easily transported sand and silt.

Sand Dunes

Sand dunes form when prevailing winds are strong enough to push, roll, or bounce sand-sized particles across the landscape. Sandy beaches or river floodplains in arid parts of the Pacific Northwest are typical environments with enough sand for dunes to form. Sand dunes come in all sizes, ranging from small ripples less than a centimeter tall to massive dune fields where individual ridges reach over 100 feet high. Many sand dunes are asymmetric, with one gently sloping face and one steeper face. The gently sloping face is the windward face of the dune, where sand particles are blown upward before falling down the steeper lee or slip face. The slip face will always be facing downwind, so if you can determine the steeper face of a dune you can estimate the prevailing wind direction that formed the dune to begin with. Over short, human timescales, dunes aren't stable landscape features. Sand is constantly being moved up the windward face and down the lee face causing the dune to migrate downwind. Vegetation such as trees or grasses can help stabilize the

of Seattle, was transported to its current location from bedrock in the San Juan Islands during the last glacial maximum. Just south of Seattle in Des Moines, a van-sized granodiorite boulder matching the composition of rocks in the North Cascades and the Coast Ranges of British Columbia was found on the Highline Community College Campus and is known as the Highline Erratic.

Sand dunes along the Oregon coast, looking west along the crest of a dune. The windward face is to the north (right side of the photo) and the steeper slip face on the south, indicating that the prevailing winds here are north to south.

dune, but they can also trap windblown sand making a dune grow larger.

Sand dunes are common features along most sandy beaches on the Pacific Coast of Oregon and Washington, with some of the best (and largest) examples between the towns of Florence and Coos Bay in Oregon. In the Columbia Basin, the Juniper Dunes Wilderness northeast of Kennewick are an example of dunes created from sand initially transported by the Columbia and Snake Rivers.

Loess

Also known as wind-blown dust, loess is wind-blown silt previously deposited by glaciers or glacial processes. Loess begins as glacial flour within larger deposits of glacial outwash or drift, but because of its small size it's easily mobilized and transported by aeolian processes. Loess-capped hills, such as the Palouse region of the Columbia Basin, tend to have smooth, convex ridges with gently sloping sides.

Loess in the Palouse region (appropriately named Palouse Loess) was deposited when prevailing southwest-to-northeast winds blew silt from glacial drift and other soils in northern Oregon into southeast Washington. Some of the younger glacial drift originated from giant glacial floods that originated in Montana (more on these on page 284). Today, the Palouse Loess covers an area of approximately 19,000 square miles in the Columbia Basin and can be up to 250 feet thick.

Centimeter-scale ripples on the windward face of a sand dune

Loess covers much of the Columbia basin and provides the base for soils excellent for growing wheat or alfalfa crops throughout eastern Washington.

A typical Pacific Northwest coast landscape—rugged headlands, sandy beaches, and almost everything in between

Coastline Features

In the Pacific Northwest we don't say we're going to the beach—we say we're going to the *coast*. Maybe this is because the coastlines of Oregon and Washington are some of our most rugged, geologically and geomorphically diverse regions. From sea cliffs hundreds of feet high that extend straight out of the water to wide sandy beaches and almost everything in between, coastal landforms in the Northwest are textbook, literally—they are commonly used as examples in geology textbooks.

The coastline of the Pacific Northwest is considered an active margin, meaning that the continental shoreline lines up with an active plate boundary, in this case the Cascadia Subduction Zone. As the Juan de Fuca and North American Plates collide, the rocks of the Coast Ranges are being squeezed and pushed up as a part of the accretionary wedge. Rocks that were deposited or formed on the ocean floor are now exposed above sea level. You can think of the Coast Ranges as slowly emerging from below sea level over geologic time.

At the coast, rocks along the shoreline are subject to erosion by nearly constant wave action. The crashing of ocean waves provides the bulk of the energy needed to erode and transport sediment, shaping the landforms we can observe today. As with glacial landforms, we can divide coastal landforms into erosional and depositional categories.

Erosional Features

Imagine taking a rock and hitting it repeatedly with a small hammer. One hit with the hammer might not do much, but over time and constant hitting, the rock will begin to break apart. Now replace the hammer with an ocean wave—imagine how effective endless waves are at hammering apart rocks exposed at the shoreline. Rivers do most of their erosive work during high flow or flood events, but waves can reach the shoreline nearly every minute of every day. Wave erosion of bedrock at the coast produces specific features that form in a distinct progression.

Headlands are rock outcroppings, large or small, that stick out into the ocean past the adjacent shoreline. Headlands can be as large as small mountains with over 1300 feet of relief between the ocean and the highpoint, but they can also be much smaller ridges of erosion-resistant rock that stick out into the ocean. Some large examples include Cape Flattery on the northwest tip of the Olympic Peninsula, which is the northwesternmost point in the continental United States, and Cape Meares and Cape Lookout on the northern Oregon coast. Smaller examples are abundant along the entire coastline between California and Cape Flattery, including Cape Blanco in Oregon, which is also the westernmost point in the continental United States.

Because headlands stick out into the ocean beyond the adjacent shoreline, they receive a larger proportion of wave energy than their surroundings. Wind-driven waves traveling across the open ocean will have their crests arranged in a semi-straight line. In an ideal wave, all points on this crest line are moving in the same direction at the same speed. However, when a wave approaches a headland, only part of it crashes into the rocky outcropping, while the rest bends or refracts around the point of contact. Where the wave refraction is the greatest, the erosive energy of the wave is concentrated. This concentrated energy produces a few other coastal-specific landforms.

Sea caves form when the sides of a headland are undercut by wave erosion. If two sea caves on opposite sides of a headland erode toward each other, they can meet and form a tunnel through the headland, which becomes a sea arch. Sea arches abound along the Oregon and Washington coastline. Some spectacular examples include Three Arch Rocks near Oceanside, Oregon, and the appropriately named Point of Arches, just south of Cape Flattery in Washington. Of course, once an arch forms, it's not immune to further erosion by wave action.

Sea stacks are blocks of rock isolated from the shoreline. Once connected to the shore by headlands, sea stacks form when a sea arch collapses or the original headland erodes away. Some sea stacks can be quite large, such as the famous Haystack Rock near Cannon Beach, Oregon, but many are smaller and dotted all along the coastline.

In the tidal zone near a steep sea cliff you can find flat or horizontal exposures of bedrock called wave-cut benches. It's not just headlands that are subject to erosion—any bedrock exposed at a coastline will be affected by waves. However, waves

Heceta Head(land), Oregon

Sea arch at Devils Punchbowl State Natural Area, Oregon

Sea stacks near Bandon, Oregon

Erosional progression (right to left) of a headland, sea arch, sea stack along the Olympic Peninsula coastline

An expansive wave-cut bench at Sunset Bay State Park. Note the sea cliff and sea stacks in the background.

can only reach up to a certain level, so any erosion on a sea cliff will be concentrated between the high and low tide levels. As waves erode the base of a sea cliff, a wave-cut notch will form. This notch eventually undercuts the cliff, causing the overlying material to collapse. As this material is then eroded away, the bedrock *underneath* the notch is unaffected by erosion. Over time, progressive erosion of wave-cut notches and collapse of the overlying material causes the sea cliff to migrate inland leaving behind a flat bedrock surface that shows us approximately where sea level met the cliff in the past. Sunset Bay State Park near Coos Bay, Oregon, has some of the best examples of wave-cut benches anywhere on the Oregon or Washington coastline.

Low-relief, flat strips of bedrock at elevations above sea level are called marine terraces. Marine terraces begin as wave-cut benches, but through tectonic uplift the wave-cut bench is elevated above the reach of wave erosion to become a more permanent feature of the landscape. If tectonic uplift has been going on long enough, multiple generations of marine terraces can be found in the landscape; the oldest being at the highest elevation.

Like many coastal erosional landforms, marine terraces are present all along the Pacific Northwest coastline. The Sunset Bay and Cape Arago area of Oregon has great examples of marine terraces. The headland and sea stacks of Cape Flattery and Tatoosh Island in northwest Washington are capped by marine terraces.

This sea cliff near Coos Bay, Oregon, is capped by a flat marine terrace—the perfect spot for a lighthouse.

Depositional Features

Imagine the journey of a typical piece of sediment. It begins somewhere in a mountainous region on the continent as a product of physical weathering. Angular-shaped, it is transported by hillslope processes into a stream channel, where it's bounced around with other sediment as it travels downstream. During stream transport, the sediment becomes smaller in size and rounder in shape. Eventually, it turns into numerous sand-sized grains and is deposited when the river flows into the ocean. But this isn't the end of the journey! Ocean currents and waves can further transport the sand from the mouth of the river along the coastline to create depositional landforms.

Beaches are probably the best-known example of a depositional landform—strips of loose sediment parallel to the coastline adjacent to the ocean. Notice that we don't say *sand* when describing beaches, but *sediment*. Yes, there are many sandy beaches along the Pacific Northwest coast, but there are also beaches composed of gravels and cobbles and mixtures of all sizes of sediment. Regardless of its size, this sediment will always be very round. Continuous waves breaking on the shore roll sediment up and down the beach, knocking off any sharp corners. Most sediment on beaches is locally sourced, either through erosion of headlands and local cliffs or from nearby rivers.

While beaches exist all along the Oregon and Washington coastline, the Long Beach peninsula just north of the Columbia River in Washington is the longest,

A sandy beach near Coos Bay, Oregon

A cobble beach at Yaquina Head near Newport, Oregon

Netarts Bay on the Oregon Coast. The Cape Lookout headland is in the background, the tidal flat and estuary in the foreground, and the Pacific Ocean is to the right.

nearly 30 miles of uninterrupted sand. Most beaches are a mixture of sand and larger sediment and can look different depending on the season. During winter months, more frequent storms and larger, more powerful waves reach the coast. These larger waves can remove sand from the beach and store it offshore in sandbars, leaving larger rocks behind on the beach, which will have a steeper slope. Smaller, less powerful waves during summer months will move the sand back to the beach, giving it a lower slope.

Sand spits are long strips of sand that stretch from the shoreline out into a bay or across an inlet. Spits are connected to the mainland at one end and formed of sediment that's transported parallel to the shoreline—their finger-like shape points in the direction of transport. A great example of a spit is the Ediz Hook in Port Angeles, Washington. If a spit closes off an inlet or bay, it is renamed a baymouth bar. These are rare in the Pacific Northwest because the volume of water flowing out of rivers into the Pacific Ocean is sufficient enough to remove any sediment that may block its path. Also, humans often modify the shoreline to prevent bays or inlets from being closed off for economic and commercial reasons.

Estuaries are wide, low-relief areas where one or more rivers carrying a high amount of sediment flow into the ocean. The sediment is deposited in tidal flats—flat regions of sand and mud in between high- and low-tide levels. Rivers flowing into estuaries and through tidal flats typically have a meandering channel shape, with the channels best exposed during low tide. Most estuaries will also have sand spits or beaches protecting the tidal flats from the open ocean.

In the Pacific Northwest, estuaries are commonly referred to as bays. For example, Willapa Bay in Washington is the estuary formed where the Willapa River flows into the Pacific Ocean—it's separated from the open sea by the Long Beach peninsula. Tillamook Bay in Oregon is the estuary formed behind the Cape Meares headland and Bayocean beach peninsula where the Wilson and Trask Rivers meet the sea.

Landscapes Unique to the Pacific Northwest

There are a couple specific landscapes in the Pacific Northwest that are unique, with very few other places in North America or the world quite like them. The Channeled Scablands of eastern Washington hold evidence for floods of monstrous proportion, and the Columbia River Gorge is one of the only places on Earth where a river cuts through an active volcanic arc without help from glaciers. These are very different yet geologically linked landscapes.

Missoula Floods and the Channeled Scablands

Rarely in the geologic record do isolated events impact and shape huge portions of the landscape without being related to volcanoes or earthquakes. However, large swaths of eastern Washington and the Columbia Basin were sculpted just this way, through a series of cataclysmic floods that took place toward the end of the last glacial maximum around 13–15,000 years ago. Called the Missoula Floods, these enormous glacial outburst flood events

were the result of collapsed ice-dammed lakes in Montana.

During the most recent glaciation in North America, most of northern Washington, Idaho, Montana, and British Columbia were covered by a giant continental glacier known as the Cordilleran Ice Sheet. The southern end of this ice sheet wasn't one continuous face—instead, various lobes or fingers of ice extended southward through valleys into the Puget Sound, Okanogan Highlands, and other places in Idaho and Montana. In the area that became present-day Montana, the Purcell Lobe of the ice sheet grew south until it blocked the Clark Fork River, forming an ice dam and flooding the river valley upstream. This flooded valley became Glacial Lake Missoula, which held approximately 500 cubic miles of water behind the ice dam. As the lake filled, water pressure on the ice dam built, eventually causing its catastrophic failure—sending the entire volume of Glacial Lake Missoula downstream into the Columbia River. Estimates on the amount of water discharged reach 15 cubic miles per hour, moving at speeds up to 80 miles per hour. This immense volume quickly overwhelmed the channel of the Columbia River, and the flood water spilled out across the eastern Washington part of the Columbia Plateau.

As the Missoula Floods raced across eastern Washington, the water stripped soil and material from the landscape and carved deep channels, called coulees, into the underlying Columbia River Basalts. Areas that were stripped or carved by the floods are now called the Channeled Scablands, named for the large river-less channels and bare bedrock swaths left

Grand Coulee in central Washington. This almost 600-foot-deep gorge was carved as the Missoula Floods tore through the Columbia Plateau. The modern Columbia River channel is north of here; the water in Grand Coulee is the reservoir of Banks Lake. The sandbar in the foreground contains giant ripples that formed from sediment transported during the floods.

behind. Grand Coulee, Moses Coulee, Frenchman Coulee, and Dry Falls are all large valleys carved by the Missoula Floods. Presently, these valleys don't contain any permanent rivers, only lakes and small streams that flow during the rainy or snowmelt seasons.

Eventually, the flood reached Wallula Gap near the present-day Tri-Cities in southeast Washington, where the water backed up and formed a temporary lake. This lake spilled through Wallula Gap before becoming backed up again on the eastern side of the Columbia River Gorge. During the short lifespan of these lakes,

floodwaters deposited fine-grained silt and clay, forming the modern Touchet Beds near Walla Walla.

The constriction of the Columbia River Gorge funneled the Missoula Flood water through the Cascade Range and into the eastern part of the Portland area, where the water had enough force to strip material from cinder cones in the Boring Volcanic Field down to their necks. It inundated the Portland area and flooded the Willamette Valley as far south as Corvallis and Eugene. Ultimately, the flood continued along the path of the Columbia River into the Pacific Ocean.

Panoramic photo of Dry Falls, south of Grand Coulee. During the Missoula Floods, this 3.5-mile-wide waterfall would have been full of water moving at up to 65 miles per hour.

The formation of an ice dam on the Clark Fork River, filling of Glacial Lake Missoula, and subsequent flooding wasn't a single, isolated event. Based on individual silt deposits in the Touchet Beds and stacked deposits on the floor of the Pacific Ocean at the mouth of the Columbia River it's estimated that this process repeated as many as forty times, with individual flood events occurring between 13,000 and 15,000 years ago.

In addition to the Channeled Scablands and Touchet Beds, there is plentiful evidence for the Missoula Floods and their likely source. Scattered throughout the Willamette Valley and eastern Washington are various dropstones, rocks that were rafted in ice blocks during flood events and deposited once their ice raft melted. Dropstones are considered a specific type of glacial erratic, ones with an additional style of transport. Many of the Missoula Flood dropstones have origins in the Canadian Rockies or Idaho and are very different in composition from the basalts that make up most of the Columbia Plateau or the volcanic and clastic rocks that make up the Cascades and Coast Ranges. One particular dropstone with a particularly erratic and famed

history is the Willamette Meteorite, which you can read about on page 207.

The Columbia River Gorge

The Columbia River is the largest river in the Pacific Northwest, fourth largest by volume on the North American continent. Its headwaters are tucked away in the Rocky Mountains of British Columbia, where the river begins flowing north before bending in a sharp arc to flow south and west through eastern Washington and finally west to the Pacific Ocean. For a long stretch of its lower section, it serves as the geographic border between Oregon and Washington. The Columbia River Gorge proper (also known simply as the Gorge) was formed as the river cut through the Columbia Flood Basalts and Cascade Volcanic Arc, roughly between the towns of Roosevelt, Washington, and Troutdale, Oregon. Throughout this entire stretch, I-84 parallels the river and allows for amazing access to the geography and geology of the Gorge.

The Columbia River Gorge in its present form is quite young, with most of the major events that shaped the modern landscape taking place within the last 15–17,000 years. However, the Columbia

Looking east into the Columbia River Gorge

River, or some ancestral version of it, has been a feature in the Pacific Northwest for over 40 million years. How do we know this? The answer lies within some sedimentary rocks of the Coast Ranges. The Eocene-age Tyee Sandstone in the Oregon Coast Ranges is composed of sediment that was originally part of large granitic intrusions in present-day Idaho. These sediments would have been transported into the Pacific Ocean between 56 and 34 million years ago by an ancestral Columbia and Snake River system. Deposition of the Tyee Sandstone was happening at approximately the same time as the growth of the early Cascade Range, so the river system carrying the sediments that would become the Tyee Sandstone must have been cutting through the growing volcanic arc.

Another clue to the longevity of the Columbia River Gorge is the extent of the Columbia Flood Basalts. These massive sheets of basalt flows are ubiquitous to the Columbia Basin and much of the Blue Mountains, but are also present within the Columbia River Gorge, the Willamette Valley, and portions of the Coast Ranges adjacent to the modern channel of the Columbia River. Since the flood basalts most likely did not flow up and over the Cascade Range, their path took advantage of a preexisting "gorge" through the Cascades that would have existed between 17 and 14 million years ago.

Even more evidence for a long-lived Columbia Gorge comes from Pleistocene (less than 2 million years old) river gravels known as the Troutdale Formation that were deposited near present-day Troutdale, Oregon, and Camas, Washington. These gravels were deposited by an older Columbia River on top of Columbia Flood Basalts and have since been cut into by the modern river channel.

The Gorge as we know it today has been shaped by three main geologic processes. First, the flood basalts and other rocks that make the walls of the Gorge are tilted and sloped generally toward the south. The tectonic process that produces this tilting has been happening for a long time and is still happening today—we can tell because older rocks in the Gorge are tilted more than the younger rocks that lie on top. Second, the Missoula Floods roared through the Gorge between 13 and 15,000 years ago on their way to the Willamette Valley and Pacific Ocean. Third, large portions of the northern (Washington) side of the Gorge have collapsed in landslides. The most recent was the Bonneville Slide, which occurred around 500 to 1000 years ago and entirely blocked the Columbia River near the present-day site of Bonneville Dam and the town of Cascade Locks, Oregon.

The deepest part of the Gorge, between Hood River and Troutdale, is quite asymmetric in shape. Its southern (Oregon) side is much more steeply sloped than the northern side—a direct result of the tilting of the rocks and subsequent landslides. The layers of basalt flows that the Gorge is cut into are stacked on top of each other similar to layers of sedimentary rocks. Because a significant amount of time passed between each basalt flow, the top of an older flow had time to weather producing a small weak zone. When a newer basalt layer flowed on top, it would sandwich the weaker, weathered layer in between the two flows. As these layers become tilted over time, the weak layer acted act as a Slip 'N Slide, allowing the layers above to collapse and slide downslope. Much of the old landslide debris has been carried out of the Gorge

The iconic Multnomah Falls on the Oregon side of the Columbia River Gorge

by the Columbia River, but this process eventually left behind a more gently sloped northern side.

The steep southern side of the Gorge, which is less prone to large landslides, is home to other features for which the Gorge is famous—its waterfalls! Streams draining into the Columbia River from the high topography on its southern side cascade over the southern side of the Gorge producing numerous waterfalls, some over 600 feet high.

TELLING THE STORY

Solid as a rock. Still as stone. From a human's perspective, rocks seem eternal and unchanging. Yet they are changing constantly. Over the Earth's lifetime, countless mountains have risen and crumbled, ocean basins have opened and closed, and pieces of the mantle have cycled up to Earth's surface and gone back down again.

Many of these processes happen so slowly they cannot be observed directly. (There is no time-lapse video of the Coast Range's 50-million-year rise from the sea.) Yet we state confidently that such things are so. Why?

Consider two rocks. One, the oldest mineral grain on Earth, is a zircon crystal dated at 4.4 billion years old. That's almost as old as the planet itself—aged 4.5 billion years.

The other is Earth's youngest rock. How old do you think that might be?

Whenever you are reading this, no matter the date, the youngest rock on Earth is being formed right now. A volcano is erupting somewhere, making ash deposits or lava flows. Sediment in an ocean basin is being buried, compacted, and cemented into sandstone and shale. Mountain belts are compressing and heating rocks beneath their weight, transforming basalts and mudstones into

greenschists and gneisses that may, once the mountain above them has eroded away, one day reach Earth's surface.

We can understand where old rocks came from by looking at the processes that make new rocks today. One of the most powerful principles of modern geology is uniformitarianism—the notion that the present is the key to the past. Put another way, this means that the processes creating and destroying rocks in the present are the same processes that have been at work inside Earth for billions of years. Because of uniformitarianism, we can study the characteristics of lava flows that cooled last week and use them to understand the genesis of basalt layers that are millions of years old.

This principle scales all the way up to the notion of plate tectonics, geology's grand unifying theory, which we explored in this book's first chapter. Modern science has mapped the boundaries and distribution of today's tectonic plates in great detail, even tracking their motions in real time with sophisticated GPS. We can determine which plates are converging, which are moving apart, and which are sliding side by side, and we can look at the rocks and landforms around those boundaries to understand what kinds of geologic features these plate interactions create. Then, when we see evidence of similar features in older rocks, we can begin to work out the tectonic forces that put them there.

This chapter begins by demonstrating how to put your feature identification skills together to see the story in a rock. It goes on to discuss our region's tectonic story as it's currently understood through the collaborative efforts of hundreds of scientists over decades of study, pointing out some key features that have led to this understanding. Be aware, however, that the geology of this region is still a subject of vigorous study, and in years to come new discoveries that challenge our current models undoubtedly await.

Looking at Outcrops

Most of Earth's surface is covered by sediments, soils, and plants. Yet these familiar features are only a thin layer of material covering what we call bedrock—the fully coherent (hard and solid) bodies of rock that make up Earth's crust. Locations where bare bedrock is exposed at the surface are called outcrops.

Outcrops are windows into the geologic architecture otherwise hidden beneath our feet. They help us learn what the underlying crust is made of and find clues about how it was assembled. They can range from kitchen-table sized to a bare, rugged mountain peak or tall cliff face.

To understand an outcrop, you must identify its geologic features and look for information about how they relate to one another. This means identifying minerals, rocks, structures, and geomorphic presentation. The following steps can help guide your observations.

Step one View the outcrop from far away. Take in the big picture. Is the outcrop all one color and texture, or are there different zones? Are there any features like layers or stripes? Does the outcrop look like a solid, vertical wall? Or are some sections crumbly, sloped, or even horizontal? Based on these observations, estimate how many different rock types you think you can see.

Step two Get closer. If you think there is more than one rock type, go look at each one. Be sure you're looking at a rock surface that hasn't been altered by weathering, what's known as a *fresh face.*

Step three Describe each rock, starting by identifying the texture. If you can see any large individual mineral crystals in the rock, test and describe their physical properties and try to identify them.

Step four Try to name each rock based on its texture and visible mineral content. Some rock types will be obvious, but others may be more ambiguous, especially if they are fine-grained.

Step five Back up again. Look at the big picture in the context of your detailed rock and mineral IDs. What do you see now? Perhaps a basalt flow, or a bed of sandstone, or a twisted schist? You may need to go back and forth between the big picture and the detailed one to work it all out. Hint: If you have a rock that's hard to identify, see if the form of the overall outcrop helps narrow it down. For example, a fine-grained black rock might be basalt, iron-rich sandstone, or shale, to name a few. Each of these rock types will have a different appearance at outcrop scale.

Step six Look for structures like cleavage, faults, dikes, folds, and veins. Large structures may be obvious at first glance,

WHY IS EARTH'S OLDEST MINERAL YOUNGER THAN THE AGE OF THE EARTH?

Because Earth recycles! All new rocks are made from old rocks: melted metamorphic rocks become igneous plutons; eroded granite mountains become beach sand, which becomes sandstone; mudstone compressed beneath a mountain becomes a schist. The processes of plate tectonics are constantly consuming old rocks to generate new ones. Because this tectonic remodeling is so widespread and efficient, very few of Earth's oldest rocks remain undisturbed.

Though the world's oldest mineral crystal is very old, it came from a rock that had already been recycled from Earth's original crust. So far, no definitively original crustal material has ever been found. However, we are still able to gauge Earth's age from fragments of other rocky planets that landed on Earth as meteorites. Despite coming from the interiors of many different celestial bodies, most of which were broken up by collisions long ago, these fragments all have the same age. This led scientists to the understanding that the rocky bodies in our solar system, including Mercury, Venus, Earth, and Mars, all formed at the same time, 4.5 billion years ago.

A representative Pacific Northwest roadcut outcrop

WEATHERING RINDS

Weathering alters the minerals near a rock's surface and creates a strange-looking zone that surrounds the rock like the rind of a fruit. If a rock is originally black, weathering rinds will often be yellow-orange to brown. Other weathering rinds may be gray, tan, or white and have an overall washed-out appearance. To identify a fresh face, make sure the rock color and pattern go all the way through the outcrop. You may need to break open a piece of rock to check.

A fresh face contrasts with dark weathering on a clast of crystalline rock.

---

and smaller structures may appear when you get up close.

Step seven If you've identified more than one type of rock in the outcrop, characterize how the rock types are in contact with one another. Are they layers deposited one on top of the other? Is there granitic pluton intruding a different rock? Have different rock types been brought together by a fault?

Step eight Using your knowledge of how each of the elements you've identified can form (hint: the rock, mineral, and structure entries can help with this), tell yourself a story about how these rocks all came to be together in this place. Compare your story with a friend's. Argue with each other in front of the outcrop—now you're acting like real geologists.

Storytelling at Work

Let's see how this process plays out in an idealized setting. The figure on the following page shows an illustration of a giant block cut out of Earth's crust like a slice of sheet cake. A real-life outcrop might only show a single face of this cube, but the cartoon shows how features on one face are related to the geometry of that whole section of crust. Let's walk through the numbered features in the order they formed to help us understand what they mean.

1. The lowest part of the cube is a metamorphic gneiss with wavy dark-and-light compositional banding. These stripes belong to a single body of rock. During the gneiss's formation deep within the Earth, pressure squeezing at its sides bent its banding into folds. If you could pull one of the folded layers out of the cube, it would look like a wavy tin roof.

2. Here, the folding in the gneiss is interrupted, and the gneiss body has a flat

A Block of Earth's Crust

upper boundary. The rocks above are sedimentary rocks deposited on what was once Earth's surface. This tells us that after the gneiss formed within the Earth, all the rock above it eroded away. Erosion also cut into the gneiss and removed some of it, ultimately making a flat exposure. Identifying erosion can be tricky—because erosion takes rock away, you must look for what is missing (here, the tops of the gneiss folds).

3. Layers of sandstone and mudstone are stacked on one another, demonstrating sedimentary bedding. The contact between the sedimentary rocks and the underlying gneiss is a depositional contact, and so are the contacts between each sedimentary layer. From this, we know that layers of sand and mud were deposited one on top of the other. They were then buried, compacted, and turned into tabular bodies of sedimentary sandstone and mudstone. (Note: As these rocks are now exposed again at Earth's surface, the layers that once

buried them had to have been eroded away at some point, too.)

4. A body of granite shaped like a blob with arm-like offshoots and irregular edges is found within both the gneiss and the sedimentary rocks. This is a classic example of an intrusive pluton—a rising felsic magma body forced its way into the older rocks and cooled slowly into coarse crystalline granite. We know it is younger than the other rock types because it couldn't have intruded into them if they weren't already there.

5. The whole block has been cut by a fault, which is identifiable by the offset in the sedimentary layers and gneissic banding. The hanging wall has slid downward relative to the footwall, creating a normal fault geometry. A normal fault indicates that changing forces in Earth's crust put our rock cube under tension, pulling it apart.

Quick Note This chronology states that 4 (granite intrusion) happened before 5 (normal fault), but based on the information we have, those events could have happened the other way around, too. The granite and the fault don't touch or cross-cut each other, so we have no way of knowing which happened first.

Overall, the story of this block of rock goes like this: a gneiss formed and folded deep within Earth's crust was then uplifted to the surface as the rocks above it eroded away. Eventually, the process driving erosion stopped, and this area instead became a place where sediment was deposited. Layers of sand and mud accumulated. Over time, these layers were buried deeply enough for pressure and heat to turn them into sandstone and mudstone. Next, a rising body of magma intruded the gneiss and the sedimentary rocks, cooling into a granite pluton. At some point, the surrounding region began to experience tectonic tension, pulling at the block until it broke and slid along a normal fault. Finally, renewed erosion, in part from the river, removed the material that had previously buried the sandstone and mudstone layers, exposing them to the surface again.

The Northwest's Tectonic History: An Overview

The story of the Pacific Northwest is a story of geological creation. Five hundred million years ago, Oregon and Washington (and California, for that matter) didn't exist. Idaho and Nevada were beachfront property on ancestral North America, a landmass known as Laurentia. The Northwest we know today was assembled in four interconnected phases: continental rifting, tectonic accretion, volcanism and uplift, and surficial erosion and deposition. This section begins with a brief overview of these phases before discussing each in more detail, highlighting specific ways you can see this story in the landscape. You may wish to refer to earlier figures, particularly the regional map on page 17 and the geologic map on page 131, as you read on.

Each phase of creation leading to today's Pacific Northwest was driven by plate tectonics. The first phase, rifting, began in the Precambrian, when newly formed divergent plate boundaries broke apart the ancient supercontinent of Rodinia, creating the proto–North American landmass of Laurentia. For a couple hundred million years, the Laurentian coast remained tectonically quiet, slowly accumulating sediments and sedimentary rocks.

In the Mesozoic, changing plate motions initiated a series of subduction zones off the Laurentian coast and kicked off phase two, tectonic accretion. As discussed in chapter one, subducting ocean crust has two major effects: it creates volcanic arcs, and it brings things together. In this case, the volcanoes developed as a series of offshore island arcs that may have resembled the modern-day Philippines. Some volcanoes arose on the fringes of the continent, too. As the ocean plate continued to subduct, sinking down into Earth's interior, the island arcs were dragged closer and closer to continental shores. Eventually the arcs collided with Laurentia and stuck there; they were too large and buoyant to be subducted themselves. The layers of sediment that ringed the islands and blanketed the continental coast got caught up in the collisions, too, and some experienced types of metamorphism unique to zones of subduction and collision.

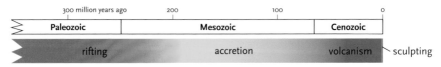

*Note that rifting began about 750 million years ago.

Each distinct package of rock swept up onto the continent is known as a terrane. The foundations of the Pacific Northwest are made of many terranes that arrived at the continent over the course of millions of years. These foundations are exposed today in areas like the Klamath and Blue Mountains of Oregon and the Okanogan Highlands and North Cascades of Washington.

Just over 50 million years ago, an oceanic basalt plateau known as Siletzia became the last terrane to dock with North America. Since then, the tectonic configuration of the Northwest coast has looked very similar to the geometry we see today: a single convergent boundary in the Pacific Ocean where ocean crust is subducting beneath the continent. Today we call this the Cascadia Subduction Zone.

In the third phase of the Pacific Northwest's assembly, this long-lived subduction zone created several generations of continental volcanoes, which erupted periodically and built layers over the continent's accreted foundation. The location of volcanic activity moved over time as the subduction zone's exact configuration evolved—flexing of the downgoing plate shifted the zone where magma was generated, sometimes giving rise to volcanoes close to the coast and other times farther to the east. This process is still going strong today; the active volcanoes of the modern Cascade Range are only the most recent volcanic mountains built by Cascadian subduction.

In addition to generating volcanoes, the convergent margin also generated stresses that continue to act on the North American Plate. Near the plate boundary, compression is squeezing the accretionary wedge at the leading edge of the continent, causing the Olympic Peninsula

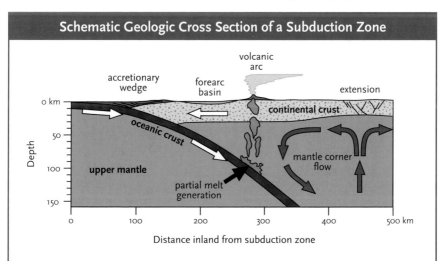

Schematic Geologic Cross Section of a Subduction Zone

This diagram is roughly to scale vertically and horizontally, and it highlights where many subduction zone–related processes take place. These processes include where partial melt and a resulting volcanic arc is generated; development of an accretionary wedge; and mantle corner flow resulting in extension.

and Coast Ranges to rise and the Puget Lowlands and Willamette Valley to drop. As the coastal zone is deformed, it's also being tugged away from the stable, central mass of North America; this has placed the central and eastern areas of the Northwest under tension and created a system of faults.

The convergent margin is not the only phenomenon that built up the Northwest landscape—volcanism from other sources played a significant role. Beginning at least 16.7 million years ago, a plume of magma rose from deep within the Earth's mantle and began to generate enormous outpourings of lava at the surface. The mechanisms behind this "hot spot" volcanism are still an area of active research, but we can easily see its effects in the form of the extensive Columbia River Basalts and other associated rhyolites covering much of eastern Oregon and Washington.

The fourth phase of the Northwest's development has actually been at work all along, acting in concert with the first three—this is surface sculpting. As long as rocks are exposed at Earth's surface, they are subject to the weathering and erosion that wears down mountains and carves river valleys. The clastic sediments these activities generate are transported by gravity, water, and wind to fill in basins and cover beaches. In the Pacific Northwest, this created large stacks of sedimentary rock, now exposed from compression and uplift along the coast, as well as sedimentary beds interspersed with the volcanic units of central and eastern regions. The fossils these units contain tell us much about our region's past, from what kinds of plants and animals

inhabited the area to what kind of climate they experienced.

The Northwest's modern topography has been heavily influenced by two major erosion events: the continental and alpine glaciations of the last ice age and the glacial dam outburst floods (the Missoula Floods, see page 284) that occurred during the same time. From the Puget Sound to the Palouse Hills and from Steens Mountain to the Columbia Gorge, we have these events to thank for much of the landscape we know and love—a landscape that is still evolving today.

The following sections contain more detailed information about each of the Northwest's four phases of development. We also invite you to "see the story" by giving examples of rock units and geographic features affected by each phase.

Phase One: The Great Rift

Notable Localities: OKH

In the ancient past, the configuration of continents on Earth looked very different from the seven landmasses we know today. Many people have heard of the supercontinent Pangea, in which all the world's major landforms were connected as one body. But Pangea is only one of several supercontinents that have come together and broken apart throughout Earth's history, and the story of the Northwest begins with a much older one called Rodinia.

Almost one and a half billion years ago, as Rodinia was assembling, the continental crust in the area of what would later become Idaho and Montana consisted

Rifting: Development of a Divergent Plate Boundary and Passive Margin Sedimentation

This figure depicts rifting and sedimentation during the breakup of Rodinia in four stages:

1. Initial stretching forming lake basins and the deposition of Belt Supergroup rocks

2. Full rifting of Rodinia, beginning stages of oceanic crust formation, and deposition of clastic Windermere Group rocks

3. Development of a passive margin off Laurentia, and deposition of shallow marine carbonates and dolomites of the Metaline Formation

4. Laurentian continental passive margin and proto–Pacific Ocean basin; deposition of sediments that would become the Ledbetter Slate was taking place in the ocean basin

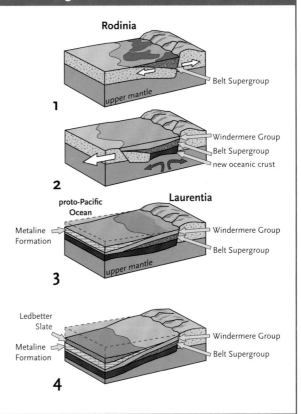

of ancient crystalline basement rocks covered by enormous lake basins filled with sediments. These sediments were compacted into sedimentary rocks and, in some places, buried deeply enough to experience metamorphism over the course of about 70 million years. The suite of related rocks, known as the Belt Supergroup, is greater than 9 miles thick and outcrops today between modern-day Idaho, Montana, British Columbia, and portions of the Okanogan Highlands

in far northeast Washington. All of the Belt Supergroup rocks in Washington have also undergone varying degrees of metamorphism and exist today as slates, greenstones, and some gneisses exposed in areas around Spokane.

Around 750 million years ago, Rodinia began to rift apart into separate tectonic plates, breaking up into multiple continents surrounded by seas. This rifting separated the proto–North America continent Laurentia from the landmasses that would later become Antarctica and Australia. The Laurentian side of the rift margin is considered the edge of true basement rock, or craton, of the modern North American continent and at present stretches roughly north-south from British Columbia in Canada through Idaho and into Nevada. During the breakup, this boundary was a coastline on a growing ocean basin.

Over time, sediments shed into the new ocean as it formed between Laurentia and the rest of Rodinia, building up an underwater continental shelf or passive margin sequence made of clastic sediments in the form of shallow marine rocks and carbonates. In Washington's Okanogan Highlands, these rocks are known as the Windermere Group, an over-5-mile-thick stack of shales, slates, carbonates, and minor volcanic rocks that lie on top of the Belt Supergroup. Later tectonic activity metamorphosed these rocks, so today the Windermere Group includes low-grade metamorphic slates and phyllites, quartzites, and metamorphosed mafic igneous rocks (greenstones) exposed along US-395 north of Spokane.

Sedimentation continued along the passive Laurentian margin for quite some time following the deposition of the Windermere Group. The new ocean basin was fairly shallow during Cambrian and Ordovician times, and thick deposits of limestone and dolostone known as the Metaline Formation accumulated as the basin continued to expand. When the basin deepened, these carbonate layers were covered by fine clays that over time became layered mudstones. Like the Windermere Group, these rocks later experienced metamorphism—the Metaline Formation now is largely marble, and the mudstones metamorphosed into our present-day Ledbetter Slate and Maitlen Phyllite. This suite of rocks is exposed along US-395 and in and around the town of Metaline Falls, Washington.

The Laurentian margin was tectonically quiescent for the bulk of the Paleozoic era and into the early Mesozoic. Sediments continued to accumulate on the ocean floor in an ever-thickening stack of clastic and carbonate rocks. The story of how these rocks, formed on the ocean floor, got to be metamorphosed and exposed at high elevations in the Okanogan Highlands is the next phase in the geologic history of the Pacific Northwest.

Phase Two: Tectonic Accretion

Notable Localities: OKH, NC, KM, BM

During the early Mesozoic, the tectonic environment of the Laurentian coast drastically changed. After over 300 million years of rifting, passive margin sedimentation, and the development of an ocean basin, plate motion changed direction. The Laurentian margin became an active subduction zone.

The downgoing oceanic plate carried its package of Paleozoic passive margin sediments back toward Laurentia, where they were ultimately pushed up onto the edge of the continent. Over the next 100 million years, many other rock formations would meet the same fate. Segments of volcanic island arcs, scraps of ocean floor, and packages of sedimentary and volcanic rocks that originally formed far away

Terrane Accretion at a Subduction Zone

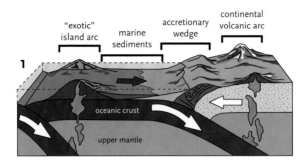

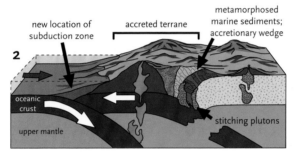

Step 1 An offshore island arc is being transported toward a subduction zone between an oceanic and continental plate. During transport and subduction, sediments are scraped off the downgoing oceanic crust and accreted onto the continent.

Step 2 Docking of the island arc. Rocks associated with the volcanic island arc are accreted to the continent and slightly metamorphosed due to tectonic compression. At the terrane boundary, the continental crust is thickened to the point of generating partial melt and a stitching pluton between the accreted island arc and the existing continental crust.

from the continent were conveyed inexorably toward the Laurentian coast and accreted. These rock groups are known as exotic terranes.

The result of this slow-motion train wreck is a patchwork of different rock types juxtaposed by faults. In many areas, the heat and pressure generated by these collisions metamorphosed and deformed the rocks, creating distinctive structures and lithologies.

Continued compression caused the newly accreted crust to thicken, and in some instances, this generated sufficient heat and pressure to make parts of it actually melt. In addition, other areas of the crust were melted by the continued subduction of oceanic plate beneath the growing continent. These zones of magma eventually cooled and resolidified into plutons. In some areas, magma bodies intruded over and over again, creating large, composite bodies called batholiths. Some plutons and batholiths are additionally known as stitching plutons because they cross the fault boundaries separating the older, distinct terranes and appear to "stitch" the terranes together (though they are not actually holding anything in place). All these plutonic features are especially important to our region's human history because they are responsible for generating mineable deposits of copper, zinc, and gold.

During and after accretion, weathering and erosion also got to work creating new sediment, which eventually covered the terranes and later became sedimentary rock. These rock units are sometimes called overlap sequences because they overlap the fault boundaries between terranes, almost like a geologic bandage. They represent the first "local" rocks formed in place on the new edge of the continent.

Because the rocks in these regions are the oldest in the Northwest, they have also been affected by all the geologic events that happened after their formation and accretion. This means that some terranes have been completely covered by young volcanic and sedimentary rocks; others have been chopped up and shifted by movements on younger faults; and still others have been carved by glaciers or largely eroded away. Even with these missing pieces, the geologic puzzle can still be put together by a dedicated and patient hand.

See the Story: Terrane Types
Accreted Island Arcs Evidence of island arcs formed off the coast of Laurentia can be found in several areas. In the North

Cascades, the Chilliwack River Terrane is made up of low-grade metamorphic rocks like greenstones, phyllites, and recrystallized limestone. These rocks represent ancient basaltic volcanoes and the muddy sediments and limestone reefs that circled them. Their metamorphism is one part of the evidence demonstrating their participation in a collision; another bit is that many of the rock units in this terrane have been turned upside-down. Similarly, in the Klamath Mountains near Canyonville, Oregon, the igneous Rogue Formation of the Western Klamath Belt is made up of Mesozoic arc rocks. Accreted arcs in the Blue Mountains appear as the greenstones, metamorphosed mudstones, and marbles of the Wallowa Terrane, best exposed in the depths of Hells Canyon and on ridges of the Wallowa Mountains.

Ophiolites Oceanic crust has a very specific recipe: layers of igneous rock, with peridotite at the bottom, gabbro in the middle, and basalt on top. The basalt, which comes from the underwater volcanic eruptions that create ocean crust at divergent plate boundaries, forms in a distinctive series of dikes topped by pillows (globular shapes that form when basalt cools underwater). This top layer of basalt is what makes the ocean floor, and it's often covered by muddy or sandy sediments that can become additional layers of sedimentary rock. When a terrane with this precise sequence of layers is found to have been pushed up onto land, it's called an ophiolite.

The Northwest has several ophiolites. The Yellow Aster Complex at Yellow Aster Butte in the North Cascades, the Twin Sisters Dunite (a peridotite) of Twin Sisters Mountain, the Ingalls Complex south of

Mt. Stuart, and the Fidalgo Ophiolite on Fidalgo Island are all great examples. The Klamath Mountains host the Coast Range Ophiolite near Game Lake and the Josephine Ophiolite south of Cave Junction, stretching down into California. Most ophiolites have experienced some level of metamorphism, transforming basalt and gabbro into greenstone or amphibolite and peridotite into serpentinite, but in places the primary lithologies remain.

Melange Some terranes were generated by the processes of subduction and collision themselves. The most distinctive are called *melanges*, from a French term meaning "mixed." Whereas most

Sheeted dikes metamorphosed to greenstone in the Josephine Ophiolite Complex

rock units have an order or a geometry to them—layers of sandstone or basalt flows, for instance, or tabular igneous dikes intruding into a body of gneiss—melanges are zones of total chaos. Tectonic melanges may form from motion along major faults and represent areas where rock units have been thoroughly broken and reshuffled, creating a texture almost like a super-sized breccia. Broken chunks of especially hard rocks, usually igneous and medium- to high-grade metamorphic rocks, are stirred into a matrix of softer rocks, usually sandstone, mudstone, or serpentinite. The chunky pieces can be as small as a pack of cards or as large as a house. Often, wildly different rock types like amphibolite, mudstone, and andesite end up jumbled together in melange.

Melanges related to subduction have special features, including some very rare metamorphic rocks. Huge melanges can form in the accretionary wedge that builds up at the interface between the overriding and downgoing tectonic plates. When the downgoing plate drags parts of that wedge down with it, it takes those rocks to great depths and subjects them to high pressures. Because of the water saturating the wedge, however, the subducted rocks remain at a relatively low temperature. This is a recipe for turning basalt into blueschist, a hallmark of subduction zone metamorphism. Other areas of the wedge that get a little hotter make greenschist and amphibolite, and areas that get a little drier make eclogite.

Blueschists turn up in melanges within the North Cascades around Mt. Shuksan and near Bell Pass, as well as within the San Juan Islands. In the

Klamaths, blueschists were dug from a quarry and used to make the jetty in Bandon, Oregon. Back in the Blue Mountains, Meyers Canyon near Mitchell, Oregon, hosts some blueschist from the Baker Terrane melange.

See the Story: Stitching Plutons

Stitching plutons in this region include bodies of diorite, granodiorite, true granite, and a plagioclase-rich granitic rock called tonalite. They popped into existence between Jurassic and Eocene times, and wherever they bloomed, metal ore deposits followed. This is because the process of making intermediate to felsic magmas concentrates rare metals, which are then drawn out of the magmas into water-based fluids that infiltrate the surrounding rocks and settle.

The richest ore deposit in the Northwest is located in the Okanogan Highlands, associated with the Eocene Keller Butte Pluton around Mt. Tolman. It was mined for copper and molybdenum in the 1970s and 80s. Other plutons more famously related to gold deposits include the Klamath Mountains' Gold Hill Pluton, Grayback Pluton, and Jacksonville Pluton, and the Blue Mountains' Wallowa Batholith and Bald Mountain Batholith. Tonalite from the Wallowa Batholith holds up the Wallowa Mountains' iconic Eagle Cap peak.

Other plutonic bodies have been less profitable but are no less interesting. The Golden Horn Batholith in the North Cascades makes up the iconic peaks surrounding Washington Pass, including the Liberty Bell, Early Winter Spires, and Silver Star Mountain. It's a sodium-rich granite that hosts a bevy of rare and unusual minerals, including the amphiboles arfvedsonite and riebeckite.

In addition to these plutonic bodies, the region contains some areas of rock that thickened and heated but didn't quite make it all the way to melting. The North Cascades' Skagit Gneiss Complex near Diablo Dam is the best example—buried sedimentary and volcanic rocks experienced just enough heat and pressure to metamorphose into high-grade gneisses, and some areas generated small pockets of melt that developed into migmatites.

See the Story: Overlap Sedimentary Sequences

Erosion never rests. Even as the accreted terranes assembled, they were already beginning to wear away. Rocks pushed to high elevations shed material into adjacent basins, building up new sedimentary layers. These new rocks therefore overlapped the boundaries of different foundational terranes, covering them like a blanket or bandage. They represent our first locally made Northwest rocks.

In Oregon, these overlap sequences are represented by the Cretaceous Hornbrook, Hudspeth, and Gable Creek Formations, which are largely composed of marine sandstones, shales, and some conglomerates. The Hornbrook outcrops around Medford and Ashland in the Klamath Mountains, while the Hudspeth and Gable Creek are found near Mitchell in the Blue Mountains. They are roughly contemporary and, in fact, probably formed along the same coastline—a large marine embayment covered much of the western portion of the region with water during Cretaceous time, creating

Outcrop of migmatitic Skagit Gneiss in the North Cascades

a beachfront running southwest to the northeast rather than north to south.

The Hudspeth Formation is especially famous because it hosts the Pacific Northwest's only known local dinosaur fossil, a 100-million-year-old toe bone from a plant-eating ornithopod. As ornithopods live on land and the Hudspeth formed in the ocean, it's thought that the toe bone came from a carcass that washed out to sea. It's important to point out that the Northwest has had several other dinosaur finds, but they were located in rock units that initially formed in other places like California and came to the Northwest later through fault movements. The toe bone, on the other hand, tells us that dinosaurs did actually inhabit this region during the Cretaceous.

Phase Three: Volcanism and Uplift

300 million years ago	200		100		0
Paleozoic		Mesozoic		Cenozoic	
rifting			accretion	VOLCANISM	sculpting

Notable Localities: COR, OLY, BM, CAS, CB, HLP, OWY

The era of terrane accretion ended about 50 million years ago, in the Cenozoic era. When Siletzia, that vast undersea plateau of basalt, became the last exotic terrane to dock with the North America, our modern coastline began to emerge—first with the accumulation of sediment (an accretionary wedge) and then by compressing and lifting that wedge up out of the ocean to form the Coast Ranges and Olympic Peninsula. Eventually the scene resembled what we see today: a single subduction zone running parallel to the coastline where the oceanic plate dips eastward and slides beneath the continent, giving rise to volcanoes that cover the land with lava and ash. This subduction volcanism was especially important in shaping portions of the Blue Mountains and the Cascade Range.

The eastern inland portions of the Pacific Northwest were tectonically active, too. In the Okanogan Highlands, Blue Mountains, High Lava Plains, and Owyhee Plateau, the newly accreted crust experienced stretching and shearing. Some of these extensional processes created the mountains and valleys that make up Oregon's Basin and Range.

Sediments accumulated everywhere in earnest throughout this time, preserving a wealth of information about the history of life and a record of Earth's changing climate from about 60 million years ago through today. The rise and diversification of mammals, including an amazingly complete record of the evolution of the horse, is recorded in great detail, as is the region's transition from a subtropical, banana-growing climate to our modern temperate one.

About 16.7 million years ago, voluminous flood basalts and explosive rhyolites generated by an upwelling mantle plume started transforming the eastern landscape. Stacks of these lava flows cover the Blue Mountains and Columbia Basin and hold up many of the region's iconic features, from Cannon Beach to the Columbia River Gorge.

See the Story: The Rising Coast
When it docked with the continent, the Siletzia Terrane was very long, stretching from southern Oregon up to the southern tip of Vancouver Island, Canada. Scraps of the plateau are exposed in many places, including Oregon's Marys Peak, and Hurricane Ridge in Washington's Olympic Mountains.

Though the accumulation of terranes has ceased, accretion of another kind has since had a dramatic effect on the landscape—the development and uplift of a sedimentary accretionary wedge. Such wedges form when sediment shedding off the continent enters the subduction zone's ocean trench. The sediment lands on the downgoing oceanic plate but is too light to be subducted itself. Instead, the leading edge of the overriding continent acts like a bulldozer and scrapes the sediment into a wedge-shaped pile that builds and builds within the trench. Sometimes horizontal compression generates intense folding and faulting within this wedge, and sometimes entire zones remain completely undeformed.

This process built the modern Northwest coastline. Over time, as sediments accumulated and convergence and compression continued, the accretionary wedge rose out of the ocean and became the mountains of the Coast Ranges and the Olympic Peninsula. Ultra-sensitive GPS measurements show that the uplift is ongoing today.

The marine sedimentary rocks that now sit hundreds and even thousands of feet above sea level are evidence of this history. Oregon's central Coast Ranges are dominated by the Tyee formation, an Eocene-age siltstone and sandstone unit deposited on a basement of Siletzian basalts. It contains graded bedding generated by successive underwater landslides

The mouth of the Columbia River dumps sediment into the sea near Astoria, Oregon. The profile of the Coast Ranges rises in the background.

called turbidites, visible today in roadcuts along US-20 approaching Newport and many other places.

In Washington, the Hoh Assemblage makes up much of the Olympic Peninsula's western coast. It is a chaotic grouping of marine siltstones, sandstones, and conglomerates that displays zones of intense deformation, shearing, and melange from being bulldozed beneath a portion of the accreted Siletzia.

Though they have similar histories, the Olympic Peninsula is separated out from the rest of the Coast Ranges because it is noticeably taller; while the Coast Ranges average 2000–3000 feet of elevation, the Olympic Mountains top out at 8000 feet. This is because a bend in the offshore subduction zone has created an enhanced zone of uplift and compression along the Peninsula's margin. In places within the core of the Olympic Mountains there has even been enough compression to metamorphose the marine sediments. Many shales that were once on the floor of the Pacific Ocean are now exposed at elevations of over 6000 feet and display slaty cleavage and minor amounts of blueschist-grade metamorphism.

Hoh Assemblage sandstones along the coast of the Olympic Peninsula

See the Story: Volcanic Arcs Shifting over Time

Subduction zones don't just scrape up sediments—they are volcano-making machines. Once the subducting plate slides below the continent and reaches a depth of about 62 miles, it releases water from its minerals. This causes the hot but solid mantle above it to melt. The newly molten rock rises buoyantly through the overriding plate and into the crust. Some of it stalls and cools underground, creating plutons, and some erupts on the surface, forming volcanoes.

The angle of a subduction zone's downgoing plate controls the location of its volcanoes. If the plate subducts shallowly, it won't reach a depth of 62 miles until it's far away from the convergent margin, creating volcanoes that pop up inland. If the downgoing plate bends steeply downward, it reaches the dewatering depth only a short distance from the margin, generating close-in volcanoes. If you stand on the slopes of an active, subduction-generated Cascades volcano today, you know exactly where the top of the subducting slab is—within Earth's mantle, dewatering roughly 62 miles below your feet.

Our subduction zone and the geometry of its downgoing slab is responsible for much of the Cenozoic history and distribution of volcanic rocks across the region. Fluctuations in the angle of subduction shifted the location of active volcanism around over time.

The Blue Mountains hosted the volcanic arc during Eocene times, between about 54 and 39 million years ago. It produced a series of tall, majority-andesite volcanoes now called the Clarno Formation in a continental basin crisscrossed with rivers and streams near the present-day towns of Mitchell and Fossil, Oregon. This geologic environment created layers of andesite, debris flow and lahar deposits, conglomerates, mudstones, and paleosols. It also preserved many plant and animal fossils, including ancestors to the banana and palm.

Yes—banana! The whole Northwest enjoyed a warm, humid climate during

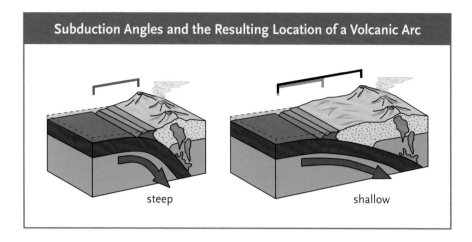

Subduction Angles and the Resulting Location of a Volcanic Arc

steep   shallow

this time, but the climate began to change toward the end of the Eocene. Proliferation of more temperate plant fossils and changes in the chemistry of ancient soils preserves the record of a global cool-down.

About 40 million years ago, volcanic activity shifted westward. This was the beginning of the Cascade Range. The modern I-5 corridor coincides roughly with the Oregon-Washington coastline at the time, and the earliest Cascades volcanoes would have risen up right near the edge of the sea. Explosive eruptions generated the mafic, intermediate, and felsic tuffs, lava flows, and mud flows of the Ohanapecosh formation near Mt. Rainier in Washington and the younger Little Butte Volcanics, now eroded and exposed along the McKenzie and Umpqua rivers in Oregon.

Interestingly, the rise of the Cascades is not only recorded by the volcanic rocks themselves—you can also see it in the plants. Recall that prior to this time the Northwest was warm and wet, with tropical flora and fauna all across the region.

As the Cascades began to rise, however, the mountains began to generate the rain shadow effect so well-known in the area today—when prevailing winds brought moisture in from the ocean, that moisture fell as rain on the western slopes of the mountains but left the eastern side high and dry. The plant fossils from contemporary sedimentary rocks west of the young Cascades include species that thrive in the damp, while those east of the mountains reflect a drier climate.

Many of these fossils are found in the John Day Basin near Mitchell, Oregon, on the dry side of the Cascades. The John Day Formation is world famous for preserving a beautiful and detailed record of plant and animal evolution during Oligocene and Miocene times, including ancestors of the modern horse. Its sedimentary beds show evidence of rivers, lakes, and extensive soils (especially evident in the vivid red and yellow stripes of the Painted Hills). The region's layers are punctuated by large pyroclastic deposits—mostly felsic tuffs—that originated from volcanic

The green-blue layers of the Turtle Cove Assemblage within the John Day Formation are made of a mixture of clay and ash. They host many spectacular mammal fossils.

vents in the Western Cascades and the Crooked River Caldera near Madras.

The Cascades are still being built up today—the High Cascades peaks, including Mt. Baker, Glacier Peak, Mt. Rainier, Mt. Saint Helens, Mt. Adams, Mt. Hood, Mt. Jefferson, the Three Sisters, and Mt. Mazama (Crater Lake), are all active volcanoes. The location of these peaks on the very eastern edge of the Cascade Range shows there has been a small eastward migration of Cascades volcanism since its initial inception. And though the overall range is venerable, each of those peaks is very young. Mt. Saint Helens, for instance, built up the

majority of its cone within the past 3000 years, and most of the other peaks are less than a million years old.

See the Story: Stretching and Sedimentation

While convergence and compression are the main themes of plate tectonics in the Pacific Northwest, some parts of the region also experience tension and extension. It may seem paradoxical, but while the leading edge of the continent is being compressed near the subduction zone, the whole margin is being pulled away from the stable interior of the continent (see the figure on page 297). This stretches the

Mt. Rainier, a quintessential Cascades volcano

crust and creates zones of normal faults. Where it occurs, bits of mantle melt and rise through the cracks, creating a scattered distribution of volcanoes over the stretched surface.

Regional extension and normal faulting also create topographic basins called grabens, a result of a normal fault's hanging wall sliding down the footwall. These grabens become local lows that tend to collect rivers and lakes—and their accompanying sediments. If extension and normal faulting continue for a long time, the hanging wall can keep sliding down and opening up more space for more sediments to accumulate, ultimately creating sedimentary packages that are thousands or even tens of thousands of feet thick.

The Chiwaukum Graben in the North Cascades is one example of such a structure. It began opening in Eocene times and filled with successive layers of conglomerate and sandstone deposited by rivers that flowed and meandered through the subsiding basin. At times, the basin environment tended toward swampy, creating thick deposits of organic material that were later compressed into coal. Volcanic tuffs make an appearance as well. This sequence of sediments is called the Chumstick Formation, and it

West

East

Exposure of mylonite at the top of a gneiss dome in a zone of large-magnitude crustal extension in the Okanogan Highlands. The slope of the hills in the photo is parallel with the foliation of the mylonitic gneiss that makes them up. Sigma clasts help confirm the foliation is sloped down toward the west indicating westward-directed extension.

is exposed today between Leavenworth and Wenatchee.

The Okanogan Highlands host more examples of extensional structures, including some that reached all the way down into the lower crust. The broad forms of Kettle Dome and Okanogan Dome, both low-lying and north-south trending, are geologic features known as gneiss domes. These are created several miles beneath Earth's surface, where rocks deform by flowing like putty rather than breaking. The dome-like shapes are both formed and uncovered by the process of extension, producing then exposing their mylonite tops.

Continued extension and ever-active erosion eventually exposed these structures at the surface, where the rocks became cold and brittle enough to break instead of flow. Additional extension added more grabens to this landscape, including the Republic Graben. The first rocks to fill the graben were felsic volcanic rocks like rhyolite and dacite. The graben subsequently filled with water, creating a large lake that collected fine-grained sediments and some periodic ash deposits from volcanic eruptions. Flower, insect, and fish fossils are spectacularly preserved within these layers. You can dig for them yourself at the Stonerose Interpretive Center and Eocene Fossil Site in Republic.

In Oregon, crustal extension enjoys some additional elements. The eponymous topographic features of the Basin

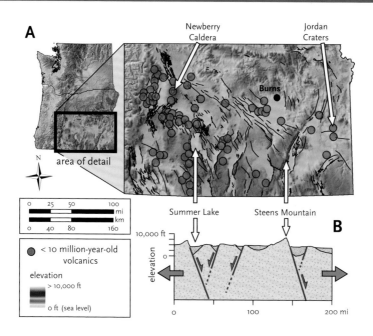

Simplified Geologic Map and Cross Section through Oregon's Basin and Range Province

A) Topographic map of the Basin and Range overlain with black lines representing Quaternary (<2-million-year-old) faults and red dots indicating locations of <10-million-year-old volcanic eruptive centers.

B) Schematic geologic cross section between Summer Lake and Alvord Desert. Normal fault geometries at depth are approximate but represent the structure of the region produced by tectonic extension.

and Range province were formed by an extensional process affecting a broad swath of the western United States, including eastern California, Nevada, Arizona, and Utah. About 10 million years ago, the evolving San Andreas Fault (as the boundary between the Pacific and North American Plates) was extending in a northwest direction. Due to the complex interplay of tectonic boundaries, much of western North America was dragged toward the northwest along with the fault's growth. This dragging caused extension of the North American crust, like the spreading of an accordion. Much of the western United States was pulled apart in a west-east direction, with the northernmost limit of the extension in Oregon at the High Lava Plains.

Basin and Range extension has created many large normal faults that have given rise to tall, north-south oriented mountain ranges with basins in between. For example, Steens Mountain reaches an elevation of just shy of 10,000 feet and towers more than 5000 feet above its adjacent basin, the Alvord Desert to the east. Numerous other parallel, north-south oriented basins and ranges are present west through Klamath Lake. This extension is still ongoing, and slip along these normal faults has the potential to generate earthquakes today. It was responsible for the 1993 Klamath Falls earthquake that rattled southern Oregon.

Volcanism accompanied this period of extension, too. There is ongoing debate about whether this volcanism is purely extension-related or whether it may have also been affected or driven by complexities related to the mantle plume discussed in the next section. Whatever the precise cause, small basaltic volcanic centers emerged in eastern Oregon just under 12 million years ago, and subsequent eruptions appeared in progressively westward locations over time. The Newberry Caldera and surrounding cinder cones, located in the High Lava Plains south of Bend, is generally considered the westernmost extent of this trend and has been active for the past 50,000 years. However, young volcanoes also exist near the Owyhee Plateau, including Diamond Craters (not a source of gems, the name comes from the shape of a local rancher's cattle brand) and Jordan Craters, which most recently erupted less than 3200 years ago.

See the Story: Flood Basalts and the Mantle Plume

There's one more major player in the volcanic systems of the Pacific Northwest. During the mid-Miocene, while the Cascade arc was active and the Coast Ranges and Olympic Peninsula were being uplifted, volcanic vents in the east released a staggering amount of basaltic lava. These rocks are known as the Columbia River Basalts (CRBs), and their formation and associated eruptive processes have had a major, lasting effect on the geology and geomorphology of the Pacific Northwest.

Most volcanoes on Earth form at plate boundaries, where the consequences of relative motion between plates cause parts of the mantle or crust to melt. Subduction zone volcanism is one familiar example. But there is another, more enigmatic source of volcanoes that can pop up anywhere on the planet, and it's called a mantle plume. Plumes are localized upwellings of incredibly warm, low viscosity material from the lower mantle. Areas where plumes reach the crust are called hot spots.

One good way to think about hot spots is to imagine a blowtorch (the plume) blasting a metal plate (the crust). The intensity of this system can generate enormous amounts of basaltic lava. Some of these eruptions create a phenomenon called flood basalts.

Flood basalts are incredibly voluminous eruptions of fluid, basaltic lava that can flow tens or even hundreds of miles from their source and, as the name implies, flood the existing landscape. Eruptions producing flood basalts are relatively fast in a geologic sense, with huge amounts of material erupting in only a few million years.

The CRBs and associated flood basalts cover over 81,000 square miles of eastern Oregon and Washington, as well as parts of the Columbia Gorge, Willamette Valley, and Coast Ranges. Beginning around 17 million years ago, a large mantle plume created a hot spot underneath the present-day Oregon-Idaho border and began to erupt basaltic lava on the surface. Over the next 2 million years, no less than 50,000 cubic miles of basalt would erupt from fissures stretching across eastern Oregon into southeast Washington. These basalts were incredibly fluid, and some of the larger flows traveled along the channel of the ancestral Columbia River, into the Willamette Valley, and eventually out into the Pacific Ocean. Smaller flows were geographically limited to eastern Oregon and the Columbia Basin but nonetheless accumulated in places to a thickness of over 2.5 miles.

The CRBs hold up many iconic and beloved geographic features in the Northwest today, such as the walls of the Columbia River Gorge, including Multnomah Falls; Haystack Rock near Cannon Beach; the waterfalls of Silver Falls State Park; the flat plateaus topping many landforms around Madras and Bend; parts of Hells Canyon; Steens Mountain; and most of the ridges and canyons of the entire Columbia Basin, including Grand Coulee and Palouse Falls.

The largest unit of the CRBs is the Grande Ronde Basalt, which accounts for about 75 percent of the total CRB volume and extends from eastern Oregon through

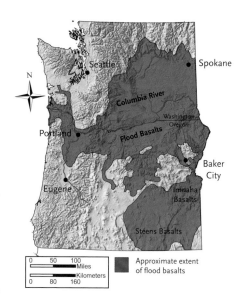

The geographic extent of the Columbia River Basalts and associated flood basalts

the entire Columbia Basin and westward to the Pacific Ocean. Smaller members of the CRBs include the Steens Basalt in the Basin and Range province, the Imnaha Basalt in eastern Oregon and the Blue Mountains, and the Wanapum and Saddle Mountains Basalts in the Columbia Basin.

There's more to the story of this mantle plume than just the CRBs. Its heat also partially melted areas of the continental crust, generating zones of felsic melt rich in silica. These melts erupted in explosive, violent, caldera-forming eruptions, leaving behind thick deposits of tuff and ash with a rhyolitic composition. At the same time as the onset of CRB eruptions, around 16.5–15.5 million years ago, the High Rocks and McDermitt Volcanic Fields on the present-day Oregon-Nevada border began

A waterfall cascades over basalt from a CRB lava flow at Silver Falls State Park in Oregon.

Stacks of CRB flows made these flat-topped plateaus at Cove Palisades State Park in Oregon.

building rhyolite-ringed calderas, which actively produced lavas and rhyolite tuffs. The Owyhee Plateau in particular features many rhyolite-ringed calderas formed during the early stages of CRB eruptions.

Caldera-style eruptions kept going for quite some time, finally ending with the eruption of the Rattlesnake Tuff approximately 7 million years ago. The Rattlesnake Tuff is the result of one of the largest single eruptions in the Pacific Northwest's history and can be found today in areas of the Blue Mountains, underlying some recent volcanics in the High Lava Plains, and south in the Oregon Basin and Range. In total, the Rattlesnake Tuff covers an area of around 18,000 square miles.

As the North American Plate has moved in a west-southwest direction, the mantle plume that generated these caldera-style eruptions and the CRBs has remained active. We can tell this by looking at a string of volcanic centers that runs from the Oregon-Idaho border to Wyoming's Yellowstone National Park. From west to east, each center is progressively younger, tracking both the plate motion and the plume's continued activity. The youngest volcanic center of all is located within Yellowstone itself—the park's famous "supervolcano." Though the civilization-ending potential of this volcano as hyped in the media is probably overstated, a new Yellowstone eruption could indeed happen someday.

Phase Four: Surface Processes and the Geology of Today

Notable Localities: CAS, COR, PLO, WV, BR

The Pacific Northwest is still being formed today. The oceanic Juan de Fuca Plate continues to subduct beneath North America along the Cascadia Subduction Zone (CSZ), driving ongoing Cascades volcanism, coastal uplift, and the development of the Puget Sound and Willamette Valley. Crustal extension continues in the east, especially in the Oregon Basin and Range. This active tectonic setting is responsible for the architecture underpinning much of our familiar geography.

But there is more to the story of our landscape's evolution. Surficial geomorphic processes have both built up the topography and stripped it down. Over the past two million years, large continental ice sheets, gargantuan floods, and some of the largest earthquakes on the planet have played a role in creating the modern Pacific Northwest.

See the Story: Down in the Valley

The Willamette Valley and the Puget Lowlands form an interrupted trough between two mountain ranges, the Coast Ranges (and Olympic Mountains) and the Cascades. The I-5 corridor runs through this trough, and it contains the majority of the human population in the Pacific Northwest, who settled here thanks to its fertile soils and abundant rainfall.

The Tualatin River National Wildlife Refuge in the northern part of the Willamette Valley—this region is typified by floodplains of the Willamette River and its tributaries, along with low rolling hills.

When convergence and compression caused the Coast Ranges to begin their rise, the Willamette and Puget Lowlands regions simultaneously began to drop or subside (imagine the bulges and valleys that form when you crinkle a piece of paper). This region of subsidence, located between a volcanic arc and an accretionary wedge, is called a foreland basin.

Over time, this basin caught many of the sediments eroded from the mountains on either side. Erosion working on the Cascades and Coast Ranges generated landslides that dumped sediments into rivers, which then transported those sediments farther into the foreland basin. Over time, the basin filled with sediment to a depth upward of 13,000 feet.

In addition, persistently wet weather encouraged the development of fertile, clay-rich soils. In today's Willamette Valley, these soils remain and support diverse and abundant agriculture. In the Puget Lowlands, however, most of these soils were buried or scraped away by glaciation during the Quaternary ice ages.

See the Story: Glaciers Give and Take
The Northern Hemisphere experienced several ice ages during the Quaternary

Period. One interesting thing about glacial periods is that glaciers do such a good
job at eroding and transporting material,
they essentially erase a lot of evidence for
previous glacial episodes. This is why we
refer to the glacial processes and features
that took place during the last glacial
maximum. In the Pacific Northwest, the
last glacial maximum was 15–20,000 years
ago. During this time, the Cascade Range,
Steens Mountain, Wallowas, Olympic
Mountains, Okanogan Highlands, and
Puget Sound were covered in glaciers,
some in excess of 4000 feet thick. While
these large glaciers are no longer present,
we can still see evidence for them from
the numerous U-shaped valleys in the
Cascade Range and other areas of higher
topography to the sediments deposited
around the Puget Sound (see page 265 for
more detail on glacial landforms).

In general, though glacial movements
may seem slow on a human timescale,
glacial erosion and deposition are fairly
rapid geologic processes. Huge volumes
of material can be removed and deposited
within a period of a few thousand years.
However, the Pacific Northwest also experienced a series of unique, transformative
glacier-related processes that each took
place over the span of only a few days. As
we learned in the previous chapter, these
are the Missoula Floods, incredibly large,
cyclical glacial outburst floods that shaped
a vast swath of the Columbia Basin and
transported sediment from eastern Washington into the Willamette Valley and
Pacific Ocean. These occurred at the end
of the last glacial maximum.

Farther south, the Quaternary ice ages
had a different effect on the Oregon Basin

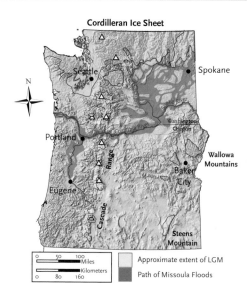

The extent of glaciers during the last glacial
maximum (LGM) in the Pacific Northwest, overlain
with the route and deposits of the Missoula Floods

and Range, filling its valleys with lakes.
The same enhanced precipitation that
helps form large glaciers and continental
ice sheets fell as rain in the Basin and
Range. This water filled in the basins and
formed large, temporary bodies of water
called pluvial lakes, which fill during ice
ages then drain after. Even though these
lakes are mostly gone today, they left
behind quite a bit of evidence of their existence. Many basins in southern and southeast Oregon are full of fine lacustrine
silts and clays and have paleo-shorelines
carved into the surrounding slopes. Salt
playas and diatomite deposits also mark
the lakes' former extent. At present, Malheur, Summer, and Klamath Lakes are
the shrunken remnants of the remaining
pluvial lakes.

Crater Lake fills the caldera of the collapsed Mt. Mazama.

See the Story: Recent Eruptions

Of course, we can't fully describe the Quaternary geologic history of the Pacific Northwest without mentioning some major volcanic events that took place within recent times. Around 7700 years ago—truly recent, geologically speaking—Mt. Mazama had its caldera-forming event, ejecting approximately 50 cubic miles of material before collapsing in on itself to form what is now Crater Lake. Ash and pumice from this eruption can be found as far away as Alberta, Canada.

To the north, Mt. Rainier experienced a significant sequence of eruptions around 5600 years ago. While it wasn't as massive as the Crater Lake–forming event, this sequence did cause a large portion of Mt. Rainier's northeast side to collapse in a giant debris avalanche. This collapse sent one of the largest lahars in recent Cascade history into the White River valley and all the way to the Puget Sound near present-day Tacoma. The Osceola Lahar, as it is named, covers an area of over 200 square miles reaching 75 miles downstream of Mt. Rainier.

Probably the best-known volcanic eruption in the Pacific Northwest is that of Washington's Mt. Saint Helens. On the morning of 18 May 1980, an earthquake dislodged the entire north side of Mt. Saint Helens, producing the largest landslide in recorded history. The landslide "uncorked" magma within the volcano, which erupted explosively in a lateral

Photo of Mt. Rainier and the Port of Tacoma, built on deposits from the Osceola Lahar

Photo of Mt. Saint Helens in 2019. The 1980 eruption removed almost 2000 feet from the top of the volcano, leaving behind an enormous crater. Inside the crater, a series of lava dome–building eruptions have taken place.

blast and vertical eruption column. The eruption ejected nearly a cubic mile of material, and ash from the eruption was found as far away as Oklahoma. Since the 1980 eruption, the mountain has also experienced a series of smaller, lava dome–building events, the most recent of which occurred in 2008.

These events represent only a small number of the Cascade Range volcanoes' Quaternary eruptions—there have been over seventy in only the past 4000 years. The next eruption could come at any time. The major hazards presented by Cascade Range volcanoes are lahar flows and ashfall. For information about how these hazards might affect your home, school, or business, and to learn about ways you can prepare, find the USGS Cascades Volcano Observatory on the web to learn more about your local volcano.

See the Story: Earthquake Country

Aside from volcanism in the Cascades, another tectonic process has been at work in the Pacific Northwest throughout Quaternary times. Sometimes violent, particularly along the coastline, these are the large earthquakes associated with the Cascadia Subduction Zone (CSZ).

Stumps of ancient spruce trees at Sunset Bay State Park in Oregon. These trees were drowned as a result of subsidence associated with a Cascadia Subduction Zone earthquake that occurred about 1200 years ago.

Often called a sleeping giant, the CSZ is capable of producing magnitude 9+ earthquakes and associated tsunamis that could flood the coast from Cape Flattery down to Northern California and travel across the Pacific Ocean basin all the way to Japan. On average, large CSZ earthquakes occur every 300–600 years, with the most recent taking place on 26 January 1700. At least thirteen additional major earthquakes occurred between the 1700 event and the eruption of Mt. Mazama around 7700 years ago.

In between CSZ earthquakes, plate convergence causes the coastal North American crust to compress horizontally like a spring. This pushes areas along the coast up in elevation. When the stress buildup is too great, or when the spring is compressed too much, the CSZ ruptures and slips, creating an earthquake with intense ground shaking. During the earthquake, those pushed-up areas along the coast rapidly subside, allowing ocean water to rush in and inundate these locations. The earthquakes also generate hundreds to thousands of landslides, both on land and underwater. Areas up to 150 miles east of the coast can experience notable shaking.

We know the history and timing of these earthquakes because they leave marks on the landscape that can be read by geologists even after thousands of years. For example, a rapid subsidence and inundation of the coast can cause entire forests to be flooded with saltwater and drown. In many places these forests are still visible, with dead, bleached trees present in marshes or tree stumps eroding out of the sand on beaches. Termed ghost forests, some great examples include the Copalis Ghost Forest in Washington and the Neskowin and Sunset Bay Ghost Forests in Oregon.

It's important to note that the CSZ is not the only source of potential earthquakes in the Pacific Northwest. Areas of active compression and extension have created smaller faults throughout the region, some of which are capable of producing events up to a magnitude 6 or 7. Even if you don't live near the coast, it's best to be earthquake-ready if you live in this region.

The Story Continues

Now that you have an idea of the big-picture narrative, we encourage you to revisit each of the feature chapters to get a better idea of how geology is expressed at different scales and how its elements are connected. If you are moved to go exploring, the Field Resources appendix is a good place to start, as is the Further Reading list.

The geology of the Pacific Northwest has been an object of fascination for over 150 years, and still more discoveries undoubtedly await. Find your piece of the story today.

ACKNOWLEDGMENTS

No author is an island, and these authors have many people to thank for making contributions to this work. The Rice Northwest Museum of Rocks and Minerals, Greg Retallack and David Blackwell at the University of Oregon, John Lindell, Raymond Lasmanis, Bart Cannon, Aaron Wieting, and Thea Stender all provided rock and mineral specimens for photography. Marli Miller, Bruce Kelley, Jeff Schwartz, Bruce Carter, the Portland State University Cascadia Meteorite Laboratory, the USGS Cascades Volcano Observatory, and Alexander Bridges provided additional photographs.

Discussions with Ellen Morris Bishop, Marli Miller, Howard Day, Raymond Lasmanis, Allan Lerner, Bruce Carter, Alyssa Morgan, and Sarah Roeske improved and clarified our manuscript. Any errors remaining in the text are our own.

Our spouses, Alexander Bridges and Lydia Garas, have supported our work in innumerable ways and we cannot thank them enough. Other family and friends have also been tremendous help, especially travel buddy Kara Sowles and new grandparents Sherry Moclock, Linda Willard, and Berch Willard, who cared for baby Rowan so editing could get done.

Last but not least, our thanks to our editors, Will McKay and Jacoba Lawson, and the team at Timber Press for the opportunity to write this book and the guidance to get it done.

APPENDIX: FIELD RESOURCES

This book contains a wealth of information about the geologic and geographic features of the Pacific Northwest. Listed below are some helpful resources that can supplement your new knowledge and help you get outside and find these features yourself.

If you are interested in . . .

Collecting Find your local rock club. The Northwest has many amateur groups dedicated to rockhounding and related activities, many of which run field trips. The American Federation of Mineralogical Societies (amfed.org) has club listings by state. If you prefer to go solo, you can acquire one of many published rockhounding books about the region to use as a guide. The website mindat.org is another invaluable resource.

Touring geology by vehicle or on foot Find a field trip guide online. Many university geology departments, state and national geology bureaus, and other professional organizations publish free, publicly available driving or hiking guides that can help you examine these rocks and regions up close. Simply do an internet search for your area of interest plus "geology field trip guide" and see what comes up.

Learning more Take a class in geology! Many community colleges and universities offer classes and short 1 to 2 day field trips to non-degree-seeking students, which can help you dive into the fundamentals of geology in a rigorous way. Of

course, there are also many other books about our region, several of which are on the Further Reading list.

For any outdoor activity, know before you go: research your region, its weather, and the condition of its roads. Some guides may lead to remote wilderness areas that require special vehicles with high clearance and four-wheel drive, or the areas may be accessible only at certain times of year. It's your responsibility to be sure you're equipped to reach your destination safely.

Tools of the Trade

For the most part, you won't need any equipment at all to study rocks and minerals in the field. Your most essential tool is a willingness for patient visual observation. However, some basics can aid your efforts.

Hand lens Sometimes referred to as a loupe, this is a small, inexpensive, 10× magnifier that can be attached to a lanyard or keychain. Hand lenses allow you to observe the properties of small minerals and fine rock textures. For the clearest view, hold the hand lens close to your eye and bring the object you are interested in up to your face until its details come into focus. A hand lens is different from a magnifying glass and will not work well if you hold it over a rock far away from your eye.

Notebook and camera Identifying rocks and minerals is a process that requires making several kinds of observations and

ROCK HAMMER DOS AND DON'TS

DO check federal, state, and local laws about "defacing" and collecting on a specific property before taking out a hammer. Generally, places like national parks are no-hammer zones, while some public federal lands allow for the personal collection of up to a certain weight of material per day. Private landowners will have their own rules.

DON'T hammer on any outcrop visible from public trails or viewing areas, even in areas that allow collecting. This is simply good etiquette.

DO hammer float first. Float is pieces of rock that have naturally fallen off an outcrop face. Float is easier to hammer than intact outcrop, and, as it's already broken, breaking it further doesn't change the landscape much.

DON'T hit a hammer with another hammer; this may cause one or both hammers to shatter or splinter. The thin, flat, pointed end of a hammer is not a chisel. If you need a chisel, use one made of hardened steel.

DO use the pointed or flat end of the hammer to dig or pry as necessary.

DON'T idly hammer or scratch at an outcrop without a purpose. Rock exposures take millions of years to form. Think about whether your reasons for hammering are really worth the destruction.

DO consider collecting with your camera instead of a pick. Collecting specimens can be a fun hobby, but be thoughtful about what you'd really like on your shelf versus what you can enjoy as a photograph and a memory.

using them to narrow down on a potential ID. Often, it's a good idea to record your observations in writing so you don't forget them or get confused or sidetracked. A notebook is also a great place to record location information and sketches of outcrops or samples. A camera is useful for sharing your finds with others, especially if you're not allowed to collect samples.

Small dropper bottle of white vinegar Some minerals fizz when they contact an acid like vinegar. Geologists prefer using dilute hydrochloric acid because it has a more vigorous reaction, but HCl is impractical for most people to obtain and vinegar works nearly as well.

Pocket knife For testing mineral hardness.

Unglazed ceramic plate For testing mineral streak. A small piece of terra cotta or the unglazed bottom of a coffee cup work well as streak plates.

Rock hammer and eye protection Though the rock hammer or pick is a ubiquitous symbol for rockhounds and geologists alike, it's also the least necessary. Rock hammers are used for breaking rocks. This can be useful if you're collecting specimens, but otherwise you probably won't need one. If you do use one, be sure to protect your eyes.

Land Use and Collecting Rules
This is a list of general guidelines for public lands managed by different agencies.

Be sure to look up each agency's collecting policies for more conditions and details.

Collecting is prohibited in:

- National Parks and Monuments, National Wildlife Refuges, and National Scenic Areas
- Tribal Lands
- Oregon State Parks and Recreation Areas (except Succor Creek State Natural Area)
- Washington State Parks

Limited collecting without a permit is allowed on some federal and state lands. In all cases it is:

- For personal, noncommercial use only
- To be collected from the surface using hand tools
- For rock, minerals, and invertebrate fossils only. Vertebrate fossils, including bones, shark teeth, and animal footprints, may not be collected from public lands. Meteorites also may not be collected. Human artifacts like arrowheads and ceramic shards are prohibited as well.

Limited collecting is also allowed in:

- Bureau of Land Management (BLM) land: collect up to 25 pounds of material per day, up to 250 pounds per year.
- USDA National Forest Service land: collect up to 10 pounds of material per day. Collecting is prohibited in designated wilderness areas.
- Oregon State Forest land: Collecting up to 12 cubic feet of rock material, excluding river rocks, is permitted in the Astoria, Tillamook, Forest Grove, North Cascade, and West Oregon districts.
- Washington Department of Natural Resources State Trust and State Forest land: Surficial collecting is permitted away from rivers, streams, and lakes, and excluding special habitats such as caves and talus slopes.

Field Safety

Viewing rocks and minerals in nature is great fun. It can take you up to mountaintops, into deserts, and everywhere in between. Lessen the risks of venturing into the wild by following these guidelines:

Tell a friend or family member of your travel plans and discuss what they should do if you are late in returning.

Carry the ten essentials: water, food, navigation tools (map and compass), sun protection, clothing to protect from cold and wet, a light source, matches or other fire starter, a knife, a first-aid kit that includes a whistle, and some form of emergency shelter. These items will help you respond to a crisis or keep you safe if you have to spend a night outside unexpectedly.

Don't rely solely on your cell phone for navigation and communication. Even popular natural areas can lack cellular coverage. Bring physical maps and make a communication plan.

Be smart about GPS. A handheld GPS can be an excellent navigation tool, but remember its limitations; it may not work under thick tree cover or in deep ravines, and it may run out of batteries.

Watch the weather and the tides. Stay alert to changing weather conditions and be prepared to leave or seek shelter if a storm begins to rise. If you are visiting the beach, check the tide tables to be sure you're not stranded when the tide comes in. Watch also for unpredictable ocean movements like sneaker waves.

Maintain situational awareness. Take care when crossing roads, train tracks, and rivers, and be sure not to stray onto private property without permission.

If you are using a rock hammer, always wear shatter-proof eye protection and keep your mouth shut (flying debris have been known to chip or even knock out teeth). Never hit a hammer with another hammer.

Familiarize yourself with minerals that can be hazardous to human health. These include but aren't limited to:

tremolite-actinolite asbestos, heavy metal ore minerals like galena, and radioactive minerals like meta-autunite. Most of these minerals are hazardous only if they are ingested or inhaled, so use caution if hammering and avoid sending mineral dust into the air.

Never enter abandoned mineshafts or quarries. Unmaintained tunnels and rock faces can collapse without warning. Human-made rock faces are much more unstable than naturally formed ones.

Avoid walking beneath rock overhangs, especially if they are human-made.

Know your limits. Be realistic about your hiking abilities and capacity for carrying weight. Drinking water and rocks are both heavy! If in doubt, turn around—the rocks will still be there another day.

DATA SOURCES

The data used for information regarding mineral and rock occurrences in the Pacific Northwest come from many sources, particularly:

- Oregon Department of Geology and Mineral Industries (DOGAMI), oregongeology.org
- Washington Department of Natural Resources, dnr.wa.gov/geology
- Rice Northwest Museum of Rocks and Minerals, ricenorthwestmuseum.org
- Museum of Natural and Cultural History at the University of Oregon, mnch.uoregon.edu
- Department of Earth Sciences at the University of Oregon, earthsciences.uoregon.edu
- Cannon, Bart. *Minerals of Washington*
- Tschernich, Rudy. *Zeolites of the World*
- Mindat.org, a comprehensive, edited crowdsourced database of worldwide mineral and rock localities
- Personal conversations with active field collectors (mostly of Washington specimens)
- Personal field trips throughout Oregon and Washington
- Selected peer-reviewed scientific journal articles and field trip guides

The data for mineral and rock formulas, properties, and identification are taken from the following sources:

- International Mineralogical Association, ima-mineralogy.org
- Deer, William A., Robert A. Howie, and Jack Zussman. *An Introduction to the Rock-Forming Minerals* (Second Edition)
- Gaines, Richard V. et al. *Dana's New Mineralogy* (Eighth Edition)
- Tschernich, Rudy. *Zeolites of the World*
- Nesse, William. *Introduction to Mineralogy*
- Bernard, Jan H. and Jaroslav Hyrsl. *Minerals and their Localities*
- Chesterman, Charles. *The Audubon Society Field Guide to North American Rocks and Minerals*
- Winter, John. *An Introduction to Igneous and Metamorphic Petrology*
- Boggs Jr., Sam. *Principles of Sedimentology and Stratigraphy* (Fourth Edition)
- Blatt, Harvey and Robert Tracy. *Petrology: Igneous, Sedimentary, and Metamorphic* (Second Edition)

A note on data for mineral names and formulas:

As scientific instrumentation such as X-ray diffraction has improved over time, differentiation among mineral species has become more and more granular. Frequently, multiple species are broken out from what would have once been considered one mineral with chemical or structural variations. These distinctions are important for researchers studying advanced geochemistry but can often muddy the waters for those identifying minerals in the field, as the physical properties of these minerals are identical. For example, "chabazite" is an umbrella term for five different mineral species that are functionally identical to the human eye as well as chemically and structurally extremely similar at a microscopic level.

As the purpose of this book is to serve as a resource for field identification, we have chosen to use mineral categories, names, and properties that are relevant at the level of direct human observation. Thus, "chabazite" is one mineral entry with one formula that encompasses the variation in chabazite minerals. Older

reference materials were sourced for several mineral chemical formulas as they frequently represent the generalized form of a group that is now differentiated.

Note that some mineral entries, such as those for plagioclase feldspar and the amphibole and pyroxene groups, do list the names of different species that are difficult or impossible to tell apart in the field. This is done in part because hobbyist mineral collectors will commonly get these minerals analyzed to determine their specific type, so many of the names (such as labradorite for a plagioclase or augite for a pyroxene) are in common usage among interested amateurs.

PERIODIC TABLE OF ELEMENTS

KEY

1	Atomic number
H	Atomic symbol
Hydrogen	Element name

Elements with gray text are man-made

- Metals
- Metalloids
- Non-metals
- Noble gasses
- Ten important elements in rocks and minerals
- Selected native metals

1																	2
H Hydrogen																	**He** Helium
3 **Li** Lithium	4 **Be** Beryllium											5 **B** Boron	6 **C** Carbon	7 **N** Nitrogen	8 **O** Oxygen	9 **F** Fluorine	10 **Ne** Neon
11 **Na** Sodium	12 **Mg** Magnesium											13 **Al** Aluminum	14 **Si** Silicon	15 **P** Phosphorus	16 **S** Sulfur	17 **Cl** Chlorine	18 **Ar** Argon
19 **K** Potassium	20 **Ca** Calcium	21 **Sc** Scandium	22 **Ti** Titanium	23 **V** Vanadium	24 **Cr** Chromium	25 **Mn** Manganese	26 **Fe** Iron	27 **Co** Cobalt	28 **Ni** Nickel	29 **Cu** Copper	30 **Zn** Zinc	31 **Ga** Gallium	32 **Ge** Germanium	33 **As** Arsenic	34 **Se** Selenium	35 **Br** Bromine	36 **Kr** Krypton
37 **Rb** Rubidium	38 **Sr** Strontium	39 **Y** Yttrium	40 **Zr** Zirconium	41 **Nb** Niobium	42 **Mo** Molybdenum	43 **Tc** Technetium	44 **Ru** Ruthenium	45 **Rh** Rhodium	46 **Pd** Palladium	47 **Ag** Silver	48 **Cd** Cadmium	49 **In** Indium	50 **Sn** Tin	51 **Sb** Antimony	52 **Te** Tellurium	53 **I** Iodine	54 **Xe** Xenon
55 **Cs** Cesium	56 **Ba** Barium	57-71 Lanthanide Series	72 **Hf** Hafnium	73 **Ta** Tantalum	74 **W** Tungsten	75 **Re** Rhenium	76 **Os** Osmium	77 **Ir** Iridium	78 **Pt** Platinum	79 **Au** Gold	80 **Hg** Mercury	81 **Tl** Thallium	82 **Pb** Lead	83 **Bi** Bismuth	84 **Po** Polonium	85 **At** Astatine	86 **Rn** Radon
87 **Fr** Francium	88 **Ra** Radium	89-103 Actinide Series	104 **Rf** Rutherfordium	105 **Db** Dubnium	106 **Sg** Seaborgium	107 **Bh** Bohrium	108 **Hs** Hassium	109 **Mt** Meitnerium	110 **Ds** Darmstadtium	111 **Rg** Roentgenium	112 **Cn** Copernicium	113 **Nh** Nihonium	114 **Fl** Flerovium	115 **Mc** Moscovium	116 **Lv** Livermorium	117 **Ts** Tennessine	118 **Og** Oganesson

57 **La** Lanthanum	58 **Ce** Cerium	59 **Pr** Praseodymium	60 **Nd** Neodymium	61 **Pm** Promethium	62 **Sm** Samarium	63 **Eu** Europium	64 **Gd** Gadolinium	65 **Tb** Terbium	66 **Dy** Dysprosium	67 **Ho** Holmium	68 **Er** Erbium	69 **Tm** Thulium	70 **Yb** Ytterbium	71 **Lu** Lutetium
89 **Ac** Actinium	90 **Th** Thorium	91 **Pa** Protactinium	92 **U** Uranium	93 **Np** Neptunium	94 **Pu** Plutonium	95 **Am** Americium	96 **Cm** Curium	97 **Bk** Berkelium	98 **Cf** Californium	99 **Es** Einsteinium	100 **Fm** Fermium	101 **Md** Mendelevium	102 **No** Nobelium	103 **Lr** Lawrencium

METRIC CONVERSIONS

Inches	Centimeters		Feet	Meters
¼	0.6		1	0.3
⅓	0.8		2	0.6
½	1.3		3	0.9
¾	1.9		4	1.2
1	2.5		5	1.5
2	5.1		6	1.8
3	7.6		7	2.1
4	10		8	2.4
5	13		9	2.7
6	15		10	3
7	18			
8	20			
9	23			
10	25			

Temperatures
degrees Celsius = 0.55 × (degrees Fahrenheit − 32)
degrees Fahrenheit = (1.8 × degrees Celsius) + 32

To convert length:	Multiply by:
Yards to meters	0.9
Inches to centimeters	2.54
Inches to millimeters	25.4
Feet to centimeters	30.5

FURTHER READING

These popular titles are excellent resources for delving deeper into mineral identification and Pacific Northwest geology.

Allen, John Eliot, Marjorie Burns, and Scott Burns. *Cataclysms on the Columbia: The Great Missoula Floods* (Revised Second Edition)

Bishop, Ellen Morris. *In Search of Ancient Oregon: A Geological and Natural History*

Bishop, Ellen Morris. *Living with Thunder: Exploring the Geologic Past, Present, and Future of Pacific Northwest Landscapes*

Bishop, Ellen Morris. *Hiking Oregon's Geology* (Second Edition)

Carson, Bob. *The Blues: Natural History of the Blue Mountains of Northeastern Oregon and Southeastern Washington*

Carson, Bob and Scott Babcock. *Hiking Guide to Washington Geology* (Second Edition)

Johnson, Lars. *Rockhounding Oregon: A Guide to the State's Best Rockhounding Sites*

Johnson, Lars. *Rockhounding Washington: A Guide to the State's Best Sites*

Kiver, Eugene, Chad Pritchard, and Richard Orndorff. *Washington Rocks!*

Lynch, Dan R. and Bob Lynch. *Rocks & Minerals of Washington and Oregon*

Miller, Marli B. *Roadside Geology of Oregon* (Second Edition)

Miller, Marli B. and Darrel S. Cowan. *Roadside Geology of Washington* (Second Edition)

National Audubon Society. *National Audubon Society Field Guide to Rocks and Minerals: North America*

Orr, Elizabeth L. and William N. Orr. *Oregon Geology* (Sixth Edition)

Pellant, Chris. *Smithsonian Handbook: Rocks & Minerals*

Romaine, Garret. *Gem Trails of Oregon* (Third Edition)

Romain, Garret. *Gem Trails of Washington* (Second Edition)

Tucker, Dave. *Geology Underfoot in Western Washington*

U.S. Geological Survey. *Field-trip guides to selected volcanoes and volcanic landscapes of the western United States*

GLOSSARY

accretion (tectonic) The process by which material (such as terranes) is added to a landmass at a convergent margin

accretionary wedge A wedge-shaped stack of marine sediments scraped off the oceanic plate at a subduction zone

active margin A continental margin influenced by an active tectonic process such as subduction

aeolian Landscape or geomorphic features and processes associated with wind

aggregate A group of particles, usually mineral crystals or rock fragments, that are gathered (aggregated) together in a rock

alluvium Sediment transported and deposited by rivers

amorphous Without definite form; without definite atomic structure or lattice

angle of repose The steepest slope a pile of loose material can hold before collapsing

angular unconformity Flat-lying rocks deposited on top of older, tilted and eroded rocks

anhedral Opposite of euhedral; a crystal that has grown poorly or been partially dissolved and does not display a clear form

anoxic Poor in oxygen

antiform Rock-layer fold where limbs are inclined away from the hinge

arete Glacial landform; steep, knife-edge ridge between two cirques

asthenosphere The ductile zone of Earth's mantle where convection takes place

aventurescence Shiny flecks inside a gem-clear crystal, as in some sunstones; also called schiller

axial surface Three-dimensional representation of all hinges in a rock fold

batholith A composite igneous body made of many plutons that have intruded into one another

beach Deposit of sediment along a coast

bedding A layer of rock formed by the accumulation of sediments over time

bedrock The fully coherent bodies and layers of rock that comprise Earth's upper crust

biological sedimentary rock A rock containing a significant component of material made by living things like plants, plankton, or bacteria

bladed A thin, flat shape with tapered edges that resemble the blade of a knife

bleb A small irregular blob

book A stack of sheeted minerals, especially micas

botryoidal A shape resembling a cluster of grapes; a surface with smooth, globular bumps

brittle A material that deforms by breaking (fracturing or cleaving)

caldera A depression in the ground caused by the collapse of a volcano

cape See headland

carbonate A family of minerals and rocks containing the carbonate molecule (CO_3)

chain silicate A silicate mineral with its tetrahedral building blocks attached together in long chains

chemical sedimentary rock A rock primarily formed through minerals precipitating from an aqueous solution (water)

cinder cone Smaller, steep-sided volcanoes composed of basaltic cinders and bombs

cirque Semicircular, amphitheater-shaped head or top of a glacial valley

clast Individual pieces or particles of sediment or rock fragments

clastic Related to broken pieces of mineral crystals or rock fragments, a.k.a. clasts; made of clasts

cleavage (crystal cleavage) Planes of weakness in a crystal's atomic structure along which a crystal readily breaks

cleavage (rock cleavage) Planes of weakness in a rock, often defined by horizons of clays or micas, along which a rock readily breaks

coarse crystalline A rock texture with large visible crystals that fit together like puzzle pieces

coast The interface between a continental landmass and an ocean

columnar A shape resembling a column, long and thin

columnar jointing Joints that form from contraction in a cooling lava flow or welded tuff and take the form of polygonal columns that fit snugly together

compositional banding Layers within a coarse crystalline rock that are defined by mineral composition, for example, light-colored layers made of quartz and feldspar alternating with dark-colored layers made of hornblende and biotite

compression Stress where a rock is squeezed in one direction

conchoidal Dish-shaped (usually referring to a type of fracture)

contact The surface at which two different rock types touch

continental shelf Area of continental crust covered by shallow ocean, flanking a continental margin

convection The physical cycling of hot and cool material in Earth's asthenospheric mantle, where warm materials rise and cooler materials descend

core The innermost layer of the Earth, comprising a liquid metal outer core and a solid metal inner core

creep Slow, almost imperceptible movement of soil downslope

crust The solid, outermost layer of the Earth

crystal An individual specimen of one type of mineral, for example, a quartz crystal

cubic Related to the shape of a cube (a box where each side is a perfect square)

cumulate layering Layers in igneous rock that form when crystals growing in a magma sink to the bottom of the magma chamber

cut bank Steep outer bank of a stream or river's meander bend

debris flow Fast downslope movement of rock material, organic debris, and water

deform; deformation To change or distort the physical dimensions and appearance of a body of rock; the act of doing so

delta Triangular or fan-shaped deposit of sediment at the mouth of a river or stream

density A measure of the mass of an object divided by its volume

deposition When transported sediment comes to rest and accumulates

dike A thin, tabular intrusion of igneous rock that usually forms at shallow crustal depths

disconformity Erosional unconformity representing a gap in time between deposition of vertically successive layers

dissolution Dissolving of rocks through chemical reaction with weak acids

dodecahedron A polyhedron with twelve diamond-, kite-, or pentagon-shaped faces that looks similar to a soccer ball

drumlin Elongate ridges of till that taper in the direction of glacial flow; sometimes called fluted ridges

drusy A surface coated with a layer of tiny, very shiny crystals (often quartz)

ductile A material that deforms by flowing, like putty

dune Ridge formed by wind-driven movement of sand particles

earthquake Shaking of the Earth's surface and crust due to energy released from rocks breaking at depth

equant Equally sized in all dimensions, like a cube or a ball

erosion Initial removal of material from its original location on Earth's surface

erratic A large boulder transported and deposited by glaciers

estuary Wide, low-relief area between the ocean and mouth of a river

euhedral Opposite of anhedral; a well-formed crystal with sharp edges and vertices that shows a clear and describable habit

exfoliation Process of crystalline rocks weathering by breaking into surface-parallel sheets

extension Stress where a rock is stretched in one direction

fabric Orderly pattern in which a rock's minerals are arranged, for example, tectonic foliation

face (crystal face) A flat surface on a crystal formed from the crystal's natural growth

face (rock face) A planar exposure in a rock outcrop

fault A plane separating two bodies of rock that have moved relative to one another

fibrous Resembling fabric fibers; mineral fibers may be rigid or flexible

fine crystalline A rock texture with crystals too small to be seen by the naked eye or low magnification (as with a hand lens)

floodplain Wide, low-relief deposits of small sediment surrounding river channels

flow banding The appearance of layers or stripes formed by the alignment of minerals in flowing, molten rock (usually lava flows)

fluvial Landforms and processes associated with rivers

fold Rock layers that have been bent (folded) due to compression

foliated Layered; specifically, in metamorphic rocks when minerals have grown or re-aligned to the same orientation, forming flat sheets

footwall Block of rock vertically below a fault

foreland basin A topographic trough between a volcanic arc and an accretionary wedge

fracture A separation within a mineral crystal or rock; may be described as planar, conchoidal, hackly, etc.

framework silicate A silicate mineral with its tetrahedral building blocks attached together in three dimensions like scaffolding

gem Any crystal that is transparent, shiny, and valued by people

geomorphology The study of Earth's surface processes and features

glacial drift *See* till

glacial trough U-shaped valley once occupied by a glacier

glacier Mass of ice that forms at high altitude or high latitude

gneiss dome A dome-shaped structure or regional exposure of gneiss formed by ductile extension

graben A basin created by the down-dropped hanging wall of a normal fault

grain/granular A particle with a shape and texture like a rice grain; a group of such particles

habit The visible shape of a mineral specimen

hackly A fracture with a rough or irregular surface

hanging wall Block of rock vertically above a fault

hardness The ability of a mineral to scratch or resist being scratched

headland Rocky outcroppings that extend oceanward beyond the adjacent shoreline

hinge Point or line of greatest curvature of a fold

horn Glacial landform; a pyramid-shaped peak surrounded by three or more cirques

horst Uplifted footwall block of a normal fault, topographic high points on sides of a graben

ice age An extended period of cool global temperatures that allows the growth of glaciers and continental ice sheets

igneous Related to rocks that form from crystals that grow in magma or lava as it cools

intrusion A body of igneous rock that has forced its way into existing rocks in the crust

joint A fracture with a planar surface

knickpoint Localized steep sections of a stream; for example, rapids and waterfalls

lacustrine Relating to or associated with lakes

lahar A debris flow that initiates on a volcano

landslide Downslope movement of material; mass movement

lapidary Related to gems and precious stones or the art of cutting them for decoration

last glacial maximum The time period corresponding to the greatest extent of glacial coverage during the most recent ice age

lateral Horizontal

lattice A description of the three-dimensional, regular, repeating patterns of atoms that make up crystals

lava dome Small felsic eruptive centers with steep sides

lava Molten rock exposed at the surface of the Earth

limb Inclined rock layers on either side of a fold

lineation Straight, linear features such as grooves on a fault or alignment of elongate minerals

lithified Descriptor for material that has been made into a rock, as when sand is transformed to sandstone; from *lithos*, Greek for stone

lithosphere The brittle, outermost portion of Earth, composed of the crust and upper mantle

loess Wind-blown silt or dust; originates as glacial drift

luster The manner in which a surface, usually a crystal face, reflects light; for example, pearly or dull

magma Molten rock beneath Earth's surface

mantle Earth's solid middle layer, comprising 84 percent of the planet by volume

massive A homogenous rock with no internal structures or features

matrix In sedimentary rock, the microcrystalline material cementing clasts together; in any rock made from components of different sizes, the body of the finer material surrounding the largest components (minerals or clasts)

meander To follow a sinuous, windy path; meandering streams

melange A mixed formation of broken rocks that are chaotically jumbled together

mesosphere Physical or mechanical term for the lower mantle

metamorphic Related to rocks that form when heat and pressure cause new minerals to grow at the expense of existing minerals in a solid body of rock

meteorite A rock from outer space that has passed through Earth's atmosphere and landed on its surface

micaceous Related to mica; a crystal habit describing a mass of small flexible sheets

microcrystalline Describes a portion of rock made from crystals too small to see without high-powered magnification

mid-ocean ridge A divergent plate boundary on the ocean floor where new crust is produced by basaltic magmatism

mineral A naturally occurring crystalline solid with a definite chemical composition

molten In a liquid state, from having been melted

moraine Ridges of till that form at the sides or front of a glacier

mylonite Recrystallized metamorphic rocks that form within ductile shear zones

native element A family of minerals with a chemical formula consisting of only a single atomic element, like gold, silver, or copper

nonconformity Depositional contact between underlying crystalline rock and overlying sedimentary rock

normal fault A fault in which the hanging wall has slipped down relative to the footwall

octahedron A polyhedron with eight triangle-shaped faces making a form like two square pyramids opposing one another

ophiolite A section of oceanic crust that has been accreted to a continent

original horizontality Principle that contacts between certain layered rocks are initially horizontal

outcrop A body of bedrock exposed at Earth's surface

oxidation Chemical reaction in which iron-rich minerals form new reddish-colored iron oxide minerals

oxide A family of minerals with a chemical formula of one or two metal atoms bound to an oxygen atom; for example, hematite (Fe_2O_3)

passive margin A rifted shoreline that is not subjected to ongoing tectonic activity such as compression or faulting

plate See tectonic plate

plate tectonics Theory that the Earth's crust is broken into numerous rigid plates which rearrange their configuration over geologic time

platy A crystal habit resembling a thin, rigid slab

pluton A body of igneous rock that has solidified underground

pluvial lake A large lake that originally filled during the last ice age

point bar Deposit of sediment on the inside of a meander bend

polish (glacial) Smooth bedrock surfaces abraded by past glaciation

polyhedron A closed, three-dimensional shape like a cube

polymorph Two or more minerals that have the same chemical formula, but different atomic structures, for example, quartz and moganite

porphyritic A rock texture with large, well-formed crystals scattered in a finer-grained matrix

potholes Small, circular erosional depressions in bedrock stream channels

prismatic A crystal habit resembling a prism (an elongate column with three, four, or six sides)

radiating A crystal habit describing an aggregate of elongated crystals that spread out from a central point

reduction Chemical reaction in anoxic environments that produces a blue-gray to green color in minerals

regmaglypt Thumb-print texture on the surface of a meteorite that can form from frictional heating as the rock passes through Earth's atmosphere

regolith Loose rocky material covering bedrock at Earth's surface (see also soil)

reverse fault Fault resulting from compression of a steep slope (greater than 45 degrees)

rhombohedron A polyhedron with six rhombus-shaped faces; resembles a slightly squashed box

rifting When one tectonic plate splits into two at a new divergent plate boundary; also when new oceanic crust forms at this boundary

ring silicate A silicate mineral with its tetrahedral building blocks attached together in rings

rock An aggregate of minerals

rosette A crystal habit describing an aggregate of tabular or platy crystals arranged like the petals of a rose blossom

roundness Measure of the shape of sediment; from angular to well-rounded

scaly A crystal habit describing micaceous sheets with irregular or ragged edges, often fitting tightly to the rock and difficult to peel away

scarp Steep cut in the landscape where motion from a landslide or other mass movement initiates

schiller *See* aventurescence

sea stack Free-standing blocks of rock isolated from the shoreline; formerly parts of headlands

sediment Loose rocky material or dissolved minerals in solution at Earth's surface

sedimentary Related to rocks that form from the accumulation of material, including clastic material, biological material, and chemical precipitates

shear Stress where one side of a rock is moved relative to the other in a sliding fashion

shear zone Localized zones of ductile deformation (shear) in the lower crust

sheet A crystal habit describing a paper-thin slab

sheet silicate A silicate mineral with its tetrahedral building blocks attached together in flat sheets

shield volcano Broad, wide volcano with gently sloping flanks

sigma clast Asymmetric growth of quartz or feldspar in a gneiss that serves as an indicator of direction of shear

silicate A family of minerals that all contain silicon tetrahedron as a basic building block

silicon tetrahedron Triangular pyramid-shaped atomic structure with four oxygen atoms at the corners connected to a silicon atom in the center

sill An igneous intrusion that is parallel to existing rock layering

slickenfibers Linear mineral growths on a fault surface

slickenlines Lineations on a fault surface indicating direction of motion

soil Layered mixture of weathered sediments, clays, and organic material covering bedrock

strain Deformation in response to stress

strata General term to describe layers in a rock or suite of rocks

stratification The process of forming layers

stratovolcano Large, steep-sided volcanoes composed of layers of lava flows and pyroclastic debris; composite cone

streak A mineral that has been reduced to powder, such as when a crystal is rubbed against a rough ceramic plate

stress A force applied over a given area; pressure

striation A linear groove on a flat surface

strike-slip fault Fault with lateral (horizontal) motion

structure (rock) End result of past deformation of a rock or suite of rocks

subduction Process of a denser oceanic plate being pushed underneath a less dense plate, continental or also oceanic

sulfide A family of minerals with a chemical formula of one or two metal atoms bound to a sulfur atom, like pyrite (FeS_2)

superposition Principle stating that in a vertical stack of undeformed rocks, the oldest rocks will be at the bottom and the youngest on top

synform Fold where limbs are inclined toward the hinge

tabular A crystal habit describing a flat slab with relative dimensions resembling a table top

talus Angular sediment produced by freeze-thaw weathering

tarn Glacial landform; the lake in a cirque

tectonic plate A portion of Earth's lithosphere separated from other portions of lithosphere by large faults or significant zones of deformation that extend down to the asthenospheric mantle

termination In elongated crystals, the shape of the crystal's end (may be flat, pyramidal, pointed, etc.)

terrace (fluvial) Abandoned floodplains elevated above the modern channel

terrace (marine) Uplifted wave-cut benches

terrane A fault-bounded fragment of crust that originated on one plate and accreted to another plate

tetrahedron A polyhedron with four triangle-shaped faces; can also be described as a triangular pyramid

thrust fault A low-angle fault resulting from compression with a shallow slope (less than 45 degrees)

till General term for sediment deposited by a glacier

transform Tectonic plate boundary where two plates are sliding laterally past each other

trench Long, narrow, deep zones along the ocean floor at a subduction zone

twin A pair of mineral crystals that grow together with a geometric relationship that has an element of symmetry; for example, two crystals may grow to be mirror images of one another

unconformity Discontinuity within a stack of rock layers

uniformitarianism The notion that modern geologic processes have been active on Earth for billions of years, allowing us to understand the past by making observations about the present

uplift When a landmass or area rises in elevation

vein Mineral deposits that infill a rock fracture, usually by precipitating from a fluid; quartz and calcite are the most common vein-filling materials

vesicle A trapped or frozen gas bubble within an igneous volcanic rock

volcanic neck Eroded remnants of the interior of a stratovolcano or cinder cone

volcaniclastic A sedimentary clastic rock made entirely of particles of volcanic rock, usually created by processes related to volcanic eruptions

volcano A surficial fissure that emits lava, gasses, or ash during eruptive events

vug A void or empty pocket in a rock

wave-cut bench Flat, planar strips of bedrock located in the tidal zone

weathering Physical and chemical processes that break down rocks at or near the Earth's surface; the series of chemical reactions between minerals exposed at Earth's surface and atmospheric oxygen and water, resulting in the formation of clay minerals, oxides, and others

wire A crystal habit resembling a wire

PHOTO AND ILLUSTRATION CREDITS

All illustrations created by the authors.

Photos by:

Alexander Bridges, pages 149, 172, 307, 310, 316, 320–321

Bruce Carter, pages 205, 206 top

D. Finnin/© American Museum of Natural History, page 208

Adrian Klein of Photo Cascadia, pages 2–3

Kevin McConnell, pages 1, 30–31, 34 top and bottom, 35 bottom, 39, 44, 45, 49, 50, 51, 52, 53, 55, 56, 57, 58, 59, 60, 62, 63 bottom, 65, 67, 68, 69, 71 right, 75 bottom, 77 right, 78 top, 79 right, 80 top, 81, 84, 85, 86, 89 bottom, 90, 92, 93, 94, 95, 96, 97 bottom, 98 top, 99 left, 102, 103, 104, 105, 106, 108, 109, 110, 111, 112, 145 bottom, 150, 151 bottom, 174 left, 211 bottom

Marli Miller, pages 107, 176, 178, 212 top, 235 top, 238

Leslie Moclock, pages 34 bottom, 35 top, 38, 43, 47, 48, 54, 61, 63 top, 64, 66, 71 left, 72, 73, 74, 75 top, 76, 77 left, 78 bottom, 79 left, 80 bottom, 83, 89 top, 97 top, 98, bottom, 99 right, 100, 128, 134, 135 top, 137, 139, 140 bottom, 141 top, 142, 143, 147 top, 148 middle, 149 bottom right, 151 top, 152 bottom, 153, 154, 155, 156, 158, 160 top, 161, 162, 164 bottom, 165, 166, 167 bottom, 169 bottom, 170 top, 173, 174 right, 175, 177, 182 top, 185 bottom, 186, 189, 190 bottom, 191 bottom, 192, 193, 194, 196 top, 197 top, 212 bottom, 213 bottom, 218 top, 219 bottom, 251, 257 bottom, 270, 275 bottom, 288

Jeff Schwartz, page 91

Jacob Selander, pages 5, 18, 19, 20, 22, 23, 24, 25, 26, 27, 28, 29 bottom, 32, 124–125, 126, 135 bottom, 136, 138, 140 top, 141 bottom, 144, 148 top and bottom, 149 bottom left, 152 top, 157, 159, 160 bottom, 163, 164 top, 167 top, 169 top, 176 bottom, 179, 180, 182 bottom, 184, 185 top, 187, 188, 190 top, 191 top, 195 bottom, 196 top, 211 top, 215, 216, 217, 218 bottom, 219 top, 220,

221, 222, 225, 227, 228, 230, 231, 233, 234, 235, 236, 237, 238, 240, 241, 242, 243, 244, 245, 246, 247, 248, 249, 250, 252, 253, 255, 257 top, 258, 259, 260, 261, 262, 263, 264, 265, 267, 268, 269, 271, 273, 274, 275 top, 276, 278, 279, 280, 281, 282, 283, 285, 286–287, 289, 290, 293, 294, 303, 305, 308, 311, 312, 318, 321, 322, 323, 325

Shutterstock, Linnas, page 87

Shutterstock, Jennifer Larsen Morrow, page 21

Shutterstock, Bob Pool, page 29 top

USGS / R.L. Schuster from USGS Professional Paper 1250, fig 406B / Public domain,, page 170 bottom

Specimens provided by:

Bart Cannon, pages 92, 105

Raymond Lasmanis, pages 69, 85

John Lindell, pages 63 bottom, 78 top, 86, 90, 93, 98 top, 99 left

Rice Northwest Museum of Rocks and Minerals, pages 1, 30-31, 32 top left and bottom, 44, 45 both, 49 both, 50 both, 51 all, 52 middle and bottom, 53 both, 55, 56, 57, 58, 59, 60, 62, 67, 68 both, 71 bottom right, 72, 74, 75 bottom, 77 right, 79 right, 80 top, 83, 84 both, 89 bottom, 94, 95, 102, 103 all, 104 both, 106, 109, 100 both, 111, 112, 150, 151 all, 205, 206 top, 211 bottom

Thea Stender, page 108

University of Oregon, pages 35 top, 38 both, 47, 48, 54 bottom, 61 both, 63 top, 65, 66, 71 top, 73 both, 75 top, 76, 77 left, 79 left, 89 top, 98 bottom, 99 right, 134 bottom, 137, 152 bottom, 155 left, 156 right, 162 top, 164 bottom, 166 middle and bottom, 169 bottom, 174 top and bottom right, 175, 177, 182 top, 185 bottom, 186 bottom, 189, 191 bottom, 192, 193, 197 top, 212 bottom, 213 bottom

Aaron Wieting, pages 81, 96

INDEX

ABOUT THE AUTHORS

Alexander Bridges

Leslie Moclock has an MS in geology from the University of California–Davis, where she taught field and laboratory geology. She held the position of curator at the Rice Northwest Museum of Rocks and Minerals in Hillsboro, Oregon, for five years, where she enjoyed many opportunities to bring science to the public.

Sarah Milhollin

Jacob Selander grew up in Oregon and holds a PhD from the university of California–Davis. He is an instructor at Highline College in Des Moines, Washington, where he teaches introductory geology, geomorphology, and geologic hazards classes, with a focus on making the sometimes-daunting field of geology accessible to everyone. When not teaching, Jacob is a landscape photographer—one who is always excited to find visual examples of complex geologic phenomena.